Everyday Reconciliation

Everyday Reconciliation

**A Guide to Action
and Change for All of Us**

Derek Aronhie:nens Montour
and Elin Sandberg Miller

HarperCollins*Publishers*Ltd

Published by HarperCollins Publishers Ltd

FIRST EDITION

HarperCollins Publishers Ltd
Bay Adelaide Centre, East Tower
22 Adelaide Street West, 41st Floor
Toronto, Ontario, Canada
M5H 4E3

www.harpercollins.ca

HarperCollins Publishers
Macken House, 39/40 Mayor Street Upper
Dublin 1, D01 C9W8, Ireland

www.harpercollins.com

Library and Archives Canada Cataloguing in Publication

Title: Everyday reconciliation : a guide to action and change for all of
us / Derek Aronhie:nens Montour and Elin Sandberg Miller.
Names: Montour, Derek Aronhie:nens, author. | Sandberg Miller, Elin, author.
Identifiers: Canadiana (print) 20260140740 | Canadiana (ebook) 20260140848 |
ISBN 9781443475648 (hardcover) | ISBN 9781443475655 (EPUB)
Subjects: LCSH: Canada—Race relations. | LCSH: Canada—
Ethnic relations. | LCSH: Indigenous peoples—
Canada. | LCSH: Immigrants—Canada. | LCSH: Reconciliation.
Classification: LCC E78.C2 M66 2026 | DDC 305.897/071—dc23

*We dedicate this book to every person who is taking steps
to learn about Indigenous Peoples and their realities.
Your efforts contribute to reconciliation and to us
sharing this land respectfully and peacefully.*

Contents

Introduction

This book is written by us—Derek Aronhie:nens Montour and Elin Sandberg Miller—two everyday Canadians. Derek is Indigenous from the Kanien'kehá:ka (Mohawk) Nation and grew up on the Kahnawà:ke (Kahnawake) reserve, south of Montreal. He has experienced first-hand the socio-economic inequalities, the intergenerational trauma, and the racism facing Indigenous Peoples in Canada. Elin immigrated to Canada from Sweden as an adult, and despite being a trained lawyer who has worked in human rights, peacebuilding, and diplomacy most of her life, she only started learning about reconciliation with Indigenous Peoples after she arrived in Canada.

We met when Derek appeared as a guest on Elin's podcast, *Everyday Reconciliation*, which she co-produced with the think tank Canada 2020. The podcast aired for ten episodes over five months in 2021–2022, with each episode discussing how non-Indigenous people can contribute to the national reconciliation process. After the podcast ended, we decided to keep our conversation going.

As we discovered, we both believe in the power of everyday reconciliation. While we had much in common, being of the same age and having both grown up in Western democracies resting roughly on the same fundamental values, our experiences were diametrically different. We came from opposite ends of the colonization process; we could just as well have come from different planets. But this difference became essential to our collaboration. And through our ongoing dialogue, which connected us throughout the writing process, we discovered that, despite our differences, the same sense of justice and responsibility to give back to our communities drove us.

Together, we wanted to explore concrete ways everyday Canadians could contribute to the national reconciliation process. While surveys demonstrated that most Canadians were supportive of reconciliation, our experience was that it was also generally viewed as an institutional endeavour, a responsibility of governments, religious entities, educational institutions, and corporations. It is true that the main responsibility rests with them: They designed and continue to uphold the many systems and practices that benefit non-Indigenous Canadians at the expense of Indigenous people. But restoring friendly, peaceful relations between our peoples—or establishing them in the first place—is a responsibility for all of us. We are all responsible for allowing the existing structures to remain unchanged and thereby the discrimination and injustices to continue. Beyond that, relationships are built by people, and it's the relationships between our peoples that must be at the centre of the reconciliation process; otherwise, we'll never understand or get along with each other. We all need to be part of building these relations, and we can all contribute. The question, of course, is how.

When we started our collaboration, there were few resources available to individuals who wanted to contribute, and it was that gap we wanted to fill with this book. We also wanted to provide information and learning grounded in Indigenous perspectives. While reconciliation is a process that must involve us all, this book speaks primarily to non-Indigenous people. Indigenous Peoples in Canada—First Nations, Inuit, and Métis—are at the receiving end of colonization. Many have already been forced to adopt the settler way of life. They communicate in either or both of Canada's official languages, English and French, and abide by non-Indigenous ways of learning and doing. They may be more familiar with the settler perspective of the country's culture and history than their own. Non-Indigenous people now need to learn the distinct histories, languages, cultural practices, and spiritual beliefs of Indigenous people. The onus of addressing the ongoing impact of colonization must rest on their shoulders, not those of Indigenous people.

We raise some unsettling and provocative questions through-out our essays, and the process of reconciliation does not come without its challenges. Yet, during the process of writing this book together, we have come across many impressive initiatives by Indigenous and non-Indigenous people alike that have posi-tively impacted our outlook. Our views are also informed by the numerous books, reports, podcasts, movies, and experts who have taught us about reconciliation throughout our research and writing process.

To make sense of what we learned, what we believe, and what we want to share, we structured the book into essays di-vided by themes, where we talk about reconciliation from our respective perspectives. Throughout the book, you'll also find brief, informative guides designed to encourage reflections and to provide simple, practical steps to start your own everyday reconciliation.

Readers will note that we sometimes use alternative terms to Indigenous and non-Indigenous, such as Indian and Aboriginal, white and settler. We do so for several reasons: The term may be reflective of a proper name, for example, the Indian Act; reflective of what is most appropriate in the context; or simply reflective of our own preferences. In the case where we're referring to a spe-cific person, we use the term that they themselves prefer, whether it's Indian, Indigenous, Native, First Nations, Métis, Inuit, Inuk (the singular form of Inuit), white, settler, non-Indigenous, or something else entirely. Readers don't have to call themselves anything that they're not comfortable with and, often, a qualifying term isn't called for at all. In the end, we are all human beings living together on this land we call Canada.

Reconciliation is a big word that means different things to different people. We are grateful to the many experts and advocates whom we have learned from. Our essays share the personal experiences that have formed our own approach to reconciliation, and you will learn more about it as you read this book. We don't speak for all Indigenous or non-Indigenous people or pretend to have all the answers. We are simply sharing what we've learned in the hope that this book will support you on your own reconciliation journey.

DEREK AND ELIN

Part I: Home

Reconciling with Hate

Derek Aronhie:nens Montour

"I HOPE WE go in and kill all them savages!"

The words hit like a punch to the solar plexus. It was the same feeling as losing my breath—I felt the pain right in my core. I froze, and for a few heartbeats, I panicked. Then, I was overwhelmed with a sense of betrayal, transitioning into a feeling of grim disappointment that things never change.

It was the summer of 1990, at the height of the Oka Crisis, and I was an eighteen-year-old private in the Royal Montreal Regiment (RMR) of the Canadian military. Our unit was stationed at the Canadian Forces Base in Valcartier, one of the largest military bases in Quebec, for my first ever summer reservist training. Meanwhile, in Kanehsatà:ke (Kanesatake), a Kanien'kehá:ka community on the north shore of Montreal, community members had erected a barricade to protect their ancient burial grounds from a developer in Oka, a nearby non-Indigenous village, who was planning a golf course expansion. Initially founded in 1717 as a Catholic mission for Kanien'kehá:ka, Algonquin and Nipissing people, Kanehsatà:ke has since become regarded as a Kanien'kehá:ka community today. After Kanehsatà:ke refused to take down their barricade, the Quebec provincial police, known as the Sûreté du Québec (SQ), surrounded the community, assaulting the blockades. During the altercation, SQ Corporal Marcel Lemay was shot. In response to the escalating situation, my community, Kahnawà:ke, located on the south shore of Montreal, erected its own blockade, cutting off the Mercier Bridge and other important infrastructure lines like the seaway and the railway.

Everyone at the training camp was talking about it, in unusually hushed voices, and I remember having a pervading feeling of anxiety about it all. It was like overhearing a story about myself, and yet it didn't quite seem like it involved me. I was in my tent fixing my gear when I heard one of the troopers outside say those words that would shake my belief in what I was doing there. I immediately went outside, but everyone stopped talking at once and just stared at me. I had no idea who said it. It didn't matter—they might as well all have said it. I walked away, ashamed of myself for not confronting them. I had never imagined that one of my "brothers in arms" could say something like that. Whoever it was, he was talking about my mom and dad, my brothers and sisters, and even my tóta, my grandmother. This was my community, my people. I was also ashamed that I was there in Valcartier while my friends and family were back home, under siege.

Growing up in Kahnawà:ke, in the Kanien'kehá:ka (Mohawk) Territory, ensured that I had experienced racism and discrimination before, so much so that such instances often faded into the background. I have always lived in the community and yet always felt like a semi-outsider, too. My dad was from the Bear Clan, and his family goes back many generations on Turtle Island, but my mom is a first-generation settler. She was born in Glasgow, Scotland, and moved here with her parents when she was three. Her only sister, Carol, was born in Canada. I have two brothers: Craig, who was ten and a half months older than me, and David, who was four years younger. We seemed to be fighting all the time, as perhaps many brothers do.

My dad had a big family, with four brothers and four sisters, and so we ended up with twenty-five first cousins of varying ages. We were always connected and would often visit each other. My brothers, cousins, and I all went to primary school in the community. We attended Kateri School up to Grade 3 and then went to Karonhianónhnha School to Grade 6. It was only once we reached high school that we started to veer our separate ways. My parents sent all three of us boys to Loyola High School in Montreal. Loyola had originated in 1896 as both a college and high school, and my dad had attended the college for a short while before he had to stop to help his family with income, so perhaps it was a way for us to follow in his footsteps.

When you grow up in an Indigenous community, everyone outside the community becomes, to some extent, foreign to you. I remember the feeling becoming embedded in me: that we were different from others outside the community—because of our race, our language, our history, our Creation Story, and even our understanding of the world. And to a large degree it felt like everyone was against us. It felt like we had to constantly fight because of who we were, whether we were playing hockey against a non-Indigenous team or simply walking on the street outside the community.

At the same time, I also often felt like an outsider within our community because my mom was from Scotland. I remember that I felt the same as all my cousins and the same as my neighbourhood friends, but once I went outside my own family and neighbourhood, I wasn't quite sure. Membership and residency have always been very contentious issues in our community, and different families responded in different ways. I remember being called a candy cane (red and white all over) and an apple (red on the outside and white on the inside), as well as other names, by other kids in the community, and yet I also remember being called savage, redskin, and Injun, just like those peers when we were all confronted by non-Indigenous kids. I remember the constant feeling of wondering whether I would be accepted by others, even in the playground. It was like walking in the world feeling both accepted and not accepted at the same time, no matter where I was.

And then, against the backdrop of all this, came my experience in Valcartier. Not only was it a shock, but it also subsequently became a turning point in my life.

I had wanted to join the military for many years. Our nation has a history of involvement in political conflict and warfare across the northeast of Turtle Island (this land we call North America) that dates back to time immemorial. The word "Kanien'kehá:ka" means "People of the Flint," and our people say this name is appropriate to describe us for two reasons. One, our ancestral homelands in what is now known as upstate New York and into Canada had an abundance of flint rock, which led to advantages in toolmaking and, of course, warfare. This leads to the other interpretation of our name: that our tempers could spark very easily, just like striking a flint stone against dry tinder.

The Kanien'kehá:ka Nation (Mohawk) is part of the Haudenosaunee Confederacy, known by settlers as the Iroquois Confederacy, which spanned an area of land, roughly the shape of a triangle, from Albany, NY, to Montreal, Quebec, with Kahnawà:ke on Montreal's southern shore, and along up the St. Lawrence past Niagara Falls. We were considered the Keepers of the Eastern Door because we were on the far eastern part of the Confederacy's territory. The Seneca Nation (Onöndowa'ga) was the Keepers of the Western Door; the Onondaga Nation (Onoñda'gegá), located in the centre, was considered the Keepers of the Central Fire. The Oneida Nation (Onyota'a:ka) was between the Onondaga and us. Meanwhile, the Cayuga Nation (Gayogohó:nǫ) was between the Seneca and the Onondaga. Later, the Tuscarora Nation (Skarù:rę) joined us, following an influx of settlers into their territory (what is now known as Virginia and the Carolinas). Although the Confederacy's Traditional Territory was located primarily in New York, our people sent out hunting and war parties as far as the Saguenay River and Lake Mistassini to the north, Florida to the south, the Atlantic coast to the east, and the mighty Mississippi to the west.

Given our people's wide range of influence, combined with our long history of warfare, long-standing enmity was bound to occur. And it did. At one point or another, members of the Haudenosaunee fought with the Mahicans (also spelled Mohicans) to the east, the Algonquin and Wendat to the north, and the Erie and Shawnee to the west. In fact, the word "Mohawk" itself comes from our historical enemies, as does the word Iroquois. It is said to mean "flesh eaters" or "cannibals" in the Algonquian language and can likely be traced back to the Narragansett Nation, which originates from what is now known as the New England area of the United States. Sometime after the settlers first arrived on these shores, they learned of the Haudenosaunee from the Nations they befriended, which were often in conflict with us. The word Iroquois was also likely taken from Algonquin speaking nations and may mean "black snake" or "terrible man". The word "Mohawk" and "Iroquois" have been with us ever since, although I try to correct people that I meet with our proper name, Kanien'kehá:ka or Haudenosaunee, whenever I can.

Our community is also proud of our long history of formal military service. At least one contingent of Kahnawa'kehró:non (meaning "someone from Kahnawà:ke") has fought in every major conflict or war, including the War of 1812, when Kahnawà:ke warriors were instrumental in stopping an American-led attack into

Canada at the Battle of Châteauguay. We served despite receiving fewer benefits and less compensation than non-Indigenous veterans, and we have served in both the Canadian and American forces. I remember hearing stories of my uncles, Andy, Chester, and Roddy, serving in the American Army, Navy, and Marines during Vietnam.

My Uncle Andy was in the 101ˢᵗ Airborne during Vietnam, and I was told he was present in 1969 during the infamous battles in the A Shau Valley, which was a major entry point for North Vietnamese forces. It resulted in some of the fiercest and costliest combat engagements of the war. Even as a kid, I was a history enthusiast. I remember reading stories of the exploits of different service members, and I always wondered what life would be like when in battle. I was enthralled with that sense of adventure. I wanted to learn to fight and defend myself, to defend our home, to shoot weapons, jump out of airplanes, and run and crawl through obstacles. I was always physically fit, so it felt like I *could* follow in my uncles' footsteps, but I would never really know until I tried.

By the time I joined the RMR, two of my cousins, Landon and Kevin, had already joined the United States Marine Corps with some of their friends, and I knew other young men my age who were in the Canadian Reserves while attending college or working. As I'd gotten closer to graduating high school in June 1989, my mom and dad had encouraged me to do the same. I decided to try the reserves first, while also attending college for business administration (because I couldn't think of anything else), and to see which I liked more.

I officially signed up for service in the Canadian Reserve Force while I was in my first year of college, along with several other men from Kahnawà:ke. From the start of our first training operation, I was hooked. We were on a winter exercise, probably in January or February of 1990, and had to ski and snowshoe out with all our heavy gear to set up camp. The goal of the training exercise was to learn to set up camp in the snow, care for our gear, build stamina, and, of course, respond to threats. In the middle of the night, our instructors staged an attack. We quickly ran out of the tents, set up our fighting positions in the snow, and prepared to defend our bivouac site. I loved this kind of adventure: It was camping in the woods but with automatic weapons!

I also liked the RMR. The leadership treated me equally and valued my involvement, and I jumped right in. It felt like I was joining a privileged group, a brotherhood, one in which I earned the right to be there through my own sweat and determination. It didn't matter where you were from, or what your background was, or who you knew. It felt like as long as I could do my job well, I would be accepted.

I can admit that I was a somewhat self-absorbed, oblivious teenager. Before tensions spiked that summer, I was aware of the unrest in Kahnawà:ke and other Kanien'kehá:ka communities, but politics were not at the top of my priorities. Yet, the unease had been building since before I was born.

In the 1970s and 1980s, many political issues surrounded our communities as we were asserting our rights against the residual colonial governments of Quebec and Canada. These constant outside political pressures exacerbated the existing internal pressures of intergenerational trauma, consistently insufficient funding, loss of language and culture, unresolved grief, and rampant addictions. During this period, we were confronted with several pieces of damaging legislation, including Bill 101 in 1977, which forced the French language on people living in the land that is called Quebec—despite some of us already having been forced to speak English at the expense of our own Kanien'kéha language.

In 1951, changes to the Indian Act under Section 88 allowed provinces to apply provincial child welfare legislation in First

Nations communities; it did not implement any accountability for providing those services. This decision to apply provincial jurisdiction for Indigenous child welfare led to atrocities such as the forced sterilization of Indigenous women; the destructive consequences of the Sixties Scoop, which removed Indigenous children from their homes and communities at record rates; and even the then-new child welfare laws, which made it even easier to remove our children, actively destroying our communities. Added to all this was a continuous refusal to acknowledge our land claims.

By the end of the 1980s, tension was high. The RCMP raided my community of Kahnawà:ke, alleging illegal tobacco distribution and smuggling of tobacco across the Canada–United States border. Meanwhile, the FBI raided another Kanien'kehá:ka community, Ahkwesáhsne (Akwesasne), located on the border where Quebec, Ontario, and New York meet, this time claiming illegal gambling sites. I say "alleged" and "claiming" because we did not perceive either practice—the sale of tobacco or gambling—as illegal, but rather as a right based in trade. I understand that both practices were not being federally or provincially taxed, and yet some First Nations communities throughout North America have benefited greatly from these industries. At the time, our communities were also regularly involved in conflict with the provincial/state or federal governments, including the killing of twenty-eight-year-old David Cross by the Sûreté du Québec in his own backyard in 1979, and so the state of tension (and even targeted danger) seemed almost normal to me as a teen.

I had joined the Canadian Armed Forces with the full knowledge that I might be called upon to give up my life in service one day. Yet, I had never imagined that I would be called upon to attack another Indigenous person in Canada. At the time, I wondered how Quebec premier Robert Bourassa could ask Canada to call in the army to invade my community. Didn't the military only invade the territories of enemies? Would that not mean that

First Nations people are truly viewed as "the enemy" of Quebec and of Canada? And how could then–Prime Minister Brian Mulroney agree to do that? How could this happen in my lifetime? After I overheard that trooper say those fateful words, I realized I had to take a side. But which side was the so-called right side of this fight, if there even was such a thing?

I talked with my fellow Kahnawa'kehró:non. Six or seven of us were at the training in Valcartier, and after we talked, we all went to our superiors to request special leave to go back home. Fortunately, it was granted. All of us young Kanien'kehá:ka men left the training and made our way back. Although I no longer remember specifics of our trip, other images have stayed with me. The mobilized police force outside the community. The concertina wire surrounding the roadways. The crowds counter-protesting our barricades. The dug-out tank traps our community made along the roadways. The men on patrol within the community and in defensive positions, surrounded by sandbags or reinforced steel. I remember my parents were joyous to see me, and I also remember feeling tense. My two brothers and I did our best to act tough and be brave, but the truth is that we were expecting the military to invade, and we were nervous and scared.

Starting in early August, over 4,000 Canadian military troops mobilized in Kanehsatà:ke and Kahnawà:ke. For comparison, the Canadian peak troop deployment in the Persian Gulf War was only 2,700, with a total of approximately 5,100 troops deployed over the course of the war. There were machine guns everywhere I looked, helicopters buzzed overhead, and I saw soldiers in armoured vehicles patrolling around outside the community. It looked like a warzone, and that's because it was. As a military attack began to feel imminent, our community leaders started to evacuate people. My mom worked for the Kahnawà:ke Shakotiia'takehnhas Community Services (KSCS) at the time, and they were setting up a shelter in Dorval at one of the hotels, and so she left to help. The priority was to evacuate our elderly, women, and children. My parents insisted that my brothers and I go with them to, as they told us, "protect the family."

I felt a profound sense of shame for having to leave and also a sense of relief that perhaps I wouldn't die there. We joined the other evacuees leaving from the Kahnawà:ke Marina to ferry across Lake St. Louis in a small boat to Dorval. John Ciaccia, then–provincial Minister of Native Affairs, owned land there, and he worked with his son, Mark, to erect a dock to help bring in much-needed food, gas, and medical supplies. I remember that another group of community members, including some of my aunties and cousins, attempted to leave by car and bus across the Mercier Bridge but were confronted by an angry mob. They were pelted with stones, clubs, and other objects.

Some memories become imprinted in our bodies, our minds, and our hearts. Some of these memories are like shining lights that we can come back to: perhaps the birth of our child or winning an award we worked so hard for. Other memories are hurtful, and they leave a dark stain in our soul. Those memories cloud our vision, block our ears, and steal our voice. Clinically, psychologists say this stain is called trauma. The Centre for Addiction and Mental Health defines trauma as a lasting emotional response that often results from living through a distressing event. "Experiencing a traumatic event can harm a person's sense of safety, sense of self, and ability to regulate emotions and navigate relationships." Its definition adds, "Long after the traumatic event occurs, people with trauma can often feel shame, helplessness, powerlessness, and intense fear."

Sometimes we experience big trauma, sometimes little trauma, but in the end, all the trauma we experience adds up. Trauma can break a person. If that happens, suffering comes, whether through mental wellness challenges, addictions, spiritual afflictions, or other forms of negative coping. Trauma can make a person become disconnected from reality or simply apathetic to their own life. And sometimes if you are not broken by the trauma but are able to become resilient—yet without really healing—you become inured to the trauma. You learn to live with it.

The trauma I felt, and that many other community members felt, during the Oka Crisis was an accumulation of all the racist and hateful events we'd previously experienced. These incidents live in our bodies, but we often try to force them to fade away so that we can function. It is not normal to have the Canadian Army surround our community. It is not normal to have soldiers, armoured vehicles, and concertina wire on display. It is not normal to evacuate our homes by boat to live in a hotel, all the while wondering if non-Indigenous people would assault us there, too. It is not normal to be attacked with stones and clubs and see burning effigies and hear horrible things about your people on the news. And yet we had to keep going on as if it was normal.

Hate can be loud and obvious, but it can also be subtle. When a person hates you simply for who you are, you can sense it—even if you can't always clearly put your finger on the specifics. Experiencing hate is an insidious type of trauma. You learn to live with the hate because you are exposed to so much of it, systemic and personal, over generations. That kind of hate can numb you until you don't even realize what is considered trauma anymore.

We also become inured to hate and other trauma because, at times, we are exposed to love from people who are, in essence, our allies: people who have reached out to help our communities; those who have built positive relationships with us; and individuals who are part of the community without being Indigenous themselves. These caring people have brought some balance to the feelings of hate.

Our collective Indigenous-settler history in North America is replete with this traumatic duality of hate and love; alliances and conflicts; treaties and broken promises; optimism and pessimism. It is striking to me how similar this is to an abusive intimate partner relationship and the constant shifting between pain and love that can keep an abused partner in thrall.

On August 29, 1990, Kahnawà:ke warriors negotiated an end to their barricades. We dismantled everything, and we all made our way back home. The warriors in Kanehsatà:ke kept their barricades up a little longer, following the cancellation of the planned golf course and the federal government's promise to address their concerns, but eventually they, too, surrendered their weapons and dismantled their blockades on September 26, 1990. After seventy-eight days, from when the SQ first assaulted the barricades and Cpl. Lemay was shot until the final barricade was removed, the Oka Crisis officially ended.

I remember the overwhelming feeling of anxiety with returning home and the wonder of what would happen next. I wondered about my role in the Canadian military, and I remember decisively choosing in my mind to join the American military instead. I was convinced that I needed to learn how to defend my community. I didn't want to feel the same shame I felt when I left my community by boat. I wondered about my next semester at Dawson College, which was supposed to start soon. I wondered how I could act as if all this was normal.

After Kahnawà:ke dismantled our barricades, the Canadian military and SQ suspected that the weapons our men used to defend Kahnawà:ke against them were buried somewhere on Kateri Tekakwitha Island. On September 18, they landed several large helicopters directly on the island and unloaded military troops to search it. Some troops stayed at the only bridge onto the island so they could hold back community members who'd quickly converged, including me. The only way onto the island was over that bridge, unless you swam or boated across, so it was a bottleneck.

There were so many people, pushing and shoving to get onto the island. We all saw the helicopters landing or hovering, and we all saw that the Canadian military was right there on the island. There were even military armoured personnel carriers on the other side of the seaway with their weapons trained on the crowd. It was like the invasion we imagined would occur while the blockades were still up. They fired tear gas, and some of us scattered, while others waited until the gas dissipated. Shots were fired in the air and yet the crowd continued to protest the military's presence. Eventually, by 9 p.m. that night, they left. It was a very tense moment for all of us and still leaves a sour taste in our mouths.

So when they say the Oka Crisis ended in a peaceful "resolution," the lingering question remains: How do Canadians and Indigenous people *reconcile* something like that?

The Merriam-Webster Dictionary has several definitions for the word "reconcile":

- To restore to friendship or harmony.
- To make consistent or congruous.
- To cause to submit to or accept something unpleasant.

There are many views out there on what reconciliation is, including the belief that reconciliation is simply another form of assimilation. For me, reconciliation is not something that has an end or something that *should* ever end. It cannot be something the government puts money into and then everyone says, "Okay, have we had enough reconciliation yet?" I really believe it is a process. It is return of land. It is removing obstacles and barriers to self-determination. It is providing sufficient funding for adequate services as a form of ongoing compensation, as well as equality. It is learning and incorporating Indigenous languages and cultures across the land and not forcing English and French, two European languages and cultures, onto everyone else. It is true consultation and partnership in decisions for what happens on and with the lands.

To get to the idea of reconciliation, we need to first have conciliation, or establishing peace. To establish peace now, after all these years of suffering, we must acknowledge, and name, the wrongs that have happened, and then do something about them. Step by step, day by day, action by action. And I mean everyone must do something about them. Everyone has a responsibility. We must understand the dire situation that Indigenous communities face every day and why this situation is the direct result of the laws, policies, and practices put in place by Canada and its provinces. These policies, laws, and practices are not only historical; they continue to exist and dominate our lives.

We must do more than simply acknowledge in our history books that relations between Indigenous people and non-Indigenous people around the world were not based in peace; we must actively reverse, or change, the damaging effects of this still-existing power imbalance. We must change our society.

My hope is that we, both the Indigenous people of this land now called Canada and the non-Indigenous settlers who arrived here, can figure out a way to have peace, either by *creating* friendly relations (conciliation) or restoring them (reconciliation) for the sake of our children, our children's children, and for the next seven generations. I believe it is possible, but attitudes don't change on their own. I believe that you picked up our book for a reason, and you are reading it for a reason. As corny as it may sound, we all need to become change agents, and that takes conscious action every day. And I believe Elin and I wrote this book for exactly that reason: to help everyone become a change agent together. We're all responsible for the changes we hope for.

Below the White Surface

Elin Sandberg Miller

BRIGHT COLOURS EXPLODED in the air, lighting up the dark, cold sky over Parliament Hill. It was New Year's Eve 2016, and I had recently moved to Ottawa from Montreal with my husband and our three young children. I was watching the spectacular firework show from the Rideau Falls, near where we lived, bundled up to keep warm in the cold winter evening. I soon got caught up in the excitement around me and joined the chorus, saying "ooh" and "ahh" at the loud bursts of vivid green, red, yellow, and purple light high above me. The fireworks show was the beginning of what would be a year-long celebration of Canada's so-called 150th anniversary, marking one hundred and fifty years of confederation. Festivities went on across the country throughout 2017, but nowhere as elaborately as in Canada's capital, with Parliament Hill at its epicentre.

By then, I'd been in Canada for eight years. I first came here from Sweden as an exchange student to study international law at the University of Montreal. That's when I met my Canadian husband, and after living abroad with me for a few years, he was eager to move back home. When we settled in Montreal,

I thought I was coming to live in a country known internationally as a bastion of multiculturalism, human rights, and inclusion. And in many ways, that's exactly what Canada felt like to me. Yet I would soon discover the many other ways in which it felt the opposite.

Not long after moving into our new home, I was baffled to discover that the city was close neighbours with two First Nations reserves—Kahnawà:ke across the Saint Lawrence River to the south and Kanehsatà:ke on the North Shore. I thought the reserve system and its segregation of peoples was a thing of the past and wondered about their parallel existence, governed by another set of rules. I had so many questions, but no one I asked could tell me the answers. They had never been to either community. I kept hearing only that the reserves were the place to go for cheap cigarettes. Whatever this setup was, it didn't sound rooted in multiculturalism, human rights, or inclusion. I decided that I wanted to learn more.

One of the first books I read was *Clearing the Plains: Disease, Politics of Starvation, and the Loss of Aboriginal Life* by Canadian scholar James Daschuk. I was in a book club in Montreal where we took turns suggesting books, and it was my turn to choose. It's not a light read, and I don't think everyone got through it, but it was a revelation to me. This was when I learned about the government's starvation tactics under Canada's first prime minister, John A. Macdonald, that were used to control First Nations and, in some cases, force them onto reserves. I also learned about the introduction of the pass system, meant to confine First Nations people to their reserves. While the pass system was long gone by the time I read about it, First Nations people were still living on reserves and under very different conditions than what I saw around me in my Montreal neighbourhood.

When I later moved to Ottawa in 2016 with my family, after my husband was elected to the House of Commons in the 2015 federal election, I started working as a public servant at Global Affairs Canada. This was not long after the Truth and Reconciliation Commission had published its report and 94 Calls to Action, and the federal government had made reconciliation with Indigenous Peoples a priority. At Global Affairs Canada, I was working on renewing Canada's national action plan to advance the Women, Peace, and Security agenda. This agenda is based on a resolution adopted by the United Nations Security Council that calls on UN member states to increase women's participation in conflict resolution and peacebuilding processes and to end sexual violence in armed conflicts. During the process of renewing the action plan, the foreign minister's office asked my team to engage with National Indigenous Organizations and to include their perspectives in the plan.

This became an eye-opening experience for me, as I soon realized how little I still understood of Indigenous realities. I remember too well a large meeting my team organized to hear from these organizations: Could we build on their experiences to inform our international peace and security efforts? It was the first time we met with them, and we were in a large room, leaving us all sitting far apart. We had asked a manager to deliver a land acknowledgement, which was a first for my team. But we didn't invite an Elder or include any icebreaking activity. Probably the whole setup was wrong: It was too austere, and I remember being nervous. Our guests, however, were very gracious about it all and kindly acknowledged that there could be room for collaboration. But, they continued, before we turned outward, what about peace and security for Indigenous Peoples in Canada, and protection from sexual violence against Indigenous women? Didn't we want to address this, too?

I was mortified. On top of that, an Indigenous participant let us know afterward that the land acknowledgement had been delivered too perfunctorily. The person delivering it did their best, but this was new territory to us. We had the right intentions and were trying to do the right thing, but there was little guidance available, the Protocols were new to us, and our knowledge gap was immense. Given the government's track record of 150 years of violations and broken promises, there were some pitfalls and general skepticism to navigate, and we were not equipped for this. After that meeting, I enrolled in some courses on reconciliation and Indigenous issues offered by the Canada School of Public Service.

The training improved my knowledge and understanding. I specifically remember one online course on Missing and Murdered Indigenous Women and Girls, where all participants were asked to make presentations. I did a small presentation on the Highway of Tears in British Columbia. The Highway of Tears refers to a section of the highway between Prince Rupert on the northwest coast of British Columbia and the central interior city of Prince George, an area characterized by poverty, lack of public transportation, and several First Nations reserves. During my research, I started to better understand how socio-economic factors and inequalities create vulnerabilities, fuel racism, and lead people to exploit other human beings.

Around this time, I also did what's called the "Blanket Exercise," provided by KAIROS Canada, a Christian human rights organization. KAIROS initially developed the Blanket Exercise to introduce Canadians to the findings of the Royal Commission on Aboriginal Peoples (RCAP). The half-day exercise aims to raise awareness of the continuing injustices and impacts of colonization and to promote further learning.

The exercise started off by positioning me and the other participants, all colleagues at Global Affairs Canada, on blankets laid out on the floor, one next to the other, symbolizing Turtle Island, which is what some Indigenous nations call or used to call Canada. One of the facilitators read a text that narrates the relationship between Indigenous Peoples and settlers as it developed from pre-contact until today. As the narrator announced the number of First Nations, Métis, and Inuit who died along the way from smallpox, tuberculosis, war, or malnutrition; were moved onto reserves or otherwise relocated; were sent to residential school; or were taken from their communities in the Sixties Scoop, another facilitator asked a representative number of people to step off their blankets. Those of us who remained were forced to huddle closer and closer together as the facilitators folded up one blanket after the other, eventually pushing us off altogether. The numbers were shocking, and as we were put in the shoes of Indigenous Peoples, the messaging made its way effectively through the formality of bureaucratic dress code and workplace culture and hit us right in the heart. It was a powerful experience. Some of my colleagues left the room in tears.

In another two-day training I took on Indigenous treaties, we read and discussed different types of treaties and the government's intention behind them. We also talked about the fact that a treaty was never signed for the Ottawa area, which is why the typical land acknowledgement there talks about the *unceded* territory of the Anishinaabe Algonquin Nation. In other words, as I learned, the Algonquins in the Ottawa valley never gave up their land, not even after they had to leave it to survive. The course instructor also told us a story about Parliament Hill that I believe everyone should know. It is a tragic story that has been passed down orally through several generations of Algonquin women and more recently captured through the artistry of Algonquin painter Janet Kaponicin, which she named *The Tragic History Behind the Parliament Building*.

Of all the important and moving things I learned while taking those courses, this story has perhaps stuck with me the most. Its version of Parliament Hill sharply contrasts with what many

Canadians are taught is a symbol of unity and celebration. I wish I had known about this story that night I stood watching the fireworks on New Year's Eve. In hopes that more people will learn the truth behind the national symbol, I reached out to Janet Kaponicin to ask if I could share her story, and the story of her painting, in this book. She generously agreed.

Janet grew up in Ottawa, where she was raised by her grandmother. She still paints, in addition to her day job, but she now lives in Vancouver to be close to her daughters and to help out with her grandchildren. We met over a video call. Janet patiently answered all my questions, as she explained the real-life story behind her piece. There are actually two paintings; after the Canadian Museum of History in Ottawa bought the first and promptly put it away in storage, she painted a second, as her grandmother wanted the story known. In both versions of the painting, which are otherwise quite different, a girl is sitting on a tree trunk near the shore of the Ottawa River, birch bark canoes pulled up in front of her, and the Peace Tower of the Parliament Buildings rising high above her. Both paintings also include the girl's spirit, overseeing the scene. (The paintings are made from acrylic and birch bark, which Janet started using in honour of her grandmother, who came from a long line of birch bark canoe makers, and some of Janet's beautiful art is made completely from birch bark.) Janet heard the story from her grandmother, who in turn heard it from her great-grandmother, who was there when it took place.

Before she began sharing the story, Janet sent me a photo from approximately 1900 that depicted four generations of Kaponicin women, from her grandmother to her grandmother's great-grandmother, both named Angelique. The older Angelique, born in 1820, is a small, serious-looking woman sitting in the middle of the picture, with Janet's grandmother standing behind her and the other two women on each side. There's also a small child in the picture, who would have been Janet's uncle. The older Angelique, who was roughly age eighty when the picture was taken, was just a child herself when the events of *The Tragic History Behind the Parliament Building* unfolded in the 1820s, only forty years before confederation.

On that day, a group of Algonquin families, among them the older Angelique, were paddling up the Ottawa River, heading back to their traditional hunting grounds north of Maniwaki. They were returning from the Lake of Two Mountains outside of Montreal, where many Algonquins and other First Nations gathered during the summer months. They stopped at an Algonquin camp site below Barrack Hill, the site of British army barracks during the 1826–1832 construction of the Rideau Canal, which was a military defence project supervised by Lieutenant-Colonel John By. Janet believes the events took place around 1826 or 1827, as the circumstances indicate it was early in the construction phase. (The Algonquins had another name for Barrack Hill, Janet told me. They called it Kijik Pikwadin, or, in English, Cedar Hill, named after the large cedar trees that used to grow up there.) When the Algonquin families arrived at the camp, they were upset to find that the British soldiers had cut down many of the trees and left the place a mess, ruining much of its beauty and wildlife.

While at the camp, one of the mothers in the group realized that her daughter, a girl in her early teens, was missing. She went looking for her and spotted her from a distance, sitting on a birch stump, her hair flowing in the wind. She knew then that something was wrong, as her hair would normally be tied up in a braid or a bun. Getting closer, she saw soldiers climbing back up Barrack Hill. A group of Algonquins went to investigate and discovered that the girl was dead. She had been raped and killed, then impaled on the stump so she would sit upright. Janet explained to me that her murderers did this to give the impression that she was still alive, to give them time to escape up the hill.

Shocked and enraged, the Algonquins wanted to confront the soldiers and hold them accountable, but a Chief in the camp urged calm. He wanted to avoid an escalation and possible war. He told his people that they would instead leave that place and never return. No good would ever come of the land where this happened. And, because of the horrific way she was killed, the Algonquin girl would take care of these men herself: her spirit would haunt them. A few decades later, the Parliament Buildings were constructed on that same hill.

We think we know the places where we live, but the story about the Algonquin girl—in effect one of the first Murdered and Missing Indigenous Women and Girls—taught me that I didn't. Ottawa was founded only a few generations ago, while archaeological findings tell us that Indigenous Peoples have lived in the region for at least 6,000 years. Until settlers arrived, the Anishinaabe Algonquin people—Janet's ancestors—and other First Nations moved freely here, navigating the river, fishing, hunting, foraging, and trading. This land was their home and their livelihood. The colonial government never negotiated a treaty with the Algonquins living here or offered them compensation. After hearing Janet's story, I understood better what it must have been like for Indigenous Peoples in Canada when settlers showed up and claimed their land. And it certainly drove home the point that by living in Canada's capital, I was also living on unceded Algonquin land. There was a lot to unpack.

As I learned more about my new country, I could also better see the parallels to the colonization process in my native Sweden. Nobody spoke about reconciliation or colonization in the Swedish context while I was growing up. In fact, as the story went, Swedes had always lived in the southern part of the country and the Sami in the north—as if everyone was simply minding their own business. It was only after I started working in the International Law and Human Rights division at the Swedish Ministry for Foreign Affairs, fresh out of law school, that I learned about the ongoing land conflict between Sweden and the Indigenous Sami people. (This would have been different in the north, where the conflict between Sami and non-Sami Swedes was present in everyday life, manifesting itself in different forms. My close friend Annette, a non-Sami, grew up there, and we have since spoken much about the prejudice and overt racism against the Sami.)

The Sami people have a rich history in my homeland, but just like here, most Swedes, me included, grow up without learning about Sami culture and language, without knowing any Sami people, and with only a hazy idea at best of contemporary Sami realities. Until recently, I'd argue, the same was true of Canada.

Official discourse about reconciliation in Canada didn't really begin until 1998, when the federal government responded to the RCAP report. This excellent report outlined the persistent socio-economic inequalities between our peoples, discussed the legacy of the residential school system, and made recommendations to restructure the relationship to one based on the inherent right to Indigenous self-determination. But few of the report's recommendations were implemented, and it wasn't until the Truth and Reconciliation Commission (TRC) published its report and 94 Calls to Action in 2015 that the national reconciliation process truly took off.

When I started working at Global Affairs Canada in Ottawa, and after my team's first stumbling efforts to contribute to reconciliation, I searched these reports for guidance. I wanted to know how I could contribute to reconciliation as an individual and avoid making mistakes along the way. However, the reports are primarily directed at the federal, and to some extent, provincial governments, laying out the steps that they and other institutions, such as schools and churches, must take for reconciliation to happen. This was in 2018 or 2019, when I was taking most of the courses the department had to offer. I was learning a lot from the training, but it didn't provide the concrete guidance I wanted.

For example, since we lived on unceded territory, should my family move or even hand over our house and the land it sat on? Should white folks be giving land acknowledgements? Ought I refer to myself as a settler? I had so many questions, but even during my training, I held back. I worried my questions were stupid and my ignorance offensive. When I talked to friends and colleagues, I realized I wasn't alone. Lots of people wanted to learn and do something but were afraid to say or do the wrong thing, or they didn't know where to start. There simply wasn't much guidance available for individual Canadians at that time.

That's why I came up with the idea of *Everyday Reconciliation*. Initially, I thought of it as an online resource depository, housed on a website, which would point people like me in the right direction. I started talking to better-informed people about it and approached a couple of different organizations to see if they would be interested in housing it on their websites. Then, in 2020, I got the opportunity to present my idea to the think tank Canada 2020, which liked the idea but suggested I do a podcast instead. I was not a trained journalist and had never done anything similar, but I also didn't want to miss out on the opportunity to realize my idea. So, as scary as it was, I agreed to a ten-episode podcast that I would host and co-produce with Canada 2020. The first episode aired on September 30, 2021—Orange Shirt Day and the first National Day for Truth and Reconciliation.

In each of its ten episodes, I spoke with Indigenous leaders and experts about reconciliation and how non-Indigenous people like me could contribute to the process. Together, we focused on simple acts that anyone could do. It was a humbling experience. During our conversations, I often felt dim. I was especially embarrassed about a conversation I had with Indigenous law professor Val Napoleon about the concept of individual human rights within Indigenous legal orders. Blinded by my own perspective of human rights law as firmly anchored in the UN system or regional organizations, like the European Union or the Organization of American States, I didn't understand how they were enforced in Indigenous legal systems. I struggled to grasp her explanation and could sense her losing patience with me, but I swallowed my pride and asked again. It had been part of the plan with the podcast that I would put myself out there, and I finally had a forum to ask all my questions and allow other people to learn from them, too. I didn't want to squander it, so I asked a third time. I finally grasped that while they wouldn't have been called "human rights," and they lacked the hierarchical or international aspect that we see in our legal system, Indigenous legal orders protected individual rights, such as the right to participate in decision-making, and there was a responsibility to act on them, depending on how the community was organized.

I was grateful that my guests welcomed the opportunity to share their experiences and advice, and the only questions I regret are the ones I didn't ask. Still, planning the podcast, I was concerned that I, as a white person, was stepping into an area where I didn't belong. Many of the non-Indigenous people I spoke with expressed similar reservations, telling me I wouldn't have credibility to talk about reconciliation or that the endeavour itself could be seen as colonial. I never got this reaction from the Indigenous people I consulted about the concept, who were all supportive of the idea. And I didn't pretend to have all the answers; to the contrary, I was there to learn.

I do believe, however, that, as non-Indigenous people, we must be very careful in what we ask from Indigenous people in this process. One of the most important things that I came to understand during the podcast conversations is that raising awareness about colonization and its impacts on Indigenous Peoples cannot be the responsibility of Indigenous people. While my guests shared their time and advice, others may not be able to. Many Indigenous people are overburdened as it is and often tired of explaining the basics repeatedly. And let's face it, they are not the ones who caused this mess or closed their eyes to it for so long. Learning the truth is the first step in a reconciliation process, and it is our job as non-Indigenous people to do so.

During my research for the podcast, I did a lot of reading. I delved into reports and books about the past and, increasingly, books by contemporary Indigenous authors. I remember my husband, Marc, who in 2019 was appointed Minister of Indigenous Services, coming home with a pile of books he had been gifted, which had made CBC's Canada Reads 2020 short list. I enjoyed all five of them, but the two I liked the most were *From the Ashes* by Jesse Thistle and *Son of a Trickster* by Eden Robinson, both Indigenous writers. *From the Ashes* is a memoir that tells the story of how Thistle came to struggle with addiction and ended up homeless, living in the streets for years, including in Ottawa, before he found his way back to his Indigenous family and culture. After reading it, whenever I saw an Indigenous homeless person in Ottawa, I would think of Thistle's story and the hardships that had brought him there.

Son of a Trickster is a fictional story about an Indigenous teenage boy who grows up in a wacky family in British Columbia and must fight all kinds of supernatural creatures while his grandmother, in not a particularly helpful way, insists he's the son of a trickster, a dangerous shapeshifter. Robinson's story reminded me of the magical realism in some of my absolute favourite books from my late teens or early twenties, and I couldn't put it down. It is the first in a trilogy, and I eagerly continued with the next two. From there, I discovered one Indigenous author after the other—there are so many excellent ones—and I learned a tremendous amount about Indigenous realities and culture from reading their fiction.

It was only after I started my own reconciliation journey that Marc was appointed federal Minister of Indigenous Services and later of Crown-Indigenous Relations. While my desire to find out more about Indigenous Peoples and reconciliation was unrelated to his role, I started learning through him as well as I tagged along with him to events and even on a few trips. While I drew a strict line between his role and my work on the podcast and later this book, I had the opportunity to meet many more Indigenous people than I otherwise would have thanks to his work. Most importantly, as I planned my podcast, he suggested that I invite this guy from Kahnawà:ke, whom he knew from his time in the Canadian Armed Forces. That guy was Derek.

Six months after the last episode of my podcast aired, I took another important step on my reconciliation journey when I started learning more about the Indigenous history of the Ottawa area and the place where I lived. This was in 2022, on the National Day for Truth and Reconciliation, which falls on the same date as Orange Shirt Day. My colleague and friend Elisabeth organized an outing for our team at work to honour the day and learn more about the past. We took a self-guided walk through a trail called Chief Pinesi's Portage. Chief Pinesi lived between 1768 and 1834 and fought throughout his life to get recognition of the Algonquin's right to their ancestral lands, correctly arguing that Algonquin land that had never been ceded or sold was, by the word of the British Royal Proclamation of 1763, to remain theirs. (Although some officials were sympathetic to Chief Pinesi's claims and nobody contested the Algonquin's right to the land, in the end, all his petitions were ignored.)

Before the construction of the Rideau Canal and founding of Ottawa, Chief Pinesi and his people lived a semi-nomadic life where they spent summers in the Algonquin village at the Sulpician mission of Oka, or Lake of the Two Mountains, and travelled up the Ottawa River in the fall to their hunting grounds. His family hunting grounds were located to the south of the Ottawa River, likely centring around the confluence of the Ottawa and Rideau rivers where Ottawa sits today, possibly extending as far south as Kemptville.

Chief Pinesi had to travel farther and farther west along the Ottawa River to pursue his traditional livelihood of hunting and fishing as non-Indigenous settlements expanded along the Ottawa River and the forests were cut down, driving away bears, deer, and other animals on which they depended for food and clothing. The construction of the Rideau Canal must have been disastrous, with its dams flooding large areas and destroying fishing, a crucial Algonquin food source. The flooding of the Rideau River also destroyed burial sites, camping sites, and regional meeting locations on the islands and along the shoreline.

The trail I walked on Orange Shirt Day follows an Algonquin portage route where the Rideau and Ottawa rivers meet, around the Rideau Falls. The trail was re-created by a group called Kichi Sibi Trails that is working to revitalize traditional Indigenous routes in eastern Ontario and western Quebec. The route starts and ends in Stanley Park, where a beautiful mural was installed as part of the initiative. The mural, which was created by Algonquin artist Doreen Stevens and her daughter Charlotte, commemorates various aspects of Indigenous life and is the first Indigenous artwork to be permanently displayed in Ottawa's New Edinburgh and Rockcliffe Park neighbourhoods.

What is so striking about Chief Pinesi's Portage, besides the pretty views of the Rideau and Ottawa rivers and the forested areas along the way, is that it runs next to Rideau Hall. The Algonquins used to portage their canoes right across the land where the Governor General's official residence now sits. The Governor General is the highest representative of the state in Canada and of the colonial power that once forced Chief Pinesi and his people off this land, robbing them of their livelihood and violating them in so many ways. It was difficult to reconcile the area's beauty with its history.

Walking Chief Pinesi's Portage route gave me unique insights into Ottawa's history from an Indigenous perspective—as did Janet's story of the Algonquin girl. Today, I see the city with other eyes, often imagining what it looked like to the Indigenous Peoples who once lived here. When I pass Rideau Falls or catch a glimpse of Parliament Hill from the water side, I can almost see Algonquins paddling up the river in their birch canoes. But I know that for many people the opportunities to gain those insights into the Indigenous past of what is now known as Ottawa are rare. Canada's capital is rife with commemoration of Canadian history, but it's all about the colonizers.

When I walk around the downtown core of a Canadian city, or any Western city, I always encounter numerous statues of white men, often elevated above the rest of us on a pedestal or a horse. I'm so used to this that, until more recently, I never thought of questioning it. There are other population groups who are severely underrepresented in this display of noteworthy citizens, including women, but for a country like Canada that is built on Indigenous dispossession, it is striking that so few statues or monuments have been erected to honour and remember Indigenous leaders and events. This seems both offensive and unnatural to me, as we have, I would argue, effectively whitewashed the past.

It is typical that I found it hard to find information about Chief Pinesi. Because he was Christian, baptized as Pierre Louis Constant, and the priests in Oka liked to keep track of their "children," as they called them, it is known that he had eleven children, five of whom died before the age of ten. His father was also a Chief, as was at least one of his sons. It is likely that Chief Pinesi fought alongside the British in the War of 1812: The government keeps track of the medals it hands out, and Chief Pinesi was awarded a Peace Medal by King George III for his efforts in that war. It is also known that the British bestowed him the title of "Grand Chief" in 1830 in honour of his leadership, although this was not an Algonquin title.

In the records from the Oka mission, it is also noted that he died there by the Lake of Two Mountains—and yet his grave isn't marked. In fact, it is believed that he was buried in an area that has since been paved over. Meanwhile, the grave of his contemporary, Thomas MacKay, one of the private contractors who led the building of the Rideau Canal under Colonel By's supervision and who purchased parts of Chief Pinesi's former land with the profits he made from this, is well marked. His grave at the Beechwood Cemetery in Ottawa has been adorned with a large plaque to inform visitors about this "Great Canadian Profile."

If we care about reconciliation, we need to bring Indigenous history and perspectives to light. In some places this is already starting to happen. Take, for instance, the growing efforts to restore Indigenous place names that were previously changed by settlers and colonial surveyors. In Ottawa, for example, Elder Albert Dumont from Kitigan Zibi Anishinābeg First Nation successfully spearheaded a push to rename the scenic Sir John A. Macdonald Parkway in 2023. The parkway is a major traffic artery that runs along the Ottawa River. Thanks to the efforts of Dumont and others, it was renamed Kichi Zībī Mīkan, which means "the Great River Road" in the Algonquin language. Indigenous leaders and community members from Kitigan Zibi and the Algonquins of Pikwakanagan First Nation, the two Algonquin reserves near Ottawa, chose the name in a consultation process organized by the National Capital Commission, a federal Crown corporation. The choice is indicative of the important role the river once played for Anishinaabe Algonquin people.

Thousands of drivers now pass by the Kichi Zībī Mīkan sign every day, and many more people see the name on maps and in addresses. Renaming the road provides recognition of Algonquin history, culture, and language, and of the continuing existence of the Anishinaabe Algonquin people on this land.

I had the opportunity to reflect on the importance of acknowledging Indigenous culture and history during a family trip to Mexico in 2022. There, the Indigenous heritage feels much more present, including in Mexico City. The enormous Museum of Anthropology, for example, is one of the most visited landmarks in the city and focuses on Mexico's pre-colonial heritage. There were many interesting exhibitions, but we didn't make it past the first floor, where the enormous Aztec Stone of the Sun left us all in awe. The stone, also known as the Calendar Stone, measures twelve feet in diameter, weighs twenty-five tons, and is a representation of the Aztec cyclical concept of time and the relationship between gods and humans. While it is one of the most iconic artifacts of the Aztec culture, it has become a symbol of Mexican identity.

There are other examples of demonstrating Indigenous culture elsewhere in the world, too. Two years after our trip to Mexico, I listened to a talk by journalist and former chairperson of the Canada Council for the Arts Jesse Wente, who is Anishinaabe on his mother's side. He described his joy when he landed in New Zealand for the first time and heard Māori spoken all around him. When he visited the Museum of New Zealand in Wellington, he was struck by the focus on Māori heritage. But if you think about it, he said, it's only natural, as the Māori have lived there for so much longer than settlers. I looked up the museum online when I got home. The website is fully bilingual, in English and Māori, and the museum's Māori name, *Te Papa*, figures more prominently than its English one.

I couldn't help but compare that to Ottawa, where a person taking a stroll through town might easily get the impression that Indigenous Peoples haven't played any role in either the area's or the nation's history, contributed to the country's well-being, or perhaps even lived here. Not only is this a false narrative, but also, I imagine, one that's hurtful to the many Algonquins who are still living here.

The names we give places and the monuments we raise tell us about our history, our role in it, and our connection to these places. I think of my hometown in Sweden, Linköping. The name and city landscape meant something to me when I was growing up. For example, the large statue in the middle of the town square depicts a man on a horse who, according to my dad, is my ancestor, and the name Linköping refers to the city's origin as a marketplace—*köping* meaning just that.

When the Europeans arrived in the land we now call Canada, the mountains, rivers, lakes, and villages already had Indigenous names that conveyed a relationship between the people and the land. These names meant something to the Indigenous people who lived here and often reflected historical facts, ecological knowledge, or cultural teachings. They could also be critical for navigation and wayfinding. Yet, the Europeans deliberately renamed them, resulting in a near erasure of Indigenous place names.

Sometimes, settlers gave places names that were derived from Indigenous languages, but this doesn't mean that these were the names Indigenous people would have used. The name Ottawa, for example, is believed by historians to originate from the Algonquin word *adawe*, meaning *to trade*. After the War of 1812, the British government decided to improve its military preparedness and sent Colonel John By to build the Rideau Canal. All the construction activity resulted in the creation of a new settlement named Bytown. In 1855, it was renamed Ottawa after the Ottawa River, which had earlier been named so by settlers, presumably in reference to the river's importance as a waterway for trade. It appears as if none of the settlers thought to ask the Algonquins for the name they used. If naming the river wasn't enough, French explorer Samuel de Champlain was credited with *discovering* the river in the early 1600s, as if nobody knew it was there.

I'm an immigrant to Canada, and the longer I live here, the more I crave a sense of belonging. It's partly because I miss my family and friends in Sweden, as well as that wider network of relatives and acquaintances that make up my personal context. I also miss the sense of familiarity I felt with my physical surroundings growing up, which I took for granted. Here, even if I learned about all the names, statues, and monuments around me, they would never become part of my own background. This loss of familiarity and context has impacted me gradually over time and more than I expected when moving here.

Still, I left my homeland voluntarily, and it is still there to visit. It is very different for the people who lived in Canada for thousands of years, and continue to live here, but still lost most of their homeland. Imagine how they must feel, walking around the places where their families lived for so long, barely seeing a trace of their own history or culture. Not only would this be hurtful, but, based on what I heard from my guests on the show, I am certain they would also want Canadians to know what these places meant to their people. Sometimes, an everyday act of reconciliation may come down to learning more about where you live—and the histories hidden there.

How to Learn More About
the Place You Call Home

How much do you know about the Indigenous history and present-day realities of the land, cities, towns, and streets you call home? There are three distinct groups of Indigenous Peoples in Canada, recognized as such in the Constitution: First Nations, Inuit, and Métis. They have their own unique histories, languages, cultural practices, and spiritual beliefs. According to the 2021 Census, more than 1.8 million people in Canada identify as Indigenous, representing 5 percent of Canada's total population. Of that, First Nations make up the largest share at 1.2 million people. They are a greatly diverse group, living in over 630 communities across Canada and belonging to more than fifty Nations that speak just as many different Indigenous languages. In this book, First Nations is the group we have written the most about, since Derek is First Nations and Elin lives on First Nations territory, and we speak of our own experiences.

You might find yourself living on First Nations territory or on the historic homeland of the roughly 600,000 Métis in Canada. The word "métis" comes from the French verb "métisser," to mix races or ethnicities. But while Métis have mixed Indigenous and European ancestry, their name (with a capital M) means more than that. It refers to communities of people who developed along the fur trade routes and across the Northwest, emerging as a distinct Indigenous people with their own shared history, culture, and language (Michif) during the late 18th century. The historic Métis Nation homeland encompasses the

Prairie provinces of Manitoba, Saskatchewan, and Alberta and extends into contiguous parts of Ontario, British Columbia, the Northwest Territories, and the northern United States. In 1870, the Métis provisional government led by Louis Riel negotiated the entry of the Red River Settlement into the confederation as the Province of Manitoba.

If you're in the North, your reconciliation may begin with the Inuit, whose population numbers about 70,000 people. The word "Inuit" means "the people" in the Inuit language of Inuktut. Many Inuit in Canada live in Inuit Nunangat, which means "the place where Inuit live," or the Inuit homeland, which is comprised of four regions: Inuvialuit (in the Northwest Territories and Yukon), Nunavik (in Northern Quebec), Nunatsiavut (in Labrador), and Nunavut (its own territory). There are many dialects of Inuktut, which is the umbrella term for the Inuit languages spoken across Inuit Nunangat, including, for example, Inuvialuktun, Inuinnaqtun, Inuttitut, and Inuktitut. Inuktitut has official status in Nunavut, along with Inuinnaqtun, English, and French. Nunavut was separated officially from the Northwest Territories in 1999, and the Nunavut Land Claims Agreement provided the territory to the Inuit for self-governance.

Whether you are new to these lands, or you have been living here for generations, we challenge you to learn more about the Indigenous People(s) who lived on the lands around your home before settlers moved there—and who could live there still. You might begin by discovering the answers to the following questions:

· Were they nomadic or more sedentary? Did they grow crops or primarily trap and hunt?
· How did they interact with other Indigenous nations?
· What happened when settlers moved into the area?
· Which residential school were their children sent to?

Next, you might learn more about how Indigenous people in your area live today. For example:

· Do they live in an urban setting or in their own, separate community? If so, how and when did that community originate?
· What are their cultural and spiritual traditions and celebrations?
· Who are some well-known people from there, including, for example, musicians, athletes, scientists, or politicians?
· Who were their political leaders when settlers arrived, and who are their leaders today?
· What Indigenous language does the community speak? How do you say "hello" and "thank you" in that language?

There are many avenues to learn more about your area's Indigenous past and present, including through books and educational lectures. When you move around in your neighbourhood, look out for any signs of its Indigenous past in place names and monuments. In many towns and cities, there are organizations that offer Indigenous walking tours—take one! Most communities will have a website where you can find out more information, such as culturally appropriate opportunities to engage, including events that are open to the public. Friendship centres and urban Indigenous cultural centres may also organize activities where non-Indigenous people are welcome to participate. Be curious and respectful if you attend, and remember you are a guest in the community.

Using a community's own language, if only a few words, will help build a connection or relationship with them. In Kanien'kéha, for example, the most common way of saying "good morning" is senhniseri'iohstha (pronounced suh-nee-zay-ree-yoh-stah), "hello" is shé:kon (pronounced say-go) or kwe (pronounced gweh), and "thank you" is niá:wen (pronounced nya-wah). "Hello" in the Algonquin language is also kwe, or kwe-kwe, usually spelled kwey. "Thank you" in the Algonquin or Ojibwe language, Anishinaabemowin, is miigwech (pronounced mee-gwetch).

Taking these kinds of everyday, simple steps to learn more about Indigenous people can make a big difference in the lives of Indigenous and non-Indigenous people alike. Not only do non-Indigenous people learn more about the places they call home and the history of the land they occupy, but their search for learning also pushes our wider society to become more inclusive of Indigenous people, culture, and knowledge. The more people demand Indigenous voices and perspectives, the more our institutions adjust to provide them. So keep learning—and encourage others to do the same.

Part II: Land

The Ever-Shrinking Blanket

Derek Aronhie:nens Montour

IN DECEMBER 2020, representatives of Harjit Sajjan, who was at the time the federal minister of national defence, called me to set up a meeting. The minister wanted to discuss my potential participation on an advisory panel on systemic racism and discrimination. To say I was surprised is an understatement, but I was also interested. Minister Sajjan was passionate about creating change in Canada, particularly when it came to thoroughly investigating discrimination in the military. During our meeting, he explained that the defence team had received many disturbing reports, including of white supremacists in the ranks, incidences of sexual assaults and harassment, micro-aggression toward members of minority races, pervasive gender bias issues, and so on. We also talked of the 1990 Oka Crisis, and he expressed Canada's need to create policies to ensure that its military is not called upon to act against its own population, including against Indigenous people.

Minister Sajjan also explained that the advisory panel's role over the next year would be to talk directly with service members, both in junior and senior ranks; to review policies with an eye to identifying opportunities for improvement; and to provide concrete examples of what the chain of command could do to act against discrimination, racism, and sexism in the military. We would be required to submit a final report of our recommendations by December of 2021. I felt tentatively enthusiastic about this potential opportunity, but I also felt that sense of acceptance/non-acceptance that I spoke of in my previous essay. It was the feeling of whether I was on the "right" side or not if I chose to participate; the feeling of whether I should be ashamed of putting my name out there and potentially being judged by Indigenous and non-Indigenous people. In the end, I agreed to participate because I feel that if we do not take intentional steps to help effect change and to be optimistic about it, change will never occur.

I had the privilege of working with three amazing panel members: Major-General Ed Fitch (ret'd), Major Sandra Perron (ret'd), and Captain Door Gibson (ret'd). All three came from diverse backgrounds and were deeply invested in supporting change for all service members. A member of the Jewish faith, Ed experienced first-hand the aggression that white supremacy can bring. As the first female Canadian infantry officer, Sandra directly experienced challenges of sexual harassment and gender bias. And as a Black Canadian, Door rose through the enlisted ranks to achieve the rank of captain, despite the racism and discrimination she experienced. They each opened my eyes to new perspectives and worldviews that I would otherwise not have experienced.

At one point during the work, the four of us were having a discussion on land acknowledgements: the purpose, the value, and, for us, the big question of who should offer a land acknowledgement, a settler or an Indigenous person, and when. While we were discussing this, Ed made a comment that has stuck with me all these years later: "It is all about the land, though, isn't it?"

He was referring to the idea that without a proper land base and without resolution of the land claims and land issues, First Nations will be continually confronted with economic, social, and political challenges. And Canada will continue to be faced with conflict and discrimination in its struggle to reconcile with its colonial past. It struck me that even a non-Indigenous Canadian recognized the need to address land issues in Canada.

Throughout our year of working together on the panel, we talked a lot about where our roles on the panel began and ended, how much impact the minister of national defence can have in comparison to the Canadian Parliament, and how there is still a need for Canada, and Canadians, to grapple with the many injustices related to land and Indigenous people. In the end, our final report consisted of three sections: a brief history of how we, collectively, got to the situation we are in; a vision of what a diverse and equitable defence team could look like; and thirteen identified areas of opportunity for action and recommendations for change. We tried our best to touch on many of the areas our vast mandate encompassed, recognizing we were really only hitting the tip of the iceberg. For example, our first recommendation suggested the defence team might consider its previous forty-one inquiries, climate surveys, and reviews, which together had generated more than 240 recommendations. How had they addressed these past areas of opportunity?

We also focused on Canada's need to redefine its relationship with Indigenous people, including the need for an improved education curriculum for all Canadian school systems; the need for military leaders to seek guidance and mentorship from Indigenous people; the need to initiate dialogue on the return of land or compensation; and even, given the desire for self-determination, the need for military leaders to look at establishing alliances. Although we decided the panel's recommendations could only extend so far, we also knew that without a real conversation about land—one that honestly and openly reckons with the damage done to Indigenous people and acknowledges the stolen land—we, settlers and Indigenous people alike, will be in constant conflict and disagreement.

In the years since our panel gathered, I have thought often about Ed's comment, as well as about subsequent conversations with Elin, my co-author, which have grappled with Indigenous land issues and how to encourage understanding and subsequent action that all Canadians can take part in. I understand it can be difficult for everyday Canadians, who this book is aimed at reaching, to think about what they can do when it comes to the subject of land. It's easy, and perhaps even tempting, to say, "It's the government's problem, not mine."

When an issue appears so big, we tend to absolve ourselves of responsibility and action—we don't see how we can possibly make a difference. But there are many ways that non-Indigenous people can contribute to better land relations. The first step is seeking to understand how we got here and how colonial forces have disrupted, damaged, and reshaped Indigenous land, culture, and life. All Canadians, and those immigrants seeking to become Canadians, must seek to understand how Canada came to be and how Indigenous people are continuing to be impacted by that history.

Land was at the centre of the Oka Crisis, as it is for so many of the most contentious First Nations issues facing Canada today. Understanding land issues, and the push to act in relation to land, has sparked the Land Back movement across Canada. The movement is fundamentally about asserting Indigenous rights to self-governance, including the right to land use and resource management. The movement is seen as a vital step in decolonization by reclaiming land, water, and resources for Indigenous nations who were dispossessed through colonization and treaty violations.

Land beats at the heart of the Wet'suwet'en Nation's protest against the gas pipelines in the west; at the heart of the 2024 Supreme Court of Canada decision that found both the federal and the Ontario governments dishonourably breached their financial obligations to the Anishnaabe people under the Robinson treaties; and it's at the heart of the lobster trapping battles in the east as the Mi'kmaq Nation try to assert their right to fish for sustenance. Though I cannot know for sure, I would bet that every Indigenous community in what is called Canada has or has had a struggle with land issues, whether it's a question of "ownership" (and therefore who is occupying the land), resource extraction, commercial use, protection against pollution, or even the fight to preserve sacred lands such as burial grounds.

At the same time, many Canadians, especially ones new to the country, don't seem to understand why these struggles persist. I have heard many variations of what people seem to consider the truth. People say things like: *Didn't we beat them in a war and win the land? Didn't they give the land to us in a treaty? Didn't they sell it? Don't our taxes pay for the land already?* And even, unbelievably, *I thought this land was barely even occupied and our ancestors just moved onto empty space!*

It would take volumes of books to discuss and highlight each individual Indigenous nation's land challenges, but there is a story behind each one. While I cannot do justice to all their journeys and challenges in this small book, I can try to highlight what my relationship to our nation's land was like for me. As a teenager in 1990, our community's relationship with our land came into sharp focus during the Oka Crisis, but it wasn't until I returned to the community as an adult, after serving in the Marines for a decade, that I started to better understand our history.

My relationship with our own land is complex and not always what I would have liked it to be. I also despair when trying to think about how I can adequately describe the colonial impact on Kahnawà:ke, particularly when so many other writers have done a much better job than I could hope to do, but all I can do here is try my best, sharing with you what I've learned as an adult and the memories of my childhood that I feel distinctly colour my own growing understanding.

The history of our community is intertwined with the history of colonialism and so-called colonial progress, and I think it is important to understand some of that history. Without such context, it becomes difficult to see the impacts as they are today. What's more, I believe it is vital for Canadians to understand the link between colonialism and the land precisely because the central aspect of colonialism is disconnection. To be successful, colonialism had to disconnect people from the land, and to achieve that, its agents also had to force a disconnection from our language, culture, nations, communities, and even within our families. And the more colonized and assimilated an Indigenous nation or community became, the more conflict it experienced, and the more suffering the people experienced—until the caring for the land was not a priority anymore. Simple survival and coping were.

In my role as executive director of our Kahnawà:ke Shakotiia'takehnhas Community Services (KSCS), I have seen first-hand the conflict our people are dealing with in our lives, as well as our attempts at coping with the trauma and suffering we have all experienced. I also act as our community's representative at the quarterly health and social service directors' meetings of the First Nations in Quebec and Labrador Health and Social Services Commission (FNQLHSSC). These meetings include representatives from the twenty-eight non-treaty First Nations in Quebec, and although the representatives from Labrador have a standing invitation to join us, they usually are not present. The meetings are an opportunity to dialogue, share best practices, and lean on each other's shoulders when the going gets tough in our own communities. They also allow us a chance to see the whole forest instead of only the trees in front of us.

In addition to all this, for several years now, I've also had the honour of serving on the seven-member board of directors of the FNQLHSSC, which is elected by the health and social services directors. This has provided me with an amazing opportunity to understand what happens in other communities throughout the region and across these lands. During these opportunities to "sit around the fire," so to speak, I get a glimpse of what life was and is like for the other nations that attend. The Algonquin tell me of their trap lines, how they manage the pelts and fur, their cabins and hunting sites in the forests, and their attempts at catching walleye and bass up in Kebaowek or Pikogan. The Mi'kmaq show me how they craft amazing beaded powwow attire and share stories of salmon fishing, lobster trapping, and moose hunting in Listuguj and Gesgapegiag. The Innu tell me of their fishing, goose hunting, and chasing the caribou.

When I visited Uashat, an Innu community located within the city of Sept-Îles, several years ago, I had a chance to eat goose and caribou that one of the directors had hunted and caught. As I was enjoying our meal, I was surprised to realize I had never before eaten goose or caribou. And in fact, I have experienced a lot of firsts as I have been connecting with other First Nations communities. All across Quebec, my brothers, sisters, and cousins from other communities tell me how wonderful it was to grow up *on the land* and how much they cherish every opportunity to be out there again, especially as our communities' face so many challenges.

These conversations made me consider my childhood and my own relation to the land. While my colleagues spoke of hunting and trapping, I remembered a train bridge, an abandoned quarry, a golf course, and the dredge from the Seaway. When I think about my own relation to the land, it's hard not to also think of the challenges my community faced. I don't remember any trapping or hunting, and although I have some wonderful memories, they are all coloured by the impact of colonialism.

In Kahnawà:ke, life used to centre around the St. Lawrence River, which was vital to our way of living. The river fed us, took us places, connected our community with other First Nations communities, and gave us all the fresh water we needed. When the Seaway was built in the late 1950s, it changed everything for my people. The St. Lawrence Seaway Act was passed in 1954, and two short years later the Seaway opened, the federal government having expropriated 1,262 acres of Kahnawà:ke's land in the process. The Seaway is essentially a thirty-foot-deep, three-hundred-foot-wide water trench that allows ships to pass from the Great Lakes to the Atlantic. It is striking to see the difference between before and after. We used to be able to go directly to the river's shores, with houses built facing the river and everyone having regular access to waterside activities. After the Seaway was created, the community faced the daily passage of commercial ships, while across the river, we saw the shoreline development of non-Indigenous communities.

Although some community members were willing to negotiate with the St. Lawrence Seaway Authority (SLSA), many felt the negotiations were exploitive, dominated by a colonial-settler mindset. Everyone agreed on the tragic impact the loss of the river had on our community. We all strived to be connected to the river despite being completely cut off from it. My family was no different.

One of the happiest childhood memories I have with my dad is from when I was roughly eight years old, in 1980 or so. That day, my dad took my older brother Craig and me to the Flat Rocks to fish for the first time. The Flat Rocks are a shallow spot in the swift-running St. Lawrence River. The rocks are smooth and allow you to wade quite far out without hurting your feet. This has made the Flat Rocks a long-time popular spot for picnicking, swimming, and fishing. But now, to get there on foot, we had to walk the train bridge going over the Seaway. We would wait until the bridge was down, because sometimes ships pass throughout the day and sometimes the Canadian Pacific Railway operators didn't want to let us cross. When the rail was clear and the bridge down, we would carefully step over the tracks, tie by tie, to get across the Seaway.

We could have taken the long way around by car. To do so, we would have had to drive down to Ste. Catherine, a non-Indigenous community located immediately outside Kahnawà:ke where the seaway locks are, cross over to the North Wall, and then drive all the way back. But not only was that a twenty-minute car ride depending on whether the locks were open, and assuming you had a car, it was also not an *adventure*. Crossing the bridge was an adventure to an eight-year-old. Older kids would even jump off that bridge—later on, I did it myself a time or two—but that day, on my first crossing, I was scared out of my pants. My dad reassured us, probably held our hands as we crossed, and we eventually got over safely.

Today, I remember the feeling of accomplishment, the sense of adventure, and the joy as my dad helped us hook worms on our lines and showed us how to cast and reel. I try to imagine what our life would be like if we all had regular access to that side of the river. Thinking about it now, it doesn't seem that far away, and yet, it is like a psychological wall has been erected between our people and the river. Perhaps if the community would have developed it more and built campgrounds or picnic areas, we could have broken that wall down. I look far across the river and see the residents of the city, in LaSalle or Lachine, enjoying the shoreline all the time, and I think of how unfair it is. And yet, I am also inspired today by all the parents taking the children out and enjoying the land as best they can.

Similar feelings surface as I remember swimming at the old Bedard Quarry, located at the west end of our village. Today, the quarry is filled with water, but back when I was a teenager, the water had only reached halfway up. The quarries in Kahnawà:ke had some of the best rock for Montreal's construction needs and helped build the Lachine Canal and many of Montreal's bridges. Companies started mining in Kahnawà:ke as far back as the 1820s, and at some point, not too long before I was born, they stopped pumping the water out of the Bedard Quarry and let it fill, deserting the whole thing.

We weren't really allowed to swim at the Bedard Quarry—like other parents in the community, my mom and dad felt it was too dangerous—but we went anyway. (My parents were right; people have drowned there.) I remember some of the braver guys and gals jumping from Tarzan Cliff, one of the highest jump points, which I don't recall attempting myself. There were other jump spots that were a bit lower that I managed to get the nerve for, but no matter where we jumped from, I remember that sense of adventure climbing down the steep quarry walls.

It is striking to me now how a child's happy memory of an adventure was also the result of colonialism and the taking of resources from the land. This memory is not one of using the land in its natural state, like that of some of my friends from other First Nations communities, but is instead forever connected to a massive by-product of colonialism. The giant holes in the ground leftover from mining permanently changed the shape and ecosystem of our land. And they are far from the only scars of colonialism. My childhood is marked by this dual reality: adventure and colonialism. Too many memories of fun times also now come with the wonder, and anger, of what might have been.

The third swimming spot we often went to stay cool in the hot summer was right next to the Onake Paddling Club—and also the result of the seaway. When I think of it now, this memory does not just bring back a sense of adventure but also one of anger. When the Seaway was created, the soil they dredged to form the canal was lifted and deposited throughout the community. Some of it was placed in what is now known as the Clay Mountains on the east of the village; the area is now home to residences that could get sufficient drainage through the clay soil. Other soil was dumped in the west, where the Grand Trunk Railroad ended and the old ferry used to be. This essentially closed off Johnson's Beach, where my aunties and uncles used to swim, as the water no longer circulated and became choked with weeds.

This soil in the west became a man-made island now known as Kateri Tekakwitha Island. The island became part of our community. After being empty for several years, it became home to the marina, where the few community members who still fished would store their boats, and it hosted our Fireman's Field Day, which was a parade around the community culminating in a day of events and celebration of our volunteer firefighters. After 1990, the community started an annual powwow there as a way to create peace and positive energy within the community on the same grounds. Our paddling club, Onake (meaning "birch bark canoe" in Kanien'kéha), was founded in 1972 as a way of helping youth find a good path and stay connected to the river and was also located near there. Paddlers would circle the island as part of their training.

Next to Onake, there was the small bridge, about ten feet high, that connected the island to the mainland. This was our swimming spot. We loved to jump from the bridge, often daring each other to time it for when the ships came by. It was fun—and dangerous. When a ship comes through the Seaway, the suction from the engines pulls anyone in the nearby water toward the ship. To avoid being sucked under, you must swim as strong as you can in the opposite direction. I almost drowned there once because I was trying to hold on to the pier as the ship passed by, and the force of the water was too strong. I was sucked under and bobbed up about halfway to the ship. If not for the quick actions of my friend Allen Patton, who jumped in and grabbed my arm to pull me up, I surely would have gone under.

Today, when I think about those summers, I think about all that adventure, and I also think about the long reach of colonialism. The paddling club and Johnson's Beach are still there, but the water is stale and overgrown from the sediment that has built up over the years after the Seaway cut the area off from the fresh, fast-running water of the St. Lawrence River. We have adapted by creating a walking path and building a beach in another spot, and our environment team is planting more trees on the island to encourage wildlife. As much as we are trying to do, it is not a perfect situation. The community is adapting and rebuilding from all these impacts of colonialism, but the onus of this healing process is squarely on us, the people who were harmed, to resolve.

Of course, it isn't just our relationship with Kahnawà:ke water that has been reshaped by colonial interference. Back in the early 1900s, a group of golfers from the Outremont Golf Club wanted something bigger than their nine-hole club. They signed a ninety-nine-year lease with a community member named Meloche to acquire 65 acres of land in Kahnawà:ke. The Kanawaki Golf Club opened for play in 1914 and spans a swath of land between the road leading to the Mercier Bridge, the rail tracks for CN, and the former Grand Trunk. Much of the embankments used to prepare the rail tracks were also taken from the area, and both swampy areas and densely wooded spots all needed to be cleared.

Throughout the years, Kanawaki became a fixture in the community, and its golfers—none of them locals—received various accolades. While Kahnawà:ke community members were not allowed to play there or become members, many of us worked as caddies, in the pro shop or in the clubhouse. That has since changed, with the signing of a new twenty-five-year lease extension in December 2021, and Kahnawà:ke community members can now become members at the course. In 2046, the land the golf course sits on is expected to be returned to community control, with both common and private land ownership.

But back when I was a thirteen-year-old kid, I remember trudging across the highway in the early morning, then walking to the caddy shop to get in line, waiting for my turn to carry a bag. Often, I'd arrive only to find the older boys and men had already beaten me there. As caddies it was our job to carry the clubs, find the ball, hand the golfer his or her next club, and stay out of their way. Some of the better caddies would provide advice and suggestions to the golfer, but I wasn't one of them. I hated golf (and to be honest, kind of still do). I did like being outside, though. As kids, we would play outside every chance we got, and as a teen who was now expected to keep busy to stay out of trouble, at least I had a chance to do so outdoors.

I also liked the money. If we worked two bags in the morning and another two in the afternoon, we could usually make $50 or more, depending on tips. It was exhausting work, and I often skipped the afternoon. I always remember the feeling of how unfair it seemed: Indigenous teenagers and adults serving the rich non-Indigenous golfers who came to our land for their own recreation. And it is striking how different these experiences of "enjoying the outdoors" that I had as a child, embedded again in colonialism, are compared to friends from other First Nations communities.

The closest thing I had to the wild was going with the Kahnawà:ke Youth Center to a camp in Ste-Lucie-de-Doncaster, which we call Tioweró:ton. Like much of our land's history, the history of the camp is complex and marked by colonialism. Under the 1851 federal "Act to authorize the setting apart of lands for the use of Indian Tribes in Lower Canada," a maximum of 230,000 acres was marked for the use of Indigenous communities in Quebec and created the current location of the reserves. Even today, the act provides the ongoing legal framework for legal land issues. During the establishment of this critical legislation, despite having the opportunity to negotiate treaties in Ontario, both Canada and Quebec chose not to do so with the nations in southern Quebec. The act was forced on us. Following this, in 1853, an Order in Council established a land allotment of a 16,000-acre plot in the Doncaster Township near Mont Tremblant for Kahnawà:ke and Kanehsatà:ke to co-manage. The land was intended to provide the two Kanien'kehá:ka communities with access to hunting and fishing, although the hunting and fishing were quite limited on that territory. Given this, it was not much used at first by the communities, so much so that non-Indigenous squatters and the local municipality requested the reserved land be abolished as it interfered with colonization of their townships. The communities began using the land more frequently in the mid-1900s, and today many families have cabins and shelters to spend time in during the summer months, with some community members living there year-round. On maps and according to the government, the land is still called Doncaster despite our communities always calling it Tioweró:ton.

When I was a child, it truly felt like I had entered the wilderness. The youth centre organized trips up to the land for exactly that purpose: to allow our youth a chance to play in the woods and enjoy the land. We would play at the falls and swim in the creek, chase small animals in the woods and get eaten alive by mosquitoes and black flies. I was not able to go up there very often, as it is about an hour and a half by car, which doesn't seem that far now, but as a child felt like another country. Even today, it is our community's mini refuge. And whenever I have a chance to go up there and visit the cabins of friends, it feels the same as it did when I was a kid. Being there is a way to find peace while living so close to the city. More and more community members are asking for a plot of land, building a cabin, and spending time in the summer with their families there.

When I first became a father in my twenties and then again in my forties, I wanted to make sure my own children were somehow connected to Kahnawà:ke—especially because they were not able to grow up living there. I have two sons, and both of their mothers are not Indigenous. In 1981, our community implemented a membership policy, which later became community law, called "marry out, move out." It required community members to leave the community if they chose to marry a non-Indigenous person. I grew up always knowing that if I ended up falling in love with a non-Indigenous person and had children, I would not be able to raise my children in the community. Our community Elders have decided to limit the number of mixed families who are able to live within the community territory. Simply put, there are limited resources, especially land.

The community had to ask itself, "Where do we draw the line?" The reality is that our territory started small and only got smaller as time went on. I understand, at least cerebrally, why we as a family are not able to live in the community, but it also hurts to feel disconnected. As a natural result, we, meaning all First

Nations living outside our communities, become less involved in community events and less aware of the daily occurrences in the community. Our children make fewer friends in the community, and we make more choices to spend our time away. We become more assimilated. That is, unless we make conscious efforts to stay connected.

When I was in the Marines, I expected to spend my life away from the community, and I really didn't think about the impact of not raising a child there. When I was twenty-one and stationed in California, I met, fell in love with, and married an American woman, Kristin. Our son, Trevor Tioronhiate, was born in 1995 in California. Two years later, our family moved to Michigan when I became a recruiter for the Marines. The marriage didn't work out, and we eventually divorced. Trevor stayed living in Michigan with his mom, while I moved back home and rebuilt my life, visiting as often as I could. Trevor, and his longtime girlfriend Kati, are now married, and they have their own beautiful baby girl, Amilia, and they have chosen to build their life in Michigan, as their families are there, too. Trevor's connection to Kahnawà:ke is limited, at best; he has visited of course, and we always make his family feel welcome, but he doesn't have his roots there, and I think that makes a big difference in feeling like you belong. I think even his connection to being First Nations is more limited as his integration into non-Indigenous society is more complete.

In 2011, I started dating and quickly fell in love with Afroditi, my life partner. Afroditi, a second-generation immigrant from Greece, and I met through work and have committed to walking this life journey together. We live in Montreal, in the neighbourhood she grew up in, only a few doors from where her mom lives, and not far from her sister and her family. I travel to Kahnawà:ke every day for work, while Afroditi works to the north of the city. Our son, Achilles Karonhiahatie, was born in 2012 in Montreal.

The choices we are making on how to raise him in the best way we can are a constant source of discussion between us. Our son speaks English, French, and Greek fluently, and the three of us are learning Kanien'kéha together. We are teaching him what we can about camping and the wilderness. Every day, we also make choices about fitness and health. Choices to teach him the differences in Greek culture, Kanien'kehá:ka culture, Canadian culture, and Quebecois culture. Choices about schools and learning what is not taught in school. Choices about belief and having the freedom to believe what you want. Choices about family dynamics and how to deal with conflict.

Despite working every day to better my community and our community members and fighting for the rights of all Indigenous people, I accept that my family's path is a different one than living in the community itself. I suppose I took a cue from my father in that I chose my partner with my heart, regardless of her ancestry. My children will have their own journeys to walk, just like I have done, but I wanted them to start their journeys with their most important connection—to Kahnawà:ke. I was taught that this process starts at birth, by burying the placenta and umbilical cord in Kahnawà:ke so that a child can be grounded to the community and thus rooted to the land. This helps ensure they always feel connected to home.

When Trevor was born in California, I took a small, dried piece of his umbilical cord home with me in a small leather bag and buried it in my mother's backyard. When Achilles was born in Montreal, at St. Justine's Hospital, it was more difficult to convince the staff to let us take home the umbilical cord and the placenta. They told us it was biohazard waste. Afroditi persisted, talking to the administration and having an Elder write a letter on our behalf. She did not give up until the hospital finally relented, and we received a piece of his umbilical cord. Just like my older son's cord, we buried it in my mom's backyard, conducting a small ceremony to ask the Creator to watch over him in the coming years. Doing this was my way of saying "this is your land, too," to my sons, even if they may not be able to live there. We wanted them to feel connected to this land, its people, and their communities.

This can be a difficult task when my own understanding of our traditional ways is often spotty at best. When we performed the umbilical cord ceremony, for instance, I was not sure of all the right words. I try to grow my understanding more every day, as so many of us do, in the small ways that I can. But I am also shy and feel shame for not knowing. Many of us feel that same sense of cultural shame—the shame of not knowing our own culture. It can even make us reluctant to try to speak our language or to learn about culture and its traditions. We are all trying our best to overcome this, and it is through supporting each other and encouraging each other to keep trying that we will change and begin to feel better about ourselves.

When I was growing up, though, the cultural shame was almost palpable. As kids we felt it. Perhaps we knew we were becoming so assimilated. Instead of a naming ceremony in the Longhouse, we attended a baptism in the church. Instead of rites of passage guided by our uncles and aunties, we drank alcohol and had sex as teenagers. I remember that when my dad died, we learned that his wishes were to have both a burial feast by a traditional Elder and a Catholic ceremony in the church. I was twenty-six years old, and I found his wishes both familiar and foreign, and I struggled to understand. The church part was easy enough to get. I grew up going to church and went to a Catholic high school. But the burial feast, which would be performed by our Elder, Otsi'tsaken:ra, felt unfamiliar. I had not experienced one before that.

Otsi'tsaken:ra explained to us that when we die, our spirit travels the earth, visiting all the places our spirit wants to see again and the people we have missed. After ten days, it is important to conduct a ceremony to explain to our spirit that it is time to leave this world and all our possessions here and to travel on. We eat a meal, usually the deceased person's favourite meal when they were alive, to provide us nourishment in our journey. A plate of this food is set aside near their remains, and then whatever food is left over from the guests' meal is added to their plate. We bury the leftover food in the woods so the animals can eat as well. I remember travelling the next day, with both my brothers, to the woods, and the three of us said our goodbyes to our dad once again. It was all new to us and yet, strangely enough, somehow familiar. It was a way to reconnect with ourselves and our spirits. And to me, that is what ceremony really is: connection.

I've shared my personal history of colonialism and how it disconnected me from my community's history and land, but it's also important to consider the longer history of colonialism and how and where the roots of that disconnection began. Much early history is written of the European nations and their wars—to the point that many people have at least a general idea of what happened in the centuries between the fall of the Roman Empire and the so-called Age of Discovery. For many years, the colonial education system has reinforced such Eurocentric learning. In the land we call Canada, this has meant reinforcing the belief that the people living here when the settlers arrived were simply *savages* or *uncivilized*. Overall, schoolbooks have been written from this settler perspective, explaining this country's history largely for the benefit of other settlers. Our Indigenous history is untold or, at the very least, extremely limited.

That alternate history exists, however, and it's one that must be told more often in these lands now called Canada. It is the history of Indigenous people. Each part of this land has a different

Indigenous nation who once inhabited it, with a rich heritage and culture, their own Creation Story and history. Understanding history helps us to understand much of the current environment. The fundamentally different outlook and way of organizing our societies—namely hierarchy and supreme ruler versus egality and consensus—has resulted in irreconcilable intentions and misunderstandings when it comes to land. Settlers were used to decision-making processes in which the other party could be overruled, whereas Indigenous people assumed there had to be agreement.

Long before the first settler arrived, five First Nations joined together to form the Haudenosaunee Confederacy, making it one of the largest allied groups of nations. This moment is a significant part of our Creation Story and history, and although our oral history does not give a date based on the Christian calendar, it's believed the Confederacy was formed as early as 1142 CE. At the time, the unending warfare between the nations was destroying them, and so the Kaianerekowa (Great Law of Peace) was created to end the incessant fighting.

Together the Oneida, Onondaga, Cayuga, Seneca, and Kanien'kehá:ka helped form one of the strongest chains of nations. We supported each other through a complex system of clan-based political appointments, clan intermarriages, and consensus-based decision-making. Today, the Creation Story, the formation of the Confederacy, the formation of our clans, and the creation of the Great Law all remain essential components of how we define ourselves and how we view our world.

As I shared in "Reconciling with Hate," my ancestors, the Kanien'kehá:ka, were known as the Keepers of the Eastern Door within the Haudenosaunee Confederacy, and the land our villages occupied ranged from near Albany, New York, to Montreal, Quebec, and down past Niagara, Ontario. Our war parties ranged much farther. Some experts say our journeys stretch north to Lake Mistassini, south to Florida, east to the Atlantic, and west to the Mississippi. According to our oral history, the Confederacy has always occupied the land now called the St. Lawrence River Valley, and some experts say our Traditional Territory extended all the way up to what is now called Quebec City (or Stadacona previously)—although always in close contact with other nations that the Haudenosaunee Confederacy had to defend against, such as the Wendat, the Tobacco, the Neutral, the Mahican, and so many more.

Everything changed after the settlers arrived. French explorer Samuel de Champlain first encountered the Kanien'kehá:ka in 1609 in a skirmish where many of our people were killed. That event kicked off a conflict that lasted almost a century between the French and Haudenosaunee. Complicating all this was further shifting conflict, power plays, and alliances between the British and the Dutch. They all wanted our land and our resources—namely furs. The next century was marked by what is, in settler history, commonly referred to as the Indian Wars or the Beaver Wars. These wars involved the competition between the French, English, and Dutch for control of the very lucrative fur trade, particularly beaver pelts, by using their respective Indigenous allies against each other. These wars waged on until the American War of Independence, eventually fracturing the Haudenosaunee Confederacy in the process.

It feels like nearly every textbook today still talks of these wars and how the colonists arrived and survived in these "new" lands. Alternate historical references, important to my people, are the oral and written treaties we made with these new settlers. These treaties recognized the sovereignty of Indigenous Peoples, though it later became clear that settlers had expected Indigenous Peoples to acknowledge them as the supreme rulers of all this land, "surrendering" enormous tracts of it for European settlement. The many histories regarding these wars, and the journeys of the nations involved in them, give a sense of the shifting currents that the First Nations struggled to stay afloat in. For now, I will focus on the Haudenosaunee Confederacy and Kahnawà:ke's history because it is the one that is most closely tied to my own history.

Kahnawà:ke was established in 1667 when a band of Kanien'kehá:ka settled and established a village south of Montreal. We became one of the most well-known—then and now—First Nations communities in Canada. We have always lived by a river, for transportation, fishing, and fresh water, and we have also always been farmers with our staple vegetables of corn, beans, and squash, which we call the Three Sisters. These three vegetables grow exceptionally well together, and they complement each other's needs perfectly: The corn supports the beans by acting as a trellis, the beans add nitrogen to the soil, and squash is grown at the base of the corn to add mulch, with its leaves trapping the moisture in the ground and its prickly vine deterring pests. The three are all very nutritious and help support a well-balanced diet, and the land around La Prairie was great farming land. But the Jesuits saw it as a place to preach and convert us.

History tells us that in 1647 the French Crown granted the Jesuits the Seigneury of La Prairie to attract natives, especially Haudenosaunee, to the French cause. The Jesuits, or Black Robes as they were then called, had started travelling to what is now known as the Mohawk Valley in New York seeking converts, and they needed a home base. Given the ongoing conflict with the French, not many Haudenosaunee were ready to move north. But the Jesuits did meet some who were willing to by establishing a mission in Ossernenon, near what is now known as Auriesville, New York. Many of the First Nations people who agreed to go with the Jesuits were likely dissatisfied with the English colonists, who were encroaching on their territory, and thought the French would perhaps make better allies.

Alcohol seems to have played a part as well. The impact of alcohol on First Nations communities is well documented, and I will explore it in more detail throughout this book. But for now, it is important to underscore that it was said the Jesuits preached a different way of living and that some of the First Nations people who migrated to Kahnawà:ke were trying to escape the devastating effects that alcohol had wrought on their families and communities. As we see from history, they didn't escape alcohol in Kahnawà:ke either.

As the conflict with the French continued, the Jesuits likewise continued to influence my ancestors' way of life. In 1666, the war between the French and the Haudenosaunee reached a breaking point after the French Carignan-Salières expedition invaded and destroyed many Indigenous villages. The Haudenosaunee sued for temporary peace and, as part of the peace agreement, Jesuit missionaries were temporarily allowed to preach, and thus convert, in the Haudenosaunee territory. Prior to this, the Haudenosaunee regularly captured and tortured the missionaries who were trying to convert their people.

Jesuit missions in Quebec were established as early as 1625, so missionaries were often trying to preach to and convert many of the Indigenous nations, including within the homelands of the Haudenosaunee. Shortly after the French expedition in 1666, my ancestors travelled up what is now known as the Richelieu River and settled with the Jesuit missionaries who taught them Catholicism and French. They became known as the "Praying Indians." Not long after, in 1680, King Louis XIV of France "granted" the lands of the Seigneury of Sault Saint Louis, as they were by then called, to the "Praying Indians," or the people of Kahnawà:ke, to recognize their support in the French's struggle against the British and the rest of the Haudenosaunee Confederacy. This is believed to be the origins of the community of Kahnawà:ke (initially called Kentake). Even as I write this, I find it so strange to read that the king of France *granted* (unceded and unsurrendered) lands in North America to the Indigenous people of North America.

After a century of warfare and much conflict, suffering, disease, and death, the Beaver Wars finally ended in 1701 with the Treaty of Montreal between the French and the Haudenosaunee (alongside thirty-nine other First Nations). Although the English and the French continued their wars, the Haudenosaunee agreed to remain peaceful. And yet, they couldn't survive against the onslaught of colonization.

A little more than fifty years later, the British and French signed the Treaty of Paris in 1763, ending the Seven Years' War, with France ceding its claimed territories in North America. Shortly afterward, the British Crown issued the Royal Proclamation to announce the new laws, policies, and administrative changes. The Royal Proclamation covered the terms of peace between Britain and France, but it also set aside a huge tract of land west of the Appalachian Mountains as Indian reserve land and recognized the land rights of Indigenous people. Settlers would not be able to occupy it without approval from the Crown.

I think the British made a tactical decision to appease the French colonists due to their growing unrest, and so the Quebec Act (1774) further exacerbated the problem by giving religious freedom to the French settlers, re-establishing the French civil code and the seigneurial system of land allotment, and expanding the borders of the Province of Quebec. Well, the American colonies didn't like any of this and the act helped to accelerate the confrontation that became the American Revolution. Some First Nations sided with the British, some with the Americans, and others remained neutral. Only fifteen years after the Royal Proclamation, the Haudenosaunee Confederacy was fractured.

Remember that, by this point, Kahnawà:ke had already been established for nearly a century. History also shows, and often forgets, that Kahnawà:ke partnered with other First Nations in the lands claimed by the French. Together they formed an alliance called the Seven Fires, or Seven Nations, of Canada. Those communities included Kahnawà:ke; Kanehsatà:ke; Ahkwesáhsne, the Kanien'kehá:ka community near the border of Quebec, Ontario, and the US; Lorette, a Huron-Wendat community now located at Wendake; Wolinak and Odanak, both Abenaki communities located on the south side of the St. Lawrence River near what is now Trois-Rivières; and later La Presentation, which was established in 1749 and was an Onondaga community near what is now Ogdensburg.

These Seven Nations, via a central fire at Kahnawà:ke, near Montreal, served as the meeting place for all easterly and westerly nations seeking to meet with the French and later the British colonial authorities. The Seven Nations played a key role in the Great Peace Treaty of 1701 that ended the Iroquois, or Beaver, Wars and in ending Pontiac's War more than five decades later. They were also important allies of the British in the American Revolution, the War of 1812, and the Lower Canadian Rebellion of 1837–38. The forming of this alliance helped preserve the identity of First Nations in Quebec and, ironically enough, preserve the British-held territory now called Canada. It saddens me to think that despite this, Quebec and Canada still chose to not honour the First Nations in Quebec with formal treaties and recognition, and things didn't stay as promised in Kahnawà:ke either.

Despite the fact that the land called Seigneury of Sault Saint Louis was given for the exclusive use of our community since 1680, deliberate and consistent land encroachment, in one form or another, has occurred since that time. Our right to our land was not respected in the same way that the right to land was for non-Indigenous settlers, especially after the War of 1812, when the Crown changed its policies and started treating Indigenous people more as subjects rather than sovereign peoples. Today, Kahnawà:ke has control of less than a third of the land that was once agreed upon as ours. To be frank, the Jesuits (and the Sulpicians, the Récollets, the Capuchins, the Ursulines, the Hospitalières, and so many more), and later the various municipal, provincial, and federal governments, appear to not have had First Nations' interests at heart. Rather, the goal was conversion and assimilation. And this goes for so many other issues that I will discuss in this book.

Thankfully, things have changed since I was a child. Many of our people are now connected with other communities, particularly those that are more traditional and that haven't lost the skills required for living on the land. Others travel to far-away places to share in the hunt, and more and more we are investing in our youth to rebuild those skills before they are lost completely. But, in considering the long history of how we got here—and the corresponding impact of colonialism throughout my life and on everyone in my community—I cannot help but also think that much harm has been done in the name of progress.

As we both gaze into the past and look toward the future in the spirit of reconciliation, we must ask: *Whose* progress? Is the suffering of one group of people a necessary evil for others to advance and progress? What happened to our many treaties? What happened to the alliances that were formed? What happened to our agreements? While many of the infrastructure projects built on our lands have meant "progress" for the rest of Canada, its provinces, and its citizens, their negative impact on Indigenous communities cannot be overstated. In Kahnawà:ke's case, despite repeated protests and legal challenges by our community, the land of the Seigneury of Sault Saint Louis continues to shrink, as neighbouring municipalities and the provincial government seem to encourage continued development.

Indigenous people have not benefited from the so-called progress in the same way as Canadians have all these years. Land value, for example, is not calculated in the same way as it is outside our communities. According to the Indian Act, reserve land is still considered Crown land, not private land. This means that legally the land is owned by the federal government, while community members have only the right to occupy and use the land. At the same time, our use of the land is subject to severe restrictions. In practice, any land allotments given to community members should return to common land status when no longer in use by them or their family. But some community members have instead sold their allotment, which then creates many legal issues. Can the land actually be sold to anyone, given the obligations in the Indian Act? And what right does the Crown have to unceded and unsurrendered Indigenous land?

Our status as Indigenous people is not recognized outside our small reserves, which can also create many challenges for us, including when it comes to land. Consider that the lack of housing on reserves forces many Indigenous people to live off reserves. Many provinces, like Quebec, do not recognize status Indians living off reserves. This means they are considered the same as Canadian citizens and are not eligible for things like tax exemption on goods or services, like those living on the reserve. They are also not eligible for certain programs and services and do not have access to the same rights and benefits as someone living on the reserve. Lack of social support for those living off reserves, like specialized social services and health services, compounds the problem by isolating the Indigenous person, disconnecting them from culture and community, and not considering their particular challenges and needs. To me, it is like forced enfranchisement—the legal process of terminating a person's Indian status and conferring full Canadian citizenship.

Throughout our collective history in Canada, policies and laws were created to undermine our ability to benefit from the land in the same way as Canadians, unless we became assimilated to the Canadian population and renounced who we are. We continue to advocate and try to hold governments accountable for their duty to consult us on decisions that affect our land, but it is a constant battle. Many others have written excellently about the history of Kahnawà:ke and other communities, but I hope that my own short reflection, describing Kahnawà:ke as an ever-shrinking blanket, will inspire further reading on the history of the lands where we all live and work.

There is little so-called progress in our region that hasn't involved Kahnawà:ke land appropriation and our interests being disregarded or overruled—much of it causing direct harm to the river that was, I must repeat, central to our whole worldview. Such damaging infrastructure extends farther into the past than even the Seaway or the quarries. Much expropriation took place during the railway boom, both to build tracks and bridges. This wasn't unique to Kahnawà:ke: Railway construction was central to the formation of Canada. From one coast to the other, railways spanned across Indigenous lands—lands the new Confederation of Canada desperately needed for expansion and settlement.

Montreal's first railway, the Montreal and Lachine Railroad, opened in 1847 and was built to bypass the Lachine Rapids. At the same time, in Kahnawà:ke, the Lake St. Louis and Province Line Railway Company built a rail between Lake St. Louis and the province's border with New York. The rail started in our community and expropriated critical portions of our land. In 1850, those two railways merged and then ultimately became absorbed into the Grand Trunk Railway.

Next came a single-track Canadian Pacific Railway (CPR) rail bridge, which was completed in July 1887 and opened for passengers to Montreal the next year. The Grand Trunk Railway had already built the Victoria Bridge in 1859, which ran across the St. Lawrence on the southeast side of Montreal, as part of its competition with the CPR for domination. This new bridge was an attempt to break the Grand Trunk's monopoly on rail access between Montreal and the south shore. The new CPR bridge ran across the St. Lawrence at Lachine to Kahnawà:ke and created a second rail line within the community itself. Although the initial bridge didn't last long, a second, two-track train bridge was built in November 1913 and is still standing today. It's the one I used to cross as a kid to get to the Flat Rocks.

In 1934, yet another bridge encroached on our land. The Mercier Bridge stretches across the St. Lawrence and was funded by the Corporation du Pont du Lac Saint-Louis and built by the Dominion Bridge Company. It replaced a ferry service, creating easier access from New York, and was intended to attract American tourists to Montreal. The Mercier Bridge and the CPR bridge run parallel to each other, bisecting the community, with homes on both sides. Powerline towers sit in between the two bridges—yet another encroachment. The power grid advanced rapidly in the 1880s and onward throughout Kahnawà:ke. And while hydropower is a clean energy form that is substantially better than fossil fuels, governments and companies dot towers and power lines across our community without regard for people and livelihoods.

All this infrastructure not only shrunk what land we had, but it also fundamentally changed how we used our land. It changed how drainage occurred, how wildlife lived, how our farmland was used, and our access to different parts of the community. It also set a precedent that colonizers can do what they want with Indigenous land without consequence and, in many ways, opened the rest of the country to colonization. With the passing of the major projects legislation in 2025, Canada is accelerating infrastructure development across Canada. The impact this may have on Indigenous territory and rights—and to what extent Indigenous nations will also benefit from this "progress"—remains to be seen.

My hope is that a more complete education on the history of this land, including how the current systems were built, how Indigenous communities were formed, and how the land around them was shaped, will give Canadians a better understanding of the realities we all face. Once someone has that knowledge, they can actively take part in their own everyday reconciliation. Much of the land issues seem to be in the hands of the government, but that is not true. There are so many ways that non-Indigenous people can contribute to reconciliation and move toward more peaceful relations.

You can support the Land Back movement and our efforts to settle land claims. You can refuse to settle on Indigenous land and encourage governments to fulfill their duties in consulting with Indigenous communities for land and resource use. If you work at a company that uses the land in any way, you can become vocal in ensuring Indigenous voices and communities are heard in the projects you undertake. And you can begin using the land in less harmful ways by becoming a conscious caretaker, which is a responsibility we all have as humans.

Our protests and demonstrations, like the Land Back movement, are not intended to hurt others, but to carry a message. You can carry the same message. *This land is for all of us and our next seven generations; how do we ensure that happens?* Everyday conciliation and reconciliation are about all Canadians building and rebuilding relationships. For that, you need to ask yourself: Do I know the real story of this land?

Should We Go?

Elin Sandberg Miller

IN 2019, THE popular CBC comedy series *Baroness von Sketch Show* aired a skit about land acknowledgements that later went viral on social media. The skit takes place in a theatre, and in it a white woman is delivering a land acknowledgement to an audience before the show is about to start. She lists the names of the First Nations whose land the theatre stands on and says she's mindful of the broken treaties and the need to make it right. The camera then zooms in on a person in the audience, another white woman. She has clearly taken in the message: They're sitting on stolen land! Getting up, confused, she asks the theatre host, "Should we all go?" What follows is an awkward and darkly funny exchange. If the audience isn't expected to vacate the stolen land on which the theatre sits, what then should they do? The audience member asks whether the theatre will donate part of the proceeds from the show to the First Nations mentioned in the acknowledgement. No? But perhaps the money from the bottled water sold at the event? Not that either? How then, she wonders, do we make this right?

The clip resonated with me and so many other Canadians because land acknowledgements often seem perfunctory or virtue-signalling—or even worse, as if they are supposed to be the extent of the discussion. As in, *Yeah, it's your land, but I live here now.* Meanwhile, I'd argue, the discussion has barely started.

I cannot remember the first time I heard a land acknowledgement, but they became common at the federal government department where I worked around the same time the *Baroness von Sketch* skit aired. Yet, while the practice may seem new, it has deep roots in Indigenous cultures, from long before colonization. As one of my podcast guests explained to me, it was part of nation-to-nation Protocol of demonstrating respect when visiting someone else's land. The rather recent practice of non-Indigenous people giving them at larger meetings and events is inspired by the TRC's call for a renewed relationship based on principles of mutual recognition and respect.

Often, when such land acknowledgements first came into more widespread, regular use by non-Indigenous people by non-Indigenous people, the person delivering them would stick strictly to the script. Sometimes, they'd stumble a bit over the words, indicating a certain level of discomfort, and there was no context or commentary to go with it. I delivered a couple of those myself and cringe at the thought of it today. The standard script in Ottawa refers to "the unceded Traditional Territory of the Anishinaabe Algonquin Nation." Despite my two law degrees, I didn't know at first what "unceded" meant, or if acknowledging the fact that the land was unceded carried any legal implications. But, like the audience member in the clip, I understood it to mean that we were on someone else's land, and, to me, there seemed to be more to do than merely *acknowledging* it.

Yet what? Though the *Baroness von Sketch* skit was just that—a comedy skit—I believe there's a reason it hit home with so many of us. If we wanted our land acknowledgements to mean something, we had to consider some tough questions. We had to think about actions. If we did mean what we were saying, should we go? It's not an easy question to ask yourself, especially if you own a business or home on that land. I'm fortunate enough to own my home in Ottawa. Does the fact that it sits on Algonquin land mean that I should give it back? If so, to whom, and is it even mine to give?

In my search for answers to these questions, I knew I needed to learn more about what happened to land ownership during the colonization process and how it works in Canada today. The more I learned, the less it made sense to me. What did become clear, though, is that while the future of reconciliation depends on many interconnected things, as I had come to understand, the most important one will be how we address the conflict over land. To fully engage in reconciliation, we must consider how we, ourselves, think about land ownership and how we relate to the land.

Early on, when reading about the colonization process and land ownership, I made an overly simplistic assumption. I believed the commonly held explanations about the Doctrine of Discovery and the concept of *terra nullius*. Everyone from journalists to teachers to judges has long used these concepts to justify or explain how Canada was settled. The Doctrine of Discovery was based on 15th-century papal bulls, decrees, or orders by the Pope stating that when discovering lands of non-Christians, European nations could claim sovereignty over these lands and convert their new subjects to Christianity. The concept of *terra nullius*, "nobody's land" in Latin, essentially means that whatever is considered vacant land is up for grabs. These concepts did play a role in the colonization of parts of the world, including in South America, where they were applied by the Spanish and Portuguese, who used them to claim ownership of the land (although there were legal scholars even even at the time who questioned the legal force of the doctrine and thus the validity of these claims).

But—as I discovered after my initial assumption—these concepts did not play the same role in the colonization of Canada. The British Crown wasn't even Catholic, and, at least until the 1780s, settlers and colonial governments largely took possession of the land through treaty and purchase agreements. (Whether those transactions were fair or not is another—extremely important—issue.)

In the early days of colonization, I learned, the dominant view was that Indigenous Peoples owned the land. The earliest settlers of Massachusetts, for example, carried instructions to purchase the land from the "savages" if they claimed "right of inheritance" to it. In the colony of New York in the late 17ᵗʰ century, the British colonial government could grant licences to purchase land, but settlers had to prove that they had rightfully purchased it from the "Indians" before they became its lawful owners. By the 1750s, New York required that land purchased from "Indians" be first surveyed together with representatives of the selling First Nations to avoid future disputes. Also, the fact that both the French and British concluded treaties with Indigenous nations on a nation-to-nation basis speaks to the fact that neither applied the Doctrine of Discovery or the concept of *terra nullius* to simply seize land. To secure peaceful coexistence and to ensure that their important military alliances with powerful Indigenous groups were respected and nurtured, they treated First Nations as the rightful owners of the land with whom they needed to negotiate.

As Derek discussed in his last essay, in 1763, following the Seven Years' War and the Treaty of Paris, when Great Britain gained much of France's possessions in North America, King George III of Britain issued a Royal Proclamation to establish a new administrative structure for the recently acquired territories. He also established new rules and protocols for future relations with First Nations The king was concerned with protecting his new lands and wanted to secure the allegiance of First Nations who had fought as allies of the French in the Seven Years' War.

Through the Proclamation, he reserved a large section of land to the west of Quebec along the Appalachians for Indigenous Peoples, stating that they would keep land not ceded by or purchased from them. And so, when we say that the land is unceded in this context, it means that it was never formally transferred away from the Indigenous nation claiming it.

So where does the misperception about the Doctrine of Discovery derive from? A US Supreme Court case. Following the American Revolution, US government officials at first held on to the British policy that Indigenous people owned the land. But a shift in perception took place in the late 18th century, as lawyers and government officials went from viewing the land as *owned* by Indigenous people to being merely *possessed* by them, in a transient sort of way. This shift was rationalized by a fabricated idea that First Nations didn't cultivate the soil, at least not as Europeans did, and therefore didn't meet a European definition of acquiring and holding property. In 1823, the US Supreme Court in *Johnson v. McIntosh* introduced the Doctrine of Discovery in American law, using it as a legal basis for this view, thereby breaking with the previous two centuries of thought. In the decision, Chief Justice John Marshall held that land ownership was vested in European nations by right of discovery. This grave misrepresentation of facts later influenced Canadian courts, where it has supported the view that the Crown's underlying title to land extends to unceded Indigenous land. Today, when Indigenous Peoples want to claim their right to unceded land, they're forced to fight an exhausting and expensive legal battle, the burden of proof unreasonably laid upon them, when it once used to be the other way around.

The fact that the Doctrine of Discovery didn't apply explicitly to the colonization of North America as it did in South America is not to say that the racist assumption of superiority embodied in the doctrine didn't underpin much of Canada's colonial history. It did. And while the papal bulls did not directly apply to the Protestant Crown, who rejected outright papal authority, the doctrine was instrumental in the religious "education" of Indigenous children through residential schools. But it is important to raise awareness about how the land changed hands, which started with a nation-to-nation relationship characterized by diplomacy, alliances, and commerce rather than the pure exertion of power based on papal bulls. While Canada did dispossess Indigenous Peoples of their land, even after the 1763 Royal Proclamation reserved it for them, for example, by granting large tracts of land to loyalists in the late 18th and early 19th centuries, here, the major shift away from viewing Indigenous Peoples as rightful landowners came with confederation.

Through the Royal Proclamation of 1763, the king reserved the right of purchasing or otherwise acquiring Indigenous land for himself, the Crown, establishing the constitutional basis for future treaty negotiations with Indigenous Peoples. The British Crown, followed by the Canadian government after confederation in 1867, continued the expansion to the West largely through treaty-making. For example, through the so-called Numbered Treaties, a series of eleven treaties concluded between 1871 and 1921, the government advanced non-Indigenous settlement, resource extraction, and construction of the Canadian Pacific Railway in an area encompassing northern Ontario, Manitoba, Alberta, Saskatchewan, the Northwest Territories, and parts of British Columbia. The construction of the railroad cut across lands formerly roamed by buffalo herds and caused great harm to the Indigenous Peoples living in these areas, just as the construction of the railroad caused great harm to Indigenous communities in other parts of Canada, too, as Derek starkly illustrated.

As I had learned earlier in the course I took on treaties, the content of the Numbered (and many other) Treaties is disputed, especially in regard to whether they extinguished First Nations' inherent title to the land. But the result was that First Nations in these territories ended up confined to small parcels of reserve land, in many cases dependent on the government for their survival. In some cases, land was taken for non-Indigenous settlement without any agreement at all, including where I live in Ottawa. This is the history that the land acknowledgement I heard at work referred to, and I wanted to keep learning more, especially about the place I called home. How did the land my house sits on end up in the hands of settlers?

While you can find information about previous home ownership on land title or deed documents, going further back in time usually requires you to search through municipal records and provincial land registers or visit Libraries and Archives Canada. In my case, by pure luck, I was able to quickly trace the ownership of my house back to when it was first built in 1934. I was out gardening in the front when a neighbour walked by and told me that growing up, he spent a lot of time in our house. He kindly came back later with a legal document drafted by his grandfather, who lived there from 1934 to 1978, which showed what his grandfather had paid both to have the house built and to purchase the lot of land.

But the process of making this land available to non-Indigenous people started long before 1934. As Loyalists arrived in large numbers following the American Revolution and later the War of 1812 and Upper Canada was formed, the British Crown surveyed the area and identified properties by townships, concessions, and lots. Lots were granted to Loyalists and also became available for purchase. Thomas MacKay purchased several lots with the considerable income he made from his work on the Rideau Canal locks, among other things. Part of this land was later developed by his son-in-law Thomas Kiefer into the residential area where I came to live. The Crown thus made this land available for settlement in contravention of the 1763

Royal Proclamation and without the consent of the Algonquins or the negotiation of a treaty. As I wrote in my last essay, Algonquin Chief Pinesi fought throughout his life to get recognition of the Algonquin's right to their ancestral lands, arguing, on the basis of the Royal Proclamation, that it remained theirs. Meanwhile, the Crown, Upper Canada land administrators, and later the Province of Ontario continued to grant settlers title to this land, and in 1934, my neighbour's grandfather purchased the lot of land that I would eventually acquire title to.

I find it absolutely shocking both as a lawyer and as a human being that the land was taken from the Algonquin Nation in this way, and, what's worse, it was not an isolated incident. The land that is today the Maritimes, nearly all of British Columbia, and a large swath of eastern Ontario and Quebec, which includes the National Capital Region, was never ceded.

As I learned more about land treaties, it became clear that even when they were concluded, they weren't always respected but in fact were systematically violated by Canadian governments. To Indigenous Peoples, treaties offered a means of maintaining peaceful relationships. Their sacred and binding character wasn't found primarily in the text but in what the parties told each other during the negotiations and concluding ceremonies. For example, descendants of Indigenous signatories of the Numbered Treaties have held that the intention was never to cede the land but to *share* it. In many cases, Indigenous signatories would not have been able to read the text and had to rely on interpreters. The more I thought about these negotiations, the more I realized how imbalanced they must have been. I think of the First Nations living on the Prairies in the late 19th century, for example, weakened by diseases and almost starving to death after the near extinction of the buffalo—what leverage did they have?

Through the treaties, the colonial and later federal government made promises, usually referred to as treaty rights, in exchange for the ceded land. In the Numbered Treaties (1871–1921), the government promised the First Nations signatories that a certain size of reserve land would be set aside for them, but that they could continue to hunt and fish across the ceded (whole) land. They would also receive annual payments known as annuities, tools and equipment for farming, and education for their children, among other things. Many of these rights were violated by the government, sometimes quickly after the treaties were concluded.

Perhaps most importantly, the size and location of the land to be set aside for reserves were often not honoured. While the size of the reserves, based on the number of families, was identified in the treaty texts, the parcels eventually carved out by a government surveyor were in many cases smaller than initially promised. As opposed to the size, the *location* of the reserves was—intentionally—not identified in the treaty texts. A report from the government-appointed commission established to negotiate Treaty 8 reveals the government's reason for this. The treaty negotiation was concluded in 1899 with thirty-nine First Nations in northern Alberta, northwestern Saskatchewan, northeastern British Columbia, and the southwest portion of the Northwest Territories, making it the largest numbered treaty in terms of area. The commission believed there was no immediate need to allot the land for Indigenous use—they needed to survey their settlement needs first. And while they acknowledged that the "Indians" were averse to the reserve system, their intent wasn't to honour their treaty partners' desires.

"It would have been impossible to have made a treaty if we had not assured them that there was no intention of confining them to reserves," they wrote. "We had to very clearly explain to them that the provision for reserves and allotments of land were made for their protection, and to secure to them in perpetuity a fair portion of the land ceded, in the event of settlement advancing." In other words, the federal government wanted to secure the treaty first, before it committed to parcels for reserve land. Following the conclusion of the treaties, when First Nations presented their preferred location, a government surveyor was sent to ensure it didn't infringe on any government or settler interests, and the result was often that reserves were located in more remote areas, leaving First Nations isolated and on land that was generally less desirable than the choice pieces of land thus freed up for non-Indigenous settlement.

Today, about 0.2 percent of Canada's total land mass is reserve land. Reserves are governed by the Indian Act, which, despite its many amendments since its adoption in 1876, remains an essentially racist document. Unlike private landowners in Canada, generally, "Indians," as they are still referred to in the act, cannot sell, lease, mortgage, or otherwise dispose of reserve land; it is merely held and administered by the community while owned by the Crown.

Think about that for a second. I can decide to rent or sell my house whenever I want and expect to make a profit. The same goes for the previous owners of my house; even a small piece of property can generate considerable wealth over time. For many Canadians, purchasing their home is the most important investment they ever make, and they take good care of it. Owning your home also gives a sense of security and stability. In my neighbourhood in Ottawa, almost everyone owns their home and the land it sits on. Houses are well looked after, and we have parks, soccer fields and tennis courts, beautiful playgrounds, and great schools. I also have access to high-quality dental and health care and public transportation.

The situation in Indigenous communities is very different. When Indigenous Peoples lost most of their lands and their traditional avenues for subsistence, they were made dependent on government handouts that were chronically underfunded. Still today, First Nations reserves, as well as Inuit and Métis communities, face underfunded services and subpar education, healthcare, infrastructure, and housing.

Indigenous children growing up in Canada are overrepresented in the foster care system, are less likely to complete high school, and are more likely to end up incarcerated than their peers. For example, less than half of First Nations youth on reserve and Inuit youth graduate from high school, compared to 90 percent of their non-Indigenous peers. Indigenous children represent just under 8 percent of all Canadian children, yet they make up more than half of all children in foster care. Many Indigenous children also grow up in poverty—nearly 40 percent compared to less than 10 percent for non-Indigenous children. Given all this, it's no wonder that many Indigenous communities are fighting for their land back and for the treaties to be honoured.

It is important to remember that treaties are not relics of the past but legally binding documents foundational to our presence here in North America. Their provisions are living obligations, constitutionally protected under Section 35 of the 1982 Constitution Act. I didn't know any of this before I started to read up, and I believe that few Canadians truly understand their importance and that they are the basis for hundreds of outstanding Indigenous claims. While settlement of these claims can seem expensive and make taxpayers worry, I have learned to see them as long overdue bills.

We should also remember that these lands continue to generate wealth, although not for Indigenous Peoples. For example, in 2023, the federal government and the provincial government of Ontario agreed to pay $10 billion in compensation to twenty-one Anishinaabe communities in Northeastern Ontario for violating the Robinson Huron Treaty signed in 1850. Under the treaty, the government promised annual payments to these First Nations in exchange for the right to use their land. A clause in the treaty explicitly tied the value of the annual payments to resource revenues, yet annual payments were capped in 1874 at $4 per person, while mining, lumber, and fishing industries in the area have generated billions of dollars in profits since then. The colonization process has taken so much from First Nations. The least the government could do is honour its treaty obligations and pay what is owed.

Courts have now started to recognize Indigenous title to this land. The most famous instance so far was in 2014 when the Supreme Court of Canada confirmed that the Tŝilhqot'in Nation in British Columbia had a right to their unceded land, pre-existing colonization. It wasn't a simple—or total—victory. The burden of proof in such cases is on Indigenous Peoples, and the court required that the Tŝilhqot'in Nation demonstrate that they had occupied the land in question continuously since before colonization. While they won, they were also only able to secure a small part of their Traditional Territory.

It's true—as some people argue—that the government imposes restrictions on all land in Canada. As much as 90 percent of land in Canada is so-called Crown land, owned by the provincial governments and to a lesser degree by the federal government. The rest is privately owned but still subject to restrictions. Take fee simple title, for example. (The "fee" comes from the word "fief," which in feudal England was a landholding granted by a lord or the Crown in exchange for services.) Fee simple provides the strongest land ownership rights in Canada and is how most Canadians own their homes. Yet, it is subject to restrictions such as zoning bylaws, property taxes, hunting and fishing regulations, and the Crown's right to subsurface resources such as oil, gas, and metals, which can represent significant wealth.

But settlers and Indigenous Peoples don't have the same historic relationship to the land. Settlers acquired their land title from the Crown, and so it makes sense that the Crown could impose restrictions through the transaction process. Indigenous Peoples, on the other hand, were here before the Crown. I find it difficult to reconcile the government's supposed recognition of Indigenous Peoples' inherent, pre-existing right to their (unceded) land with its insistence on deciding how Indigenous Peoples can use that land. The government, or formally the Crown, tries to conveniently fit the concept of Indigenous land into its own way of thinking about land ownership. Its approach also seems to clash with its articulated nation-to-nation relationship with Indigenous Peoples, because what nation imposes its laws on another if they are supposed to be equal?

While it may not always be possible or even desirable for settlers to outright leave, returning land and resources is fully possible. Today, an increasing number of so-called modern treaties, or comprehensive land agreements, are being negotiated between Indigenous Peoples and the federal, provincial, and territorial governments, often to address claims relating to unceded land. Modern treaties aren't perfect, but they do represent a shift in thinking, and the government fairly sees them as a central component of its reconciliation efforts. These treaties clarify land ownership, but they aren't simple real estate transactions. They regulate land-based rights such as fishing, hunting, and resource extraction and grant ownership to portions of the covered area. They also usually include provisions to increase Indigenous self-governance, an important step toward self-determination. And if successful, they can offer us ways of sharing the land and maintaining peaceful relationships, just like Indigenous Peoples once envisioned.

Today, the government has concluded around thirty such treaties, starting with the James Bay and Northern Quebec Agreement in 1975, predating both the Royal Commission on

Aboriginal Peoples, the Truth and Reconciliation Commission, and the national reconciliation process. Modern treaties currently cover 40 percent of Canada's landmass, with the James Bay and Northern Quebec, Inuvialuit, and Nunavut agreements making up the bulk of it. While an impressive number on its surface, most of these agreements exist north of the 60th parallel, covering sparsely populated areas. This is in large part why the RCAP emphasized the importance of significantly increasing land holdings for First Nations in southern Canada, where the vast majority of Indigenous people live. An important next step would be to negotiate such modern treaties in higher population density areas.

Doing so could benefit the entire country, including non-Indigenous people. In *Valley of the Birdtail*, co-authors Andrew Stobo Sniderman and Douglas Sanderson (Amo Binashii) beautifully wrote about the complex relationship between two neighbouring communities, the town of Rossburn and the Waywayseecappo Indian reserve in Manitoba, highlighting both racism and hopeful reconciliation efforts. In the book, they put forward a strong argument for extending the practice of modern treaties to areas where treaties were concluded but have proven inadequate, which could include urban areas. They believe this could offer an efficient way of ensuring equal access to government services and help address the persistent socio-economic inequalities between Indigenous and non-Indigenous Peoples.

Indigenous people represent the fastest-growing population group in Canada. From 2016 to 2021, their population grew by more than 9 percent, almost twice as much as the non-Indigenous population. Besides it being the right thing to do, there's immense potential in bringing Indigenous people up to par with the rest of Canadians in terms of health, education, and economic prospects. The impacts of land dispossession, intergenerational trauma, underfunding of education, health care, and other services for Indigenous people, and the continuing systemic discrimination they face on everything from mental and physical health to incarceration rates are costly for all of Canada, and so far, federal investments haven't been able to close the gaps.

A large part of Canada's wealth is generated from the forestry, petroleum, and mining industries—land that belonged to Indigenous Peoples and that we recognize in our acknowledgements. If Indigenous communities still occupied their traditional lands or at the very least had control over an adequate land base and its resources, they wouldn't have to rely so heavily on federal funding. They would be in a position to close the socio-economic gaps themselves, and more sustainably, too, as they could build their economies long term.

Calculations by Statistics Canada demonstrate that the Indigenous contribution to Canada's economy is on an upward trend. Measured in Gross Domestic Income (GDI), which is the total income that all sectors of a country's economy generate together, including wages, profits, and taxes, Indigenous people earned $60 billion in 2022, an increase of 10 percent from 2021. Since 2012, Indigenous GDI has increased by 75 percent, outpacing GDI growth in the total economy. According to the Business Development Bank of Canada, the number of Indigenous entrepreneurs is expected to grow by more than 20 percent in the next decade, compared to a 10 percent increase projected for other Canadian entrepreneurs. The fact that Indigenous economies and contributions to the wider economy are on an upswing despite the hurdles—imagine what they could achieve and contribute if they had more power and self-determination.

Modern treaties can mean that people living in the affected area will see another government—an Indigenous one—come into place. This doesn't mean that non-Indigenous people would have to move, but the responsibility for decision-making, tax collection, and the administration of services would change hands.

Coexisting peacefully on this land will take incredible work, and we will have to learn to trust each other. Perhaps these new agreements can even help us change our approach to land and land ownership altogether. Canada is the second-largest country in the world by landmass. At the same time, Canada's population, at 40 million, is comparatively small. Simply put, there's enough land for all of us.

Listening to and doing land acknowledgements has made me more aware of all the issues surrounding land ownership and our relation to the land. After my first nervous attempts, I have increasingly included my own thoughts about land and what it means to me to live here when I have an opportunity to give a land acknowledgement. Sometimes I include an anecdote from my own reconciliation journey, or the questions I still have about land ownership, including my own. The Indigenous people I've spoken with have welcomed this new trend of non-Indigenous people delivering land acknowledgements, as long as they're not pro forma, and very few have credibly suggested that we pack up and leave. What they have suggested, however, is learning and concrete action.

When thoughtful, land acknowledgements can be meaningful acts of reconciliation. They provide an opportunity to reflect on our histories but also to consider what can be done to correct the past wrongs—because we must go beyond merely acknowledging Indigenous Traditional Territories. Land claims, unequal access to resources, and socio-economic disparities can be addressed, and we have the tools to do it. Indigenous people want to see change and everyone will be better off for it, without anyone having to go.

How to Give a Meaningful Land Acknowledgement

In our two essays on land, we discussed the process by which Indigenous Peoples lost most of their land and the devastating impact this had on them—and continues to have. All Canadians, and those immigrants seeking to become Canadians, should know about this. What happened is part of our common history, present, and future. Learning about it is an important part of everyday reconciliation and land acknowledgements can be an excellent starting point for that learning process. In this section, we'll offer more guidance on how to give a meaningful land acknowledgement.

Land acknowledgements have long been used traditionally by Indigenous nations to give thanks and pay respects to the land of the people they are visiting. Acknowledging that you are a visitor to someone else's territory and grateful to be welcomed there helps manage relations between nations respectfully and peacefully. Following the report of the Truth and Reconciliation Commission and its 94 Calls to Action, land acknowledgements are increasingly used by non-Indigenous people to acknowledge whose land they're on. Done properly, a land acknowledgement can be an important act of reconciliation. But this requires careful consideration, thought, and research. Without it, or if delivered routinely or strictly performatively, a land acknowledgement lacks meaning. It can even be offensive, hurtful, and harmful to our relations, as the lack of research and consideration can come across as disrespectful and even result in misrepresentations or the reinforcement of colonial perceptions.

There are no rules about when to deliver a land acknowledgement, but it is usually appropriate at the outset of a meeting, event, course, lecture, or conference to raise awareness of Indigenous Peoples, their rights and connections to the land, and of our treaty relationships. For larger meetings, you may consider inviting an Elder to perform the land acknowledgement. There are no rules for when to do this, but if you do, remember to inquire about Protocol, such as gifts to the Elder to demonstrate your appreciation and honorariums to compensate them for their time and effort. Gift giving is a common practice in all Indigenous cultures, and by asking an Elder to conduct a land acknowledgement, they are giving the audience the gift of ceremony. Providing a gift to them in return for their effort is respectful.

A land acknowledgement can be especially meaningful when participants are joining from other parts of the country or from outside of Canada, as they will likely be less knowledgeable about whose land they visit. The acknowledgement can also serve to ground the event by making connections between the land and what's being discussed, by instilling a sense of gratitude and humility about our presence here, or by reminding participants of their responsibilities toward future generations.

In other cases, a land acknowledgement may not be the best way to open a meeting, for example, in recurrent meetings with the same group of people, where it quickly risks becoming performative. In those cases, if you still want to contribute to reconciliation, consider sharing something else, such as information about an upcoming Indigenous event open to the public.

In addition to giving them orally, land acknowledgements can be provided in written format, including on websites to indicate whose land a company or organization is located on, in a report to indicate where it was authored, or in an email signature block to indicate where the sender is living or working.

There is no single or uniform traditional land acknowledgement. In fact, they are more meaningful when personalized. For example, you may want to share your own story of you or your ancestors coming to Canada, or of learning the history of the land you now live on. You may also want to reflect on the treaty in place. When you prepare for giving your first acknowledgement, it can be helpful to use an existing local land acknowledgement as a template to create your own. You can often find them on municipal or community websites, or if there's a university in your area, you may find one on their website. But make sure the text has been reviewed or created in consultation with local Indigenous communities before you trust its content, which should be explicitly indicated in connection with the text itself.

When you personalize a land acknowledgement, or draft your own from scratch, do your research and reflect on what you want to say and why. We provide some questions below to guide you. You may not find all the answers, but what you learn during the process will help you understand the point of a land acknowledgement and assist you in giving one that is meaningful to yourself and your listeners.

· Consider the context and adapt the text accordingly. For example, do you need to explain the purpose of a land acknowledgement or is that obvious to the audience?
· Research the Indigenous People(s) whose land you're on and learn to pronounce their name(s) correctly. You can sometimes find guidance online, including on YouTube. Another way is to ask a member of that nation, for example, someone working at a friendship centre, band council, or cultural centre, or call these places after hours to listen to the pronunciation in the recorded voice message.
· Include a reflection on something you have learned. For example, how did these people lose their land, is there a reserve nearby, or do most of them live in urban settings?

· Mention whether there's a treaty relationship, or if the land is unceded. Remember, however, that a treaty doesn't necessarily mean that the land was ceded. While this may have been the intention of the Canadian government at the time, the Indigenous signatories often interpreted the treaty provisions differently.

· If you reference a treaty, look up the text and consider including a reflection on a specific treaty provision that stood out to you. Treaty obligations are still in force, and the Canadian government—one of the treaty partners—represents you. This is your treaty, too.

· Identify your positionality—are you a descendant of a settler, a more recent immigrant, or a visitor to this land? Reflecting on your own reason for being here will make the acknowledgement more meaningful. For example, if your family has lived in Canada for generations, when did it arrive, and how did it interact with Indigenous Peoples? If you're a newcomer, why did you come to this land? What does this land and living here mean to you?

· Is there an active land claim related to your area? What are the grounds for claiming the land back?

· Can you find an example of people giving land back to Indigenous communities? What was the process like and what was the result?

· Consider each word you use. For example, is "acknowledge" the right word? Try something more direct and consider if that conveys a different message, such as "I am on . . ." or "I'm joining you from . . ." or "we are gathering on the land of . . ." Also try using the subsequent wording in present tense and see what difference that makes. (Past tense tends to feed into the dominant narrative that the Indigenous Peoples whose traditional land you're on don't live there anymore, which is likely untrue.)

· If you're part of a group or organization, alternate between those who give the land acknowledgement to increase everyone's learning and to diversify and enrich the messaging.

· Finally, land acknowledgements are only the beginning of a conversation—they can never replace action. Consider what you can do to contribute to reconciliation and describe the actions you are taking to carry forth those commitments. Next time you give a land acknowledgement, you can talk about what you've done!

You may also consider these tips and questions when listening to a land acknowledgement. We encourage you to become an active listener and to use land acknowledgements to learn more about the land on which you live, work, study, and play.

*Part III: Culture, Identity,
and Nationhood*

Losing Your Identity, Losing Your Soul

Derek Aronhie:nens Montour

WHENEVER I HEAR the song "Wasted Days and Wasted Nights" by Freddy Fender, I am transported back in time to the front porch of my house. It's winter, and I am about seven years old, playing and probably fighting with my brothers. I am looking inside the house at my father. He is sitting on his favourite chair, smoking cigarettes, and drinking his Labatt 50. Freddy Fender is blaring on his eight-track. I remember being cold. When my dad was in his drinking mood, we were not allowed to play inside and had to spend most of the day outside, at least until my mom got home. We caused too much noise, and we bothered him. We also didn't want to become the focus of his wrath. I am still amazed that I can go back in time like that just by hearing a song. Smelling a certain scent. Observing a certain scene. Feeling the bite of winter. Is that what trauma is?

Whenever I think of my father, I often have memories of him drinking or being drunk. The feeling of being scared, or the apprehension of whether I would become scared, comes back so sharply. The feeling of wanting him, and waiting for him, to become sober. Sometimes it's a song or simply seeing a random object and getting a flash of memory of feeling. I can see a belt and remember the feel of one striking across my legs and back as he missed my butt. I can watch old episodes with Charlie Bunker or Bennie Hill, and flash back to wondering if my dad would laugh or rage. I see a can of corned beef and hear him complain in my mind to my mom about the cabbage that came with it. Memories brought to life in the present.

When I pass by the Atwater Metro station in downtown Montreal, it always brings back the times my brothers and I had to wait outside the bar on the bottom floor of the Alexis Nihon Plaza as my dad grabbed a beer—or more. When I walk up the front stairs of my mom's house, I see the time she and my older brother Craig helped him up those same stairs when he fell down drunk after a night out at the Knights of Columbus. I remember being more scared than normal for him that time because he was bleeding as he hit his head on the cement porch. I remember the time I was woken in the middle of the night with slaps, hits, and the belt for something I did earlier in the day; I was in the top bunk of our bunk bed with my older brother and woke to the image burned in my mind of my dad hitting my brother and then turning to me. When I see one of those old-style lawn chairs—the ones that have a leg support and are made from vinyl webbing—I see my dad and my grandma Margaret arguing on the back porch and my grandma throwing the chair at him. That day the Peacekeepers, the Kahnawà:ke police force, took him away. I watched him get thrown in the back of the police car.

I have many memories like that from the first eleven or twelve years of my life. We had an alcoholic home, with my mom struggling to make ends meet and us three boys trying to figure out which way was up or down. I want to share some of my trauma in this essay not because I think I'm unique, but because I'm not. Many First Nations people have suffered from the devastating effects of colonialism and genocide, and in sharing my story I hope to relay how such events can create deep trauma and leave open wounds—wounds we may seek to cover with substance use and other harmful coping behaviours. We cope with our pain by seeking a way to not feel it, even for a brief period. I also hope to share my story with others who may be going through similar experiences to show them that there is a way through the suffering.

I do not think Canadians and First Nations people can get far in our conversation about reconciliation if we do not talk of healing first. Every individual First Nations member, family, and community is still trying to understand their trauma. Even after we do, we then must start the long journey of healing. Many Canadians that I meet are now becoming aware of the depth of our trauma and want to know what they can do for us, how they can help us, and what it means for reconciliation. One of the most important things such people can do is to remember that many of us are what I think of as the walking wounded. We are still traumatized; we need time to heal. If we don't get time, energy, support, and the proper services, then we will continue to struggle with reconciliation. We cannot ask people to move on while they are still traumatized.

For us to really talk about reconciliation, we must work together to heal the wounds in our lives and our relationships. The attempted systemic and systematic erasure of Indigenous people is very much present in all our lives. In Canada, the practice of sending our children to Indian residential schools and Indian day schools remained common until not that long ago (my own lifetime!). The trauma inflicted from that echoes every day in our lives. So, too, do the impacts of the Indian Act and all the other assimilationist acts of Canada and the provinces. The consequences of the loss of land, culture, language, environment, and even our societal values are broad and far-reaching, affecting every aspect of our lives.

In thinking about my dad now, I reflect on what changed my perspective toward him and allowed me to find forgiveness. As an adult on my own sobriety journey, I would share my story in Alcoholics Anonymous, and in the early days, there wasn't much forgiveness in my words. I was angry. But then one day I listened to a younger person, who was roughly twenty, describe how they struggled with being in a foster home during their childhood. Someone asked them why they weren't angry at their mom and dad for not getting sober, and they replied that their parents were just doing the best they could with what they knew at the time.

A flash of light went off in my head. I suddenly understood that my dad was also doing the best he could with what he knew at the time. I started to think more about his own life and realized what it must have been like for him growing up. When he was just six years old, my dad lost his father, Louis Thaientaneken, known by everyone as Louis T. He was the eldest male in a family of nine kids. They were poor and had limited resources. My dad also went through the Indian day school system, which was a federally funded school system for Indigenous people in Canada. The system was run by religious orders and had a mandate similar to that of the Indian residential school system—to erase the Indian in the child. The difference between the two was that in the day schools, the child went home at night. It made the assimilation process harder but still destructive. Considering that, I could understand why my dad heeded alcohol's easy call to oblivion.

Alcohol had been in my dad's family a long time. The day my grandfather died, he was up in Val Morin, Quebec. He had been drinking that day, and when one of my aunties slipped in the river, he jumped in to save her from drowning in a whirlpool. He managed to get her out, saving her life, but succumbed to the swirling depths himself. It was an utter tragedy for the family. He had owned a burgeoning hardware store right in the centre of Kahnawà:ke. He had eight kids and another on the way. My grandfather had grown up an orphan, so having a large family and being successful enough to own a hardware store at that time must have been a dream come true for him.

I am not sure how my tóta, Agnes Karonhienhawe, did it after his death. My tóta came from the "farm." The farm was all the land outside the village of Kahnawà:ke, mostly along Route 207 going toward St. Remi. Kahnawà:ke is only about 13,000 acres, representing what's left of the approximately 40,000 acres in the Seigneurie, with the village itself being only a couple thousand acres of that. Her family was very traditional, as many of the families out on the farm were. I often felt intimidated whenever we would go out there and I'd see cousins I seemed to barely know because I was not knowledgeable about our Kanien'kehá:ka culture and traditions.

That is, my tóta's family was *underground* traditional. While they were some of the ones who kept the old ways, or Tsi Niionkwarihotens, alive in Kahnawà:ke, the Indian Act had formally outlawed the practice of traditional ceremony. Plus, the community was founded as a mission. And so, the continued practice of traditional ceremony was not well received by many community members who wanted to fit in with the new ways; a lot of conflict occurred. But while our traditions were driven underground, they remained. Familial relationships with the rest of the Haudenosaunee communities, as well as with our sister communities of Ahkwesáhsne and Kanehsatà:ke, also helped keep the knowledge alive, even if it was only a shadow of what we once knew.

When my dad was younger, Indian residential schools and day schools were prevalent, the Church was powerful, and the Indian agent, the representative of the federal government, had a lot of control in First Nations communities. An Indian agent operated in Kahnawà:ke from 1821 to 1955, presumably to oversee the wellness of the community on behalf of the government. They instilled Canadian laws and values, often contrary to Kahnawà:ke's own laws and values. I believe my grandfather was raised Roman Catholic, and so he and Tóta lived in the village and raised my dad and his siblings in that religion as well, and then on to my brothers and me. We were the Praying Indians after all!

I don't know much of my grandfather since he died when my dad and his siblings were so young, and there was not a lot of discussion on his upbringing. My aunties told me that after my grandfather died, my tóta worked at the church cleaning the pews, the icons, and all inside the building to make ends meet. They all spent time in the church, I suppose; I always remember going there, hearing my Uncle Eddie's powerful voice in the choir, or sitting on those narrow, painful pews. I remember going to her house as a kid and imagining all the kids growing up there in that small house, wondering what it must have been like.

Even now, I try to imagine what it was like for my father growing up. He had two sisters older than him, Veronica and Geraldine, who everyone called Gerie, and his twin sister Madeline, then his younger siblings Andy, Watio, Angela, Angus, and Louis Tekaronhiake, who was still in the womb when their dad died. He was also known as Louis T., like his father. My dad did well in school, despite it being one of the Indian day schools— and despite my father being a known trickster.

All his siblings, like their parents before them, went to the Indian day school in Kahnawà:ke. The Indian day school in my father's time was pretty bad, especially if you didn't follow the strict rules the nuns expected. It was common practice to use corporal punishment, such as wooden sticks, belts, and other implements. But as bad as those schools might have been, they were not as bad as the residential schools. At those schools, the children were completely isolated from their families and communities, and it was only after they returned that they could tell their families and the community of the regular horrors of abuse, neglect, experimentation, and malnourishment they, or their friends, experienced.

Since my tóta was a single mother with so many children, and they were so poor, the Indian agent had suggested sending some of her children to one of the Indian residential schools where a lot of kids from Kahnawà:ke were forced to go. But my tóta refused to send any of her children to the residential school. Whenever she had needed help, family would step in, including my father's Auntie Towie from Detroit. At times, Auntie Towie would take one or two of the kids to spend a bit of time there to give my tóta a break, but they would always come back. My tóta did whatever she could to take care of all nine of her children.

The Indian day school that my dad, his siblings, and their parents before them attended was run by the Sisters of St. Anne, a group of nuns who have long been celebrated as education and health pioneers and visionaries. The negative impact the sisters had on Indigenous cultures and values is often left unmentioned. To put it simply, the sisters brainwashed us into believing that being Indigenous was wrong or bad; they taught us to be ashamed of being who we were. After all, the goal of the residential and Indian day school systems was to assimilate Indigenous people and eliminate Indigenous culture.

The striking thing to me is many of our people didn't seem to realize the full extent of what was happening; we wanted to be like the non-Indigenous. In many respects, we wanted to fit in, perhaps because we no longer seemed to fit in with our own culture. We were becoming disconnected. We didn't think it strange or wrong. When I read about our history, it often seems that people didn't fully see or understand the impact of colonization as it was happening. It is like the tale of the frog in the boiling pot of water; the frog would immediately jump out if placed in boiling water, but if placed in cold water and slowly heated to boiling, the frog would never notice it. Were we the frogs?

Take what happened with our language, for example. Kahnawà:ke residents were always trilingual speakers. Remember that Kahnawà:ke made peace with the French and partnered with the other Indigenous nations in Quebec to, in essence, support their colonization efforts. In many respects, we lived between the worlds of the Haudenosaunee Confederacy, the French settlers and the English settlers, facilitating trade between all. Our community used to fluently speak Kanien'kéha, English, and French so that we could facilitate trade everywhere. Yet, by the time I was a child, we mainly spoke only English. The sisters were arguably a crucial factor in that change. English was the language spoken in the school, and only at Grade 4 was French introduced as a class.

When my tóta and her generation attended Indian day school, she was forbidden to speak Kanien'kéha. When she became a mother herself, though, she always spoke it at home to her own children. By the time my dad attended school, Kanien'kéha wasn't specifically forbidden, but it was already second nature for English to be spoken in the schools. It was going to school that caused a shift in the daily spoken language in the home. First the older girls spoke mainly English in the house to practice. Then, as each child started attending school more often, the only language in the home amongst the children became English, even if my tóta kept speaking in Kanien'kéha.

By the time my generation came around, our parents didn't speak Kanien'kéha in the home. While our mom was Scottish and didn't know the language, all my cousins and all the friends I played with all grew up speaking English in their homes, too. As our parents became adults, many were able to still understand Kanien'kéha, yet could not speak it. In this way, the language started to become lost. Once they realized this, they pushed to introduce Kanien'kéha language classes in the schools. They were the same length of time as the French class: one hour a week. Most of the school day was in English. This was still truly novel and innovative for us; it was taking back ownership of our own education. This meant I grew up not hearing Kanien'kéha in our home and not speaking it regularly, but I understood a little from the classroom.

As I consider all this, I think of how difficult it must have been for my dad growing up. He had the trauma of losing his father young, of growing up in a large family with barely enough to go around for everyone, of being taught what a good Christian boy is supposed to be like, and of not being able to speak Kanien'kéha. I wonder if he was taught to be ashamed to be Kanien'kehá:ka. To make it all even tougher, he attended Loyola College after high school but needed to drop out of school after a year to work and help financially provide for the family. I never had a chance to ask him what he studied or what he dreamed of becoming by attending, but it makes me wonder now what might have been. Alcohol was a ready escape.

The liquor trade has for centuries been a tool of manipulation and abuse against Indigenous people, with recorded problems as early as the first contact with settlers and colonists. Colonizers brought alcohol with them for personal use but quickly realized its power to hurt Indigenous communities. The impact on Kahnawà:ke was no different. Although our community was designated a "dry" community for many years, alcohol often found its way inside. Some community members would buy it from elsewhere and bring it back in, and other enterprising members would sell it within the community, whether it was with the consent of the authorities or not.

Our community stopped being classified as "dry" in the 1950s, with the establishment of Royal Canadian Legion Branch 219 in 1953, following the Second World War. It was the first Legion located within a First Nations community. Returning veterans wanted a place to connect with other veterans who suffered the consequences of warfare. After that, in 1958, the Knights of Columbus was established to support the social welfare of Roman Catholics and community development. The first Knights of Columbus chapter in Canada opened in Montreal in 1897, and new chapters quickly followed throughout Canada in the early 1900s. Apparently, there was some prestige in being a member of the Knights of Columbus; they helped the war effort, they supported the Church, and they drove home good Christian values.

A large part of both social organizations' business model was the sale of alcohol. Other social clubs opened up after that, such as the Moose Lodge and Marina, to serve other community members who didn't feel like they belonged at the Legion or Knights, until these social organizations became a normal part of the community. Today, I wonder what impact it would have had if these organizations did not influence so much of community life.

My dad and his friends went to the Knights, my Uncle Andy and his army buddies went to the Legion, and my Uncle Angus and his buddies went to the Moose. I associated little good with the place where my father did most of his drinking. When I was a kid, I'd hear about the fights he got into. His nickname at the club was "Mad Dog" because apparently whenever he drank and got in a fight, he would go crazy. I'd hear about the shuffleboard matches he played, and I remember smelling stale beer and cigarettes at the club while we waited for him. A lot of us kids had to wait for our parents who were in the bar, although luckily the Knights of Columbus bar also had a bowling alley next to it. I still remember making a bit of money as a pin boy, resetting the pins after they were knocked down.

It is hard to describe a childhood in an alcoholic home to someone who did not grow up that way. I suppose the best way I could describe it is unexpected chaos followed by periods of peace. A lot of times, things seemed stable at home, but I was never quite sure if they actually were or if they would stay that way. I gained an ability to sense tension but couldn't pinpoint its exact source. Or I sensed it, but became unsure if I actually understood what was happening, doubting my own emotions. I was on edge until I knew if the drinking had started. I grew up in fear. Parents are supposed to provide a sense of security in the home so that children have the tools to manage all the insecurities that come from outside the home. But if a child's home life is insecure, they are already behind the learning curve of managing those emotions and insecurities.

I think each child in a family remembers things differently, and I've often wondered what my brothers' memories were like, although I don't recall asking them. Growing up, it seemed Craig and I had it the roughest. We were so close in age, it was like we were twins. As kids, we would all fight like cats and dogs. Looking back, I know we were taking the pain, anger, and frustration caused by our father, and the helplessness we felt because of it, out on each other. At one point, when I was about eight years old, we had to go see the school counsellor. He asked why we fought so much. I said whatever I could except the truth. I learned early on to wear a mask to feel safe and protected so that people did not know the struggles my family was experiencing.

Part of that was also a sort of guilt. I felt I would be blamed for what was happening and would get in trouble. I learned to lie because the better the lie, the less I experienced pain. I hid my real self behind the mask and presented what I thought people wanted to hear and see. I figured that if the mask were good enough, no one would need to know what I was going through. I didn't want people to know the truth because I was ashamed. Eventually, I wore a mask wherever I went. The mask could change depending on the group of people I was with, but it was never really me.

I got good at it, too. I discovered that if you believe your own lies, the mask becomes nearly impenetrable. I distanced myself from my feelings. I remember having the thought that if I was just a good enough boy, maybe my dad wouldn't drink today; if I did good enough in school, or while playing with my brothers, or with cleaning up the house, then maybe it would be an okay day. And if I knew I wasn't going to be good enough that day, then I told myself the result would be the same if I lied well enough.

As an adult, I tell myself that I was also doing the best I could. We all were. My mom worked relentlessly. Up until I was a teenager, she worked at a place called Town Distributors in Montreal, located just off the traffic-filled Décarie Expressway. As a kid I sometimes went with her to work when there was no sitter; it felt like the traffic would never end, like we were stuck between the two giant concrete retaining walls on each side of the expressway. Later, when I was about fourteen years old, she began working in Kahnawà:ke, first for a local businessman as an administrative assistant, and a couple years after that for Kahnawà:ke Shakotiia'takehnhas Community Services (KSCS), where I work now. My mom was a saviour to us in many ways, and I am amazed at what she has done. But when I was a child, I guess I blamed her, too, thinking it was my dad's fault for drinking and my mom's fault for letting it happen and not protecting me from my dad.

My father quit drinking in 1983 when I was eleven years old. The episode with the Peacekeepers was one of the last straws. My mom had enough of his drinking. He needed to sober up or she was ready to leave. It was at that point that he really started to try to quit, but it was difficult, as it is for anyone with a long-time addiction. Even his health was failing him by that point. I remember going up to the third floor of our old hospital, past the long-term care ward of our Elders with dementia, and seeing my father in a hospital bed with yellow skin. His liver was failing, and he had jaundice. The look of him shivering and staring at me with a smile still sends chills down my spine. He started on a road to recovery not long after that and, after a couple slips, was sober until he died.

I wish I knew my dad more when he was sober. But even though I was still a child when he stopped drinking, at twelve years old I was already wearing my protective mask. Today, I wonder about his journey and his struggles. He went back to school after achieving sobriety and became a well-respected electrician in the community. Although quiet, he was involved and very intelligent. He and my mom had worked through the most challenging part of their marriage and learned to live a sober life together. He used to spend so much time with my younger brother, David. He would go to all his hockey games, and they would watch sports together. My brother got to really know him. Yet not long after my dad stopped drinking, I started.

Chaos comes whenever alcohol is involved. As I'm writing these words, my son is twelve years old. I can hardly believe that I was only slightly younger than him when my dad stopped drinking—and that I was his age when I took my first drink. My cousin Landon had just got the new AC/DC album *For Those About to Rock.* I was fascinated with the cannon on the cover. Craig and I slept over at his house, and for some reason I don't remember, Landon stole some beer from my Uncle Roddy's fridge. We snuck out the back door and went to the lagoon behind their house called Turtle Bay. Turtle Bay is now the location of our Elder's Lodge, but at the time, it was a secluded spot for a teen to get up to mischief. I hated the cigarettes that we tried that night (my first), and I can't say I liked the taste of beer either. But I did love the feeling the alcohol had over me. It created a sense of euphoria, a sense where I didn't have to feel as much. It was wonderful.

From then on, I drank whenever I could. As a teen, I preferred drinking to using drugs. I started going to school in the city. Alcohol was easily available everywhere: parties in Châteauguay, parties in Montreal, parties in Kahnawà:ke. I remember often hitchhiking with my cousin Neil to Châteauguay. There, we would stop at a dépanneur and get someone to buy us wine coolers or beer. Then we would take a cab to Mercier, which is one town away, drinking as fast as we could before we got to the dance. We'd then either spend the night in a drunken stupor or get in a fight. Eventually I quit hockey because it couldn't compete with drinking and not having to *think*. I am not sure that anyone except my brother Craig knew how much I drank. I had become so good at hiding, lying, and masking the truth. Drinking alcohol shaped my worldview.

At the same time, I was also struggling with my identity and connection to culture, and the alcohol helped me not have to worry or think about that disconnection either. I was always so confused about my culture as a kid. My parents met at a factory where they both worked before my mom went to work for Town Distributors. My mom was an old hand at surviving with alcoholics in her life; both her parents died from complications of alcoholism, but my mom never took much to drinking alcohol. Her family had moved to Montreal from Glasgow, Scotland, when she was only three years old. Her father was an Orangeman, through and through. As Protestants, her family was very much against Catholicism, so I can only imagine the conversations she had with them when she and my dad started dating, him being a Catholic and an Indian to boot!

Growing up, I didn't only wonder if I was good enough: I also wondered if I was Kanien'kehá:ka enough. Even as kids in the same community, we noted the differences between us. While Kahnawà:ke had roots as a religious community, we also had a long connection to the Longhouse and the Haudenosaunee Confederacy. There were Catholic kids like me and my brothers, who had to go to get communion, penance, mass, and all that. Then there were the Protestant kids, who were sort of like us Catholic kids without having to do so many rigid things. And then there were the Longhouse kids. I was told by the other kids that they went out to a farm somewhere, the same farmland my extended family lived at, and attended something called *ceremony* at the Longhouse. I had absolutely no idea what that meant and what they actually did. It wasn't spoken of by my teachers, and my dad didn't know either—the people he grew up with weren't raised that way and my tóta didn't teach it to them.

I knew some kids who went to the Longhouse, but we didn't talk about what they did there. I just knew they were different. But were they still Kanien'kehá:ka? They all said they were, and obviously even more so than me. And it certainly seemed true because they spoke Kanien'kéha a lot better than most of us Christian kids could. Were they the *real* Kanien'kehá:ka and we were fake ones? And if all of us Christian kids were already not enough Kanien'kehá:ka, then what exactly did that make me, whose mom was born in Glasgow, Scotland? I had all these questions about myself, and the culture, and with the feeling of having no one to ask. I was left feeling ashamed that I didn't know who I was. Or perhaps it left me feeling ashamed of *who* I was, full stop. I was even confused about what to feel, and so I tried to pretend the confusion didn't bother me, creating another mask in the process.

I couldn't figure it out. What should decide if you are "enough" Kanien'kehá:ka, and what does it even mean to *be* Kanien'kehá:ka? Is it speaking "enough" Kanien'kéha? Or is it practising the cultural activities regularly, like farming, hunting, and fishing? Is it going to ceremony? And if that is the case, does it mean that all those people who practised Catholicism, Protestantism, or any of the other belief systems for all those years were not Kanien'kehá:ka anymore?

Complicating all this for me was a law that Kahnawà:ke introduced in 1984, when I was twelve years old, that required everyone to have at least 60 percent Kanien'kehá:ka ancestry to live in the community. When it was introduced, there was an exception for people who were already living in Kahnawà:ke, like me. We were allowed to stay. Yet while this exception meant I was "enough" Kanien'kehá:ka to stay, as I grew older, I couldn't help but think I was *not really* Kanien'kehá:ka because others like me (one parent Kanien'kehá:ka, one parent not) were not allowed to stay. Despite its intention, the law reinforced divisions that already existed within the community. I remember feeling like I was in limbo. I knew a bunch of other kids who were just like me, but we never spoke about what that was like. No one ever really asked or explained our identity to us; we just survived.

The dance in my mind between whether I was Kanien'kehá:ka or not never quite went away. Even now, whenever I meet someone who is also Kanien'kehá:ka, I wonder if they will accept me because I may not be *enough* for them. If I speak Kanien'kéha, I get scared that if I don't pronounce the words well enough or can't communicate well enough, I will be found out—*look, he is a faker!* And when I meet someone who is not Kanien'kehá:ka, I wonder if I am enough Kanien'kehá:ka for them to be racist toward me. When I was younger, it wasn't lost on me that for anyone outside of Kahnawà:ke, the latter was often true—and when it was, I could find myself in potential danger.

As a child, I experienced the most overt and repeated racism during my hockey games. Organized sports programs were relatively new to Kahnawà:ke at that time. Often spearheaded by motivated parents, including my mom and dad, they offered an opportunity that our parents did not have. We had Onake, the paddling club, and the youth centre, which originally started as a Boys and Girls Club, plus hockey, lacrosse, and baseball. My mom often volunteered to be on the Hockey Association, and after he got sober, when we were teenagers, my dad volunteered to referee and umpire. The trouble would happen when our teams played against neighbouring communities.

My teammates and I faced constant name-calling and aggression, with nearby Valleyfield and Verdun being the worst offenders. Fights would invariably break out, and parents would often get involved. I admit our boys were no angels, but I always saw our fighting as defending ourselves. The worst incident took place in Verdun when one day I was called up to play for the league above my age group. I was a pretty good player, decent at shooting and stick handling, but smaller in stature. I wasn't much of a fighter, though, and that night, the fights started out bad and got worse as the game progressed.

We were leading and it looked like we were winning the game; maybe that was the problem. Things escalated as the other team trailed further and further behind: more penalties, slashing, and racist name-calling, which all provoked retaliation. Finally, everything broke loose. It was a classic bench-clearing brawl, with everybody rushing onto the ice. I remember looking at the stands and seeing parents fighting parents, and my mom looking like she was screaming at a man coming toward her. One man attempted to climb over the glass and onto the ice. It was utter chaos. The police were called in, and everyone was escorted off the ice, with a gauntlet of Verdun parents screaming at us and sending beer bottles flying our way. We made it to the locker room but needed a police escort all the way out of the city. Was that normal? Does that happen to other people? I don't think so.

When I think back on these memories, I am often amazed that I had experiences like that—ones that were so closely related to my identity—while at the same time never being sure of who I *really* was. I began to wonder if all these bad experiences added up to who I really was. In other words, I wondered if I was all the things people called me and all the bad things that happened to me.

As I hit my teen years, my drinking increased. I became even better at hiding who I was—and also better at hiding from the bad things I experienced. I was increasingly putting myself in dangerous situations and going to places I simply should not have been. Attending an all-boys school didn't afford me much interaction with girls, and I eventually discovered the world of pornography and peep shows in downtown Montreal. I would sneak in the back and watch porn on little screens in a locked room until one day I did so on the wrong day.

I was about to go in one of the booths when, suddenly, a knife was at my throat. I never saw the man holding it. He forced me into a booth and assaulted me. I was sixteen. Afterward, cleaning myself from the blood and fluid, I was overwhelmed by shame. Also, weakness and fear. And I was angry, mostly at myself. There was hatred. But above all, shame. *What will people think of me now?* I thought. *How do I tell someone this?* If I was barely accepted as half Kanien'kehá:ka, I wondered what people would say when they found out I'd been raped. I wanted to make sure nobody would ever find out what had happened. Who could I possibly tell that would understand? How the hell would I survive this? *I know,* I thought, *I will drink it all away, and it will be like it never happened.*

So I drank, again and again. I tried to forget. I told myself it never happened and ignored the fact that I was having daily nightmares and that my jaw would ache in the morning from grinding my teeth. I drank whenever the feelings or the memories got too much. I was focused on trying to survive. I struggled a lot with sexuality after that. Was I gay? I was never attracted to men, but maybe that guy knew something I didn't. When I was with a woman, would she know what had happened to me?

Could you sense something like that? I made my mask stronger and pretended that I was okay, that nothing had happened.

I wrote that I joined the Canadian Army because there was a long history of service in my community. That's true, but after my assault I also wanted to learn how to fight and defend myself. I did well in the army, but after the 1990 Oka Crisis and all the racism I faced, I decided to leave and join the US Marine Corps in September 1990, right when the US was building up forces in defence of Saudi Arabia as part of Operation Desert Shield, following the invasion of Kuwait by Iraq. I wasn't afraid of getting deployed. I figured that if I got killed in combat, at least no one would ever hurt me again. I went to Parris Island on January 3, 1991, a Marine Corps training centre in South Carolina, shortly before Operation Desert Storm—the combat phase—kicked off on January 17, 1991.

By the time I finished my initial training, I was assigned to a unit in Okinawa, Japan. I never ended up in a combat zone, but I kept drinking, especially when the memories got too bad. The Marines don't mind an alcoholic as long as you can still be a good Marine. I wish I could share all about the wonderful things I saw in Okinawa, but when I first arrived there, I found a bar instead. My cousin Landon was already stationed there, and when we reunited, he introduced me to a little bar called Lemon Hearts and its owner Kay. Over the next year, I spent many a night there playing pool and trying to ignore anything called a *feeling*.

After Okinawa, I moved on to the Marine Corps base in El Toro, California, managed to get married, and had my son Trevor. All the while, I continued to hide who I was. About a year after we had Trevor, we moved to Michigan so I could work as a recruiter convincing (or trying to convince) young men and women to join the Marines. That's when things started to change. By then, my dad had been fighting throat cancer for three years, while for three years I had been mostly ignoring that he was sick. He sent me letters in an attempt to communicate, but I could only open them when I had a few drinks in me. But the end was close now, and my mom insisted that I come home to say goodbye. It was his third bout of throat cancer, and radiation and surgery were no longer effective. Chemo was the only option, which my dad refused. He had no more fight left in him.

It normally took eight hours for me to drive home, but this time I made it in six and a half hours—drinking a six-pack on my way to the hospital. My family members were all waiting on different parts of the hospital floor so they could direct me to the right room. Once I got there, my mom kicked everyone out except for my brothers and me. I remember walking up to the bed and seeing my dad look at me. He was a skeleton. His hands were shaking from the morphine, and he was holding a turtle rattle. Tears were in his eyes. During his previous bout, they'd had to remove his tongue, and he hadn't spoken a word in about a year and a half. I had so much to say. So many unsaid words over so many years. But all I could say was "I am sorry. I love you, Dad." That was it. He closed his eyes, and a few hours later, he passed on to the Sky World.

A few months after my dad died, my mom came to visit me and my family in Michigan. I avoided her and said I had to work late. But I was drinking. Whenever the memories and the grief became too hard, I shoved the grief aside with some alcohol. When it was time for her to leave and we were saying goodbye, she looked me in the eyes and said, "I know what you are doing and how much you are drinking. You need help."

I knew she was right, and yet the road to sobriety is often a long one. I spent another three years going back and forth between admitting to myself I was an alcoholic and then being convinced that I wasn't. I'd go to treatment and then tell myself I didn't need it because I was different. I'd get in trouble with the law for driving under the influence and then say it was a simple mistake. I quit alcohol to save my marriage and then told myself the marriage was not worth saving. I felt so paralyzed that when I spoke with a counsellor at the local base, he was convinced I was suicidal. I convinced the hospital that I wasn't.

And then in April 2001, I got my fourth DUI. I had managed to keep them all a secret from the Marines, but now I truly despaired. There was no way I could hide this anymore. I thought that when the Marines found out, I would get a bad conduct discharge, and I was already picturing the shame I would feel for failing. At this point, I was divorced and I barely saw my son. I was living with a friend with nothing except two bags of clothes and my Marine Corps gear. I was disconnected from family, friends, and community; I felt I had no roots anymore. I'd had enough. I couldn't imagine surviving much longer while still using alcohol, but I also couldn't imagine going through life without the alcohol to block my feelings.

So, instead of attempting to quit drinking again, I decided to make a new plan that night. I bought a few bottles of alcohol, maybe gin or scotch. Then, I made a video to explain to my son why I took my own life. I wrote a note. I drew a bath. I had every intention of drinking away the pain and then cutting my femoral artery.

And then the phone rang. It was 3:30 a.m. I answered. It was my younger brother, David. He had never called me at all before, but on this night he did. He asked what I was up to, and instead of putting up my mask to say everything was fine, I told him the truth. I didn't care to hide anymore because I was leaving and no one would know. I told David so that he would know, and maybe he could tell everyone back home why I did it. I don't remember the conversation, but it helped. Why he called that night, at that time, I truly don't know. But I am convinced the Creator, however we imagine him, her, or it, played a part.

I went back to AA the next morning. I got a sponsor. I went to meetings almost every day that I could. I did all the right things. I worked hard and I got sober. And I kept being sober. It wasn't always easy. A couple of years into my sobriety, I remember really struggling. At the time, I was a relatively new manager for our Support and Prevention Services at KSCS. I had gone to Victoria, British Columbia, for a conference on child welfare, and after the conference, I took a bit of extra time to go to Washington to visit Craig and his wife, Angelique.

We got into an argument, and I had the overwhelming desire to drink again. I was angry and frustrated, and I couldn't calm the storm in my head. I decided to take a drive to Mount Rainier. I drove all the way up the mountain, and when I got to the top of the mountain, the whole mountain was covered in fog. *AAARRGGG!* was my only thought. *The Creator was against me!* I started to drive back down the mountain, fully intending on heading to a bar. But a little whisper in my head told me to stop the car and take a walk.

I started down one of the forest trails, with fog all around me. The trail led to a ravine formed from the stones left by a glacier. I climbed over the massive boulders, just putting one foot in front of the other. I remember that at one point, I stopped and stared at a rock face. Everywhere else, I could see nothing but fog, but here was this rock face straight ahead of me, and it was clear of fog. My eyes started travelling up the face until my neck strained, and I was looking skyward. I stared and saw a pair of eagles circling each other and settling into a nest high above. I felt like the Creator made that happen for me. I was at peace for the rest of that trip. The walk made me realize that whenever my head is full of fog, my priority should be to get into the natural world. It can do wonders for my soul.

I have since learned many methods of healing. Tai chi, and especially Qigong, helped me understand how the energy inside me moved. Exploring Hinduism and Buddhism led me to various types of meditation and yoga, and I eventually became a regular practitioner of hot yoga. Meditation helped me start to understand my inner world. I started drawing and painting, and I learned about aromatherapy and Bach flower remedies. I began to exercise and even managed to complete a half marathon (which was plenty good enough for me). I started trying to eat like how we Kanien'kehá:ka used to eat, like the Three Sisters, with wild game and fresh fish.

Yet, while all these teachings helped get me closer to feeling more healed, I sensed they were still not quite *me*. It wasn't until I started learning and incorporating Kanien'kehá:ka culture that I started to make the most progress, and I began to let the masks truly slip away. Many of the challenges I experienced, and perhaps how I dealt with them, were either directly or indirectly the products of colonization. And it was with these realizations that I started my life over, this time on the Red Road, as the Oglala Sioux say. Following the Red Road signifies a deep commitment to living your best life, respecting yourself, others, and all of Creation, in addition to being free of alcohol, drugs, and anything that can damage oneself or others. While walking this road, I have used our traditional medicines and healing methods, thanks to the many Knowledge Keepers who helped me in finally finding my culture.

One of those people who helped me heal is a counsellor from Kahnawà:ke named Rakwirenhtha, to whom I'm eternally grateful. He introduced me to the "House of Pain," which is what he called the Sweat Lodge because it is where we go to face all the pain we have hidden deep inside ourselves. It would come out in that dark space, and you had to face it because there was nowhere to run. The Sweat Lodge is made by taking branches and bending them to connect with each other to create a small hut, which is then covered by heavy hide or canvas. Modern materials can be used, but it is always better to use natural tools. It is small, and to enter it a person has to crawl inside on their hands and knees. The inside is so pitch black that you can't even see your hand in front of your face. A hole is dug in the centre of the lodge and filled with rocks that were heated in a fire outside. Water is poured on the rocks and steam released, just like the Bastu, or saunas, in Sweden and Finland. I know that many First Nations use the Sweat Lodge, but I never knew about it until I went in the first time.

Rakwirenhtha helped me understand different aspects of our culture, and I also told him my story. He and Fran, his better half, as well as other healers helped me understand the context in which my relationships were formed. I started to understand that while those bad things did happen to me, they were just milestones on the way to discovering who I was. *They did not define me.* And if they did not define me, then I could figure out a way to let them go. I did not have to carry them. And the way to let them go, for me at least, was through the Sweat Lodge.

Before I went in, I would drink a big two-gallon jug of water that contained various traditional medicines. First Rakwirenhtha, Fran, and the other healers prepared them, but eventually I also learned how to do it. I was told to think hard about the issue I was going to be facing that day in the lodge so that the medicine's energy would help with the ceremony I was about to do. The medicine caused me to vomit, and shortly after, I would go inside. The healers then walked me through whatever issue or memory I was facing that day. I often relived the experiences I had, but this time from a place of safety. By walking through the memory with a guide, I was able to not feel trapped within the memory but instead obtain a sense of freedom. The healers explained to me that our spirits become trapped in these painful memories, so the ceremony is to retrieve our spirit from the memory they are tied to.

As my healing progressed, I began regularly using spiritual medicine. The healers taught me about our four sacred medicines: tobacco, cedar, sage, and sweetgrass. Many First Nations use these medicines to clean and purify their spirits. I learned that each medicine has different but related purposes. Tobacco is one of our most sacred medicines and is used as a way to establish communication with the Creator. Cedar is used as a physical, emotional, and spiritual cleansing when burned, and it can also be used as a bath or to clear the air, or even as a tea. Sage, and more specifically white sage, is used to get rid of negative energies and spirits, and it can also act as a cleanser. This is what is traditionally used in a smudge stick, which is what we use to purify our spirits of negative emotions and to connect with the spiritual world. The last of the four sacred medicines is sweetgrass. I was taught that it has an opposite effect from the sage—rather than clear negative energy, it is used to bring in positive energy. We burn sweetgrass to encourage positive feelings, movement, and energy to come into our lives, and ropes of braided sweetgrass are often used as a gift for this exact reason.

It has been a long road to wellness, and I'm still learning. Although I still feel shame at times, I fight that feeling by continuing to learn about my culture. There is a major revitalization of our culture, not just in Kahnawà:ke, but in all Indigenous communities, as we begin to realize the impact that colonization had on us. This has been a big part of my healing, and I think the healing for all Indigenous people.

As a child, I always used my English name, Derek, and my Kanien'kéha name, which was written Arienios, felt almost foreign. When I started on my healing journey, I asked an Elder what my name meant. He said that it doesn't mean anything. Others tried to guess. I eventually found out the right spelling from my Auntie Gerie: Aronhie:nens, after my Uncle Eddie's name. The priest wrote it the wrong way on my baptismal certificate, and that is how it was entered on my birth certificate. Another Elder told me Aronhie:nens means "the place where the sky and the earth meet," but recently, my Auntie Gerie confirmed that it means the place where the sky is coming down or falling from the sky. I may never know for sure; I am not a speaker.

Experiences like these have taught me that healing cannot happen in isolation. An individual heals within their family and community. If the family of birth is still in the depths of their own trauma, then a new family must be found. If the community is full of pain and suffering, then rebuilding a community is necessary. Unfortunately, many First Nations communities are in the latter situation, and much rebuilding still needs to occur. My own journey is a large part of why I have since dedicated my life to improving my community for the next generations to come. I constantly strive to learn how I can best help our people in health and social services and to provide leadership wherever I can.

This is what I hope to accomplish from writing this book as well. I am telling my journey from my viewpoint, but others will see their own journey differently. Some may be ready to make changes, and some need help. Everyday reconciliation is about achieving these everyday changes. And it is through conscious action, like supporting someone who is going through trauma and not judging them, that this everyday reconciliation will be achieved.

I maintain my sobriety every day. It has now been over twenty-three years since I had a drink. AA helped save my life, and now I can use the gifts the Creator gave me to help others. I've learned, slowly, over many years, how to take off the mask and introduce the real me to people and to accept their reactions. I try my hardest not to put the mask back on, and when I catch myself doing so—because it can be unconscious—I do my best to let it go.

We Are All Ambassadors

Elin Sandberg Miller

I STOPPED TO catch my breath. I knew the air would be thin, but I was still caught off guard. It was 2000, late August, and this was my first day in Colombia—and also the first day of my first posting as a diplomat. I was climbing up the Monserrate, a steep mountain reaching over 3,000 metres above sea level. The Monserrate summit can be reached by both cable car and a rail-based funicular, but I had chosen to walk up the range, like the many pilgrims who come here to pray and find spiritual guidance from *El Señor Caído*. In English, that translates to "The Fallen Lord," fitting for a statue of Jesus depicted as having fallen under the weight of the Cross.

I was the only blond person around; everyone I met was Colombian. They were courteous and friendly, like most people I'd meet during my time there. The lack of tourists was a result of the internal armed conflict that had ravaged the country for decades. After violent clashes between the Liberal and Conservative political parties in the late 1940s, an armed conflict erupted between the government and newly formed guerrilla groups in the 1960s. While the guerrilla groups initially fought for equality and socio-economic reforms in defence of impoverished communities, the conflict became increasingly more complex with the creation of paramilitary groups and drug cartels. Eventually, all parties, the guerrilla included, were focused on control over territory, coca production, and drug trafficking routes.

Before I left for Colombia, I had researched the country, its history, culture, and politics, and the Swedish Ministry for Foreign Affairs had provided me with Spanish language training, which I'd gladly undertaken. I knew I wouldn't be of much use as a diplomat if I couldn't communicate with my interlocutors or understand what was going on. It would also be embarrassing for a country if its representatives were clueless or committed cultural faux pas due to ignorance. I was proud to be working at the Ministry for Foreign Affairs, proud to be fresh out of the diplomatic training program, and proud to have done my homework.

Because of that, I knew that Monserrate has been a sacred site since pre-Colombian times, when the Bogotá area was inhabited by the Muisca people, known for their fine goldwork. But it wasn't until I set out to write this essay that I read up a bit more about the Muisca people. They were organized in a loose confederation of states, with most of them sharing the same language and culture. Their population was estimated at somewhere between one and three million before the Spanish invaded the area in the 1500s in search of the mythical golden kingdom, *El Dorado*. The Spanish tore down the city's Muisca temples and replaced them with Catholic buildings, including the one on Monserrate. Their arrival also led to the drastic decline of the Muisca population, along with their language, culture, and much of their history.

I wonder if I would have felt differently that day had I known more about the Muisca's history. As it was, when I reached the top after the long climb in the sharp sunlight, I felt pure delight as I soaked up the spectacular views. Bogotá is built on a plateau in the Andes, flanked by mountain ranges. Far below me, the immense city with its many vibrant neighbourhoods stretched so far that I couldn't see the end of it. The high-rises marking the city's business district shimmered in the sun as they reached for the deep blue sky. On the horizon, beyond the city limits, the sky met the lush, green hills of the western mountain range. For my first posting as a diplomat, I figured I was off to a good start.

Looking back, however, I can see that there were things I still hadn't prepared for or learned enough about. I knew very little about the Muisca or any other Indigenous people in Colombia. I didn't think of studying any of Colombia's Indigenous languages before I left in addition to the Spanish I'd learned and had only a vague idea about the extent to which they were still spoken. In truth, I didn't know much at all about the Indigenous Peoples in Colombia, what their lives looked like before the conquistadores arrived, and what they looked like when I was there.

According to the National Indigenous Organization of Colombia, as I would later learn, the Muisca people are only one of more than one hundred different Indigenous Peoples living in the land the Spaniards named Colombia. Like the Muisca, most of them were drastically diminished as a result of the conflict, famine, and disease that followed contact. Today, it is estimated that Indigenous people make up between 4 and 10 percent of the country's total population of fifty-five million. In Bogotá, a city of ten million people, there are no more than 5,700 people who identify as Muisca. There are currently efforts to revitalize Indigenous languages and cultures in Colombia, yet at the same time Indigenous Peoples continue to face marginalization and non-recognition. Many are fighting for their survival, threatened by poverty, resource extraction projects, armed conflict, and targeted killings.

During my one-year posting in Colombia, I had the opportunity to visit the Emberá people in the Chocó region in the Pacific coastal part of Colombia. I travelled there together with representatives of Swedish and Colombian aid organizations, as well as the International Peace Brigades, a non-governmental organization that seeks to protect human rights defenders, Indigenous people, and others in conflict areas by increasing visibility and exposure of any attacks against them. The Emberá historically lived in dispersed settlements along the river systems of Panamá and Colombia. While a majority have transitioned to settled communities and urban areas, the Emberá have to some extent been able to maintain their culture, in contrast to the Muisca people, in part thanks to their remote location.

To get to the small Emberá village, we took a boat from Quibdó, the capital of Chocó, which is located on the bank of the Atrato River. If I remember correctly, the community was facing the threat of either a hydro development or mining project, in addition to suffering from poverty and the impacts of the armed conflict. Despite such severe challenges, the members had prepared for our visit, proudly displaying traditional painted body tattoos, clothing, and beaded jewellery. Some of the women and girls were wearing colourful, short wraparound skirts and no tops, in the traditional way, while the men were in Western shorts and shirts. Almost everyone was barefoot, except for a few men in rubber boots. The children were shy but curious, following us around while we were given a tour of the village. There was no electricity or running water, and the dwellings were simple, mostly made from wooden boards, partly open-air, with roofs from tarp or corrugated metal.

In the middle of our visit, a group of armed men driving a Jeep stopped in the village. They had a flat tire and requested assistance. We could see that the vehicle was stolen: Someone had spray-painted the name of a guerrilla group over the official logo of the Attorney General's Office. The Emberá helped in silence as the guerrilla soldiers watched over them with their machine guns. Shortly after they left, another Jeep full of armed men stopped by—this time a paramilitary group. They wanted to know about the guerrilla group: What was it doing there, and had the Emberá helped them? The situation was tense, and I remember staying in the background, not wanting our presence there to cause our hosts any additional problems. I also recall a sense of guilt over my privilege, knowing that soon after these men were gone, I would be on my way back to my secure and comfortable life, while the people in the village would continue to face threats from all sides, with no relief in sight.

In 2016, five years after I left Colombia, the Colombian government and the largest guerrilla group, the Revolutionary Armed Forces of Colombia (FARC), finally agreed on a peace accord. Despite this, many regions in the country, including the Chocó department, remain a battleground for illegal armed groups who fight for control over coca production, illegal gold mining, and trafficking routes. The civilian population in these areas continues to get caught in the crossfire, just as I had seen with the Emberá people: No matter what they do, they get accused of siding with the enemy. They suffer from threats, sexual violence, targeted killings, kidnappings, disappearances, forced confinement, and forced recruitment, and the government is taking insufficient steps to protect them. Colombia has one of the largest internally displaced populations in the world. In 2022 in Chocó alone, over 6,000 people were forced to leave their homes, including many Emberá people, further threatening their culture and language.

My visit to the Emberá village was a powerful experience and a stark illustration of the realities of an internal armed conflict, where everyone is forced to take sides or perceived to be even when they don't. But it also clearly demonstrated how Indigenous Peoples are often—quite literally—caught in the crossfire as powerful actors fight for control over their land and resources. I wish I had known more about the Muisca, Emberá, and other

Indigenous Peoples in Colombia before I got there, to better understand what losing their culture and language meant to them, and to Colombia as a nation.

Despite my experience in Colombia, it wasn't until I found myself living in Canada years later, witnessing the marginalization of Indigenous Peoples here, that I reflected more carefully on what it would mean to lose your culture and language. During my childhood in the 1970s and early 1980s, Sweden was still a fairly homogenous culture where everybody around me spoke Swedish and celebrated the same holidays. As I've previously shared, we had the impression that the Sami lived in the north, where they practised reindeer herding, and that was that.

But I have since learned the wrongness of that assumption. Today, the Sami people live throughout Sweden—and while many Swedes think only of those Sami whose lives visibly centre on reindeer herding, which is an important source of income and traditional way of life, that population is, in fact, the minority of Sami. When I think about it, I likely encountered Sami people growing up without knowing it. For centuries, since the forced assimilation of the Sami started in the 17th century, they have faced racism and discrimination and have been persecuted for their beliefs by the Swedish government, supported by the Church, resulting in many Sami hiding their Sami identity to protect themselves.

In his previous essay, "Losing Your Identity, Losing Your Soul," Derek shared a deeply personal perspective on losing his language and culture, effectively demonstrating how assimilation policies cause harm to both communities and individuals, impacting them for generations. In Canada, the 1876 Indian Act was an important vehicle for the government's assimilation efforts. Through various amendments, it increasingly restricted

First Nations' right to conduct cultural and spiritual ceremonies such as the powwow, Potlatch, and Sundance. First Nations would sometimes hold ceremonies in secret. In 1921, the government raided a Potlatch in the Kwakwaka'wakw village of 'Mimkwamlis (also spelled Memkumlis), arrested forty-five people, and sent about half of them to prison.

In the 1921 Potlatch raid, the government confiscated hundreds of precious Kwakwaka'wakw ceremonial objects, such as drums and masks, to prevent their use. In an act of economic exploitation, they further sold many of those items to collectors and museums around the world. How ironic that while Indigenous cultures had to be suppressed in Canada, our government and others also apparently viewed them as important enough to preserve and display! The Canadian Museums Association estimates that 6.7 million Indigenous objects and human remains are still held by Canadian museums. Today, many communities are working to have their artifacts and other items returned to them, where they belong.

When I was little in Sweden, my dad would take me and my siblings to see my paternal grandmother, who lived nearby in a town even smaller than our own. During those visits, we would sometimes visit the town's little museum. This was generally a boring outing, imposed on us kids over the years, but there was one thing that drew our attention and evoked a sense of horror-infused excitement: an Indian head! We didn't know where this human head, which was intact with skin and hair, came from, how it was preserved, or the context in which it was taken; it was confusing. If there was any historical information provided, I must have missed it. I especially remember my puzzlement over its smallness, as the head's facial features were not those of a child.

When writing this essay, I finally looked up the information I missed as a child. I discovered that what I saw was likely a so-called shrunken head, a human head that some Indigenous

Peoples in the Amazon would shrink and preserve through a special process and use for trophy, ritual, trade, or other purposes. I found it deeply disturbing that this grossly misplaced cultural object was, in retrospect, my first encounter with Indigenous Peoples. (The second was through watching the TV series *How the West Was Won*, which, I can see today, was full of false and romanticized ideas about the necessary casualties of a nation's growth. The show was widely popular in Europe.) The practice of displaying Indigenous objects and human remains behind museum glass without consent is wrong in so many ways, but it has also contributed to the colonial narrative that "Indians" are a thing of the past.

This narrative would be true for Canada—had its assimilation project succeeded. But despite its efforts, the Canadian government failed: Indigenous Peoples are still here. Like other colonial governments, it did, however, manage to destroy much of Indigenous culture and render several Indigenous languages extinct and many others endangered. Many of my podcast guests stressed the importance of revitalizing and keeping Indigenous cultures and languages alive. They also stressed the importance for the national reconciliation process of non-Indigenous people learning about their culture. I'm embarrassed over how little I knew about Sami culture growing up, or about Indigenous cultures and languages when I arrived in Colombia on my first diplomatic posting. Rectifying this now, in Canada, is an important part of my own everyday reconciliation.

In the summer of 2024, I had a very special opportunity to learn about the Sundance ceremony. I was invited by Cree language teacher Doctor Kevin Lewis, a friend of my husband's, to participate in a Sundance in Ministikwan Lake Cree Nation on Treaty 6 Territory in Saskatchewan. Together with his mother, Elder

Matilda Lewis, Kevin runs the kâniyâsihk Cultural Camps, a non-profit educational organization in Ministikwan. At the camp, they offer Indigenous children, youth, and adults a place to rediscover their culture and to learn how to live off the land. Participants get to harvest and prepare herbs used for medicine, tea, and smudging; fish and hunt; tan hides; and build birchbark canoes. In 2005, guided by an Elder who was the area's last canoe maker, Kevin built the first prototype for the canoe making at kâniyâsihk. Before he reinitiated the practice, it hadn't been done in Ministikwan since the 1940s.

I had visited Indigenous communities before and attended a few powwows, but this was different. The Sundance is both more private and more spiritual, and participants are usually members of the community or those who've been specifically in-vited. It involves days of fasting, dancing, and praying. (Though there aren't many written experiences of the Sundance ceremony, Kevin and Sundance Chief Wilfrid Watherhen have given their consent for me to write about my experience here. "I think it's time," Kevin told me.)

Like other Indigenous ceremonies in Canada, Sundance was prohibited for many years. While there are sometimes more than one Sundance hosted each year in a community, the one I attended has only taken place since 2008. Today, it's now an important annual celebration, allowing older and younger generations to rediscover—or discover for the first time—their culture and to truly immerse themselves in it. At the time, I was honoured to have been invited but also a little apprehensive. I didn't know what to expect.

Before the Sundance, I flew to Edmonton, where I met with my husband, who was already out west for work. From there, we rented a car to drive the four hours to Ministikwan, which is located northeast of Lloydminster in Saskatchewan. Besides a brief visit to Banff nearly two decades earlier, I had never visited

Alberta or Saskatchewan. The drive was an experience in itself. The road was straight and the landscape flat. I had never seen such flat terrain; there was nothing that blocked my view. The bright green fields went on and on, uninterrupted all the way to the horizon, which seemed unnaturally far away. It was mesmerizing.

Eventually, though, my view was interrupted, as I spotted a concrete industrial grain elevator towering high above the road ahead of us. As we got nearer, I saw a long train snaking its way around the facility, ready to transport the grain away. It had more cars than I had time to count, but I'm guessing there were at least one hundred. I was taken aback by the size and apparent efficiency of it all. It made me think about how First Nations on the Prairies had lost their land, and it struck me that the agriculture that seemed to so strongly characterize the landscape was, in reality, a relatively new phenomenon. This land used to be covered by buffalo herds, roaming free, grazing the prairie grass, and feeding, clothing, and providing shelter for the First Nations who have lived here for thousands of years.

What really drove home the point, though, was when I realized what the squares dotting our car's GPS map represented: reserves. I thought back to the Blanket Exercise from years earlier. All this beautiful land had belonged to First Nations. Then, with the railroad, more and more settlers arrived, and their first little patches of farmland expanded until their fields blanketed nearly the entire landscape. Now it was the land reserved for Indigenous Peoples that appeared as small patches on the map. From a historical perspective, one of the oldest cultures in the world had been nearly erased in the blink of an eye.

I was still thinking about this when we arrived at the kâni-yâsihk Cultural Camps on the shore of the beautiful Lake Minis-tikwan in the early evening. Birch and poplar trees grew high on the slope leading down to the water, where sweetgrass and wild mint thrived at the water's edge. It was here that I prepared for my first Sundance together with some other visitors, including a group of Indigenous youth from Terrace, BC. I learned how to make a whistle from eagle bone and spruce gum, and I helped with grinding the dried herbs that would be used for smudging during the ceremony. Working outdoors under a large, open tent, together we turned sweetgrass, sweet pine, diamond willow, cedar, and different kinds of sage into a wonderfully fragrant powder. Many of the women also used this time to sew beautiful ribbon skirts to wear during the dancing. I had made mine before coming there, struggling for days at the sewing machine in my kitchen back in Ottawa, guided by a YouTube video.

While the women prepared back at the camp, the men were at the Sundance grounds, picking out the site for the new Sundance lodge. It was the men's role to build the lodge, which meant starting with felling the trees—it was a good day's job. First, they selected the tree for the important centre pole that would hold up the round, open structure where the praying and dancing would take place.

The night before the dancing started, I headed over with the other women from the camp to join the men for a feast at the Sundance ground. We gathered in a large field at the outskirts of the community where grass and wildflowers grew high. The remains of previous Sundance lodges were scattered around like large wooden skeletons. They are considered sacred and left to decompose in their own time. Here and there, a piece of colourful fabric had been left behind, fluttering in the wind. Kevin explained to me that the focus of Sundance participants is the Creator and the centre pole, which he called the Tree of Life. The two of them had a conversation during the ceremony, and that the tree must remain there for the animals, birds, and flowers who may need it. A new lodge allows a new discussion with the Creator.

Inside a tipi, Elders from the community, men and some women, performed a pipe-smoking ceremony. The ceremonial pipes are sacred, and smoking them, I learned, is a powerful way of communicating with the spirit world. The ceremony can take place to seal a treaty or, like on the first night I was there, to offer prayers, with the smoke from the tobacco carrying the prayers to the Creator. Outside the tipi, younger men tended to a fire, carrying the hot coals inside for smudging. It was raining and chilly, and they also used the fire to warm up the drums for the Elders, holding them over the fire until they made the right sound again.

Together with women and children from the community, I sat outside the tipi, listening to the music and song, trying to stay dry and warm. All the songs and prayers were in Cree. The women I sat next to generously explained some of it—stories about their people's history, about Earth and its various beings— but I still missed most of the meaning, and it made me feel inadequate, like a spectator rather than part of the group. When the ceremony was over, the men carried around large, steaming pots of food: soup, lard, bannock, and tea, ensuring that all of us, whether inside the tipi or listening from outside, were properly fed. Many had brought containers that they filled to the rim with food to bring back home. Nothing was wasted.

The dancing started in the early evening the next day, once the men had finished building the Sundance lodge. A small ceremony took place in which the men raised the tall centre pole made from white poplar, which I mistook for birch, while we women stood by, blowing our whistles. The lodge was a large, round structure, perhaps eight to ten metres in diameter, created from young trees staked into the ground. Branches were woven between the young trees to create two circular fences, an outer and an inner one, with a corridor about one metre wide between them. This corridor was the place for the dancers, while the large round space in the middle was reserved for the Sundance Chief and the other Elders who would drum and sing while we danced and prayed.

The men had also leaned thinner tree trunks against the larger centre pole, which looked like spokes reaching for the hub in a wheel. At the top of the centre pole, they had tied large pieces of fabric in different colours that have varying meanings, some honouring the sun and other elements of nature. The colours appeared to glow in the sunlight against the light blue sky. The lodge was beautiful, and together the smell of fresh leaves, the tall centre pole, and the brightly coloured cloth reminded me of a Swedish Midsummer celebration. At the time of the summer solstice, Swedes decorate a large pole with leaves and wildflowers, raise it through a similar effort, and dance around it. But the comparison ends there, as Swedish Midsummer, at least as it is celebrated today, lacks the spirituality of a Sundance.

During my time in Ministikwan, I learned that an important part of Sundance is fasting. There is no eating or drinking for as long as the dancing lasts. Dancing for so long is already a challenge; fasting while doing it only adds to the physical and mental effort. Kevin explained that fasting was considered an important personal sacrifice, as well as being symbolically important at the community level. As in older times, communities sometimes didn't have enough food, and the fasting was meant to teach people to appreciate when they did.

I could understand that: I still remember how good my first meal tasted after Sundance. Kevin highlighted that it's also good for your health. I found that it helped me focus on the praying. Some dancers started fasting the night before the dance, right after the feast, but I waited a bit longer, until after lunch the following day. I wanted to try the bannock dogs that were on the camp lunch menu. I don't much like hot dogs, but the warm, crispy, deep-fried bannock bread with hot dogs inside was delicious. It was the last thing I ate until the end of Sundance.

During the preparations, the other first-timers and I from the kâniyâsihk Cultural Camps were trying to figure out what to expect. I am used to reading up and being prepared when I go into new situations, and I was keen to follow the Protocols. It wasn't simply to avoid my own embarrassment but also to demonstrate respect to the Elders and the dancers. Including me, there were a few non-Indigenous people dancing, invited by Kevin, and one of them was doing her fifth year. She could see I was a bit nervous and kindly tried to answer all my questions: When would the dancing and praying start? How long would it go on for? How should I carry myself? I had also learned about the dance from my husband and my friend Diane, who had both participated before. Diane is Anishinaabe Ikwe, an Ojibwe woman, from the Eagle Clan of the Batchewana First Nation on Robinson–Huron Treaty territory. (Diane has a wonderful Anishinaabe name: Kitchi-no-aagisishe ma'iingan, which means "the voice of the wolf that howls at the full moon.") She's the one who told me to prepare a ribbon skirt and to bring coloured cloth, a blanket, and gifts, and she got me the tobacco that I would need.

But despite my attempts at preparing myself, as we all finally walked into the lodge, positioning ourselves next to each other in the circle, men on one side, women on the other, there was still so much I didn't understand. I looked at the others for guidance as I hung my pieces of fabric over the fence, one piece for each prayer, put down my folded-up blanket on the ground to kneel or sit on between dances, and set my tobacco to the side. The tobacco was for later, to be gifted to the helpers who assisted the Elders with the ceremony, as thanks for their support. One of the helpers walked around with hot coal on a shovel from a fire outside the lodge. He handed me the shovel, and I used a stick to scrape off bits of the glowing coal into a little pile on the ground in front of me. Leaning forward on my knees, taking the cue from my neighbours, I sprinkled some medicine over it. The herbs quickly turned to ashes, leaving a light, pleasantly fragrant smoke swirling upward.

I used my hands to "wash" myself as if the smoke were water. It was the first time that I smudged on my own, and I initially worried that I didn't do it the right way. That feeling soon faded, and I smudged at every opportunity, between the songs and prayers throughout the ceremony. Diane later explained to me that smudging purifies the body and soul and brings you closer to the Creator: You clean your ears and eyes to see and hear more clearly; your mouth to speak the truth; your heart to be good; and you bring the smoke over your head and behind you to chase away bad energy. It can give you a renewed sense of yourself, and, at least for me, it is calming and makes me feel grounded.

Back at the Sundance, the Elders sat in a ring in the middle of the lodge. Once they started drumming and singing, we got up to dance and pray. When the drumming stopped, we sat down, hidden behind the fence. During the dancing, the men, who were across from us, held on to eagle wings, waving them to the rhythm of the drumbeats. The women instead tied scarves to the fence that they held on to while dancing. I didn't have one; this was one of many things I hadn't known about, but a kind neighbour quickly lent me an extra.

We all moved in time with the drumbeats, bending our knees to the rhythm, us women holding on to our fabric, the men to their eagle wings. And we whistled. When I had prepared my whistle, I didn't realize how important it would be during the ceremony, but the whole time we danced, we blew our whistles to accompany the drumming. I had worried about the fasting, especially going without water, but I never felt hungry or thirsty, only dry in my throat from all my whistling. (Toward the end, though, I suddenly remembered the ginger ale I'd left in the car, and I couldn't stop thinking about it.)

Many times during Sundance, I wished there had been a written manual that explained the procedures and the meaning of it all. More than once, the helpers yelled out, "Eyes on the centre pole!" to remind us that is where we should rest our eyes to focus on our prayers. Every time, I felt guilty, knowing I had let my eyes wander. It was all new to me, and I was curious to know what was going on around me. It wasn't the only mistake I made. At one point, an elegant woman to my left, wearing an unusually beautiful ribbon skirt and exquisite traditional jewellery, told me to stop blowing on my coal as I was trying to revive my fire. "That is not the way," she said. Diane explained to me afterward that if you blow on a sacred fire, your breath can take away its essence. I was deeply embarrassed each time I got called out, and it made me feel acutely aware of my whiteness. Another time, my neighbour asked me to uncross my legs while sitting down. "Only men can sit like that," she explained. I still don't know why.

Even in the moment, I realized that my reaction was ridiculous. Here I was, in a community that traditionally relied on oral teachings, but so stuck in my Western culture that I kept wishing for an explanatory text rather than allowing myself to let go and simply immerse myself in the experience. Throughout the ceremony, I struggled with these kinds of conflicting emotions. I was also embarrassed when I felt the sting of jealousy as my husband and the other men took off to prepare the Sundance lodge, leaving us women behind in the camp. I felt held back, even though I knew that women and men had distinct roles in the ceremony that were equally important and valued. I was used to my own notion of gender equality, which to me meant that men and women could take on interchangeable roles.

We danced for two days, while praying for family members, for our communities, or other things, only taking a break to sleep between dusk and dawn, still fasting. Toward the end of the second day, the music stopped to let the dancers participate in a large giveaway for the community. Community members, many of them family members of Sundance participants, had gathered outside the lodge, and the gifts that participants had brought with them were put in a large pile at the lodge's entrance. The gifts included things like kitchen utensils, blankets, toys, and even appliances. Before they were handed out, the Elders leading the Sundance addressed us. One of them, Steve Morningchild (who has since passed away), speaking in Cree and then English, focused on us women, praising the important role we played in society and our mental strength. Referencing a pipe-smoking ceremony, he said that for every woman who smoked a pipe, you needed four men to balance her out. "That's how powerful you are," he said. He urged us to "take back control," saying it was time. I liked the sound of that!

At kâniyâsihk and the Sundance grounds, I met Indigenous people who, like me, were learning about Cree culture and ceremony for the first time. This was powerful to witness. Afterward, I realized that even if there had been a blueprint to guide me, I likely could not have prepared myself anyway. Sundance is so spiritual, complex, and deeply ingrained in culture and language that a person must experience it to understand it, and they must do so more than once. You're not considered a sundancer before you've done it four times. In other words, it's okay not to understand everything. What is important, though, is being open to learning and to follow the Protocols, whether it's to bring gifts, observe the dress code, keep your eyes on the centre pole, or something else. The importance of following the Protocols when engaging with Indigenous communities goes beyond Sundance.

In my first podcast conversation, TRC Commissioner Marie Wilson highlighted the importance of observing the Protocols in the reconciliation process and made the point that we have much to learn from diplomatic protocol. In their interactions, diplomats are expected to respect the laws and customs of the host country. They learn the language to be able to communicate properly, and they find out what's expected of them and how to carry themselves before they engage with representatives of another country. Even seemingly mundane things like how to greet or address someone, whether to kneel or bow, and where to place people around a dinner table can be important considerations. All cultures have certain protocols that anybody must observe to demonstrate respect and understanding of the significance of an occasion. Canada should apply diplomatic protocol in its own nation-to-nation relationships, Marie said, just as it does with outside countries. It made me think about my own role as a diplomat representing my country and how I had adjusted my behaviour to the culture and customs of my interlocutors during my diplomatic postings, just as I had during Sundance—her reasoning made total sense.

Diplomacy and the role of ambassadors are often thought of as Western and relatively modern concepts. But the use of envoys or ambassadors sent on behalf of nations to negotiate issues, make alliances, conclude treaties, and avoid war with other nations is a much older concept, predating the 1961 Vienna Convention on Diplomatic Relations by centuries. In fact, the art of diplomacy was an important aspect of Indigenous cultures in the Americas long before contact, as demonstrated, for example, by the Haudenosaunee Great Law of Peace that constituted the Iroquois Confederacy, also known as the Haudenosaunee or Six Nations, which Derek addressed in his essay "The Ever-Shrinking Blanket." Indigenous Peoples also brought their diplomatic skills to negotiations with the colonial governments and have continued to send envoys to communicate and represent their interests, including to the United Nations to participate in the negotiations of the Declaration on the Rights of Indigenous Peoples.

After speaking with Marie, I was curious to learn more about the role of diplomacy in the reconciliation process, and so I invited my friend Deborah Chatsis to my podcast. Deborah was Canada's first ambassador from a First Nation and a member of the Ahtah-kakoop Cree Nation on Treaty 6 territory, which is a few hours east of Ministikwan. I got to know her when we were both posted as diplomats to New York, she at the Canadian UN mission and I at the Swedish. Deborah had also been posted to Colombia, some years before me, and later became Canada's ambassador to Guatemala, a country with a large Indigenous population.

On the show, Deborah spoke about being Indigenous and representing Canada abroad and about the value of understanding culture. To succeed in negotiations with other countries, she stressed, you need to know their culture and their history so that you can understand where their governments are coming from. Her point was that what happened in Colombia in the 1500s or in Canada in the 1800s still has resonance and matters today. To develop and maintain sound bilateral relations, she said, knowing your counterpart's history, culture, and language allows you to engage successfully on a deeper level.

While speaking the language of your interlocutor is incredibly important, and I desperately wished I had known Cree when participating in Sundance, it isn't always possible. But in my podcast conversations, I made sure to greet each guest in their own language. I don't think my efforts were always comprehensible or fully accurate, but my hope is that they carried symbolic value. Interacting respectfully is crucial for building and maintaining peaceful and friendly relationships.

The Government of Canada frequently uses the term "nation-to-nation" when it speaks of its relationship with Indigenous Peoples. I don't think that government officials themselves always know what they mean by this. Internationally, a "nation" usually refers to a country or a state, as in the United Nations, of which Canada is one of 193 sovereign member states. When a country recognizes a new state or government, this generally implies a readiness to assume diplomatic relations.

When the Canadian federal government uses the expression "nation-to-nation," I think it means to say that Canada recognizes First Nations, Métis, and Inuit as equal partners. Yet, the expression rings false to me because, in practice, the government does not treat Indigenous nations as equals. When it comes to land, the issue most central to the reconciliation process, the government insists on having the last word. I'm not alone in this conclusion: The Canadian Reconciliation Barometer, an online national survey from 2022, shows that non-Indigenous respondents increasingly agree with Indigenous respondents that governments do not respect Indigenous nations.

Regardless of what the government means by "nation-to-nation," my conversations with Deborah and Marie, as well as my experiences at Sundance and as a diplomat in places like Colombia, have convinced me that we should approach the reconciliation process as a diplomatic undertaking. As such, the federal, provincial, and territorial governments would treat Indigenous nations as they would treat a foreign nation—as a true equal—and respect Indigenous laws and customs, just as when they were assuming diplomatic relations. In the same vein, we, as individuals, should observe Indigenous Protocols in our interactions. We should also take the time to learn about Indigenous cultures and languages. This could also mean that just as diplomats receive foreign language training, officials who interact with Indigenous nations receive Indigenous language training, which is not the case today.

By taking this approach, we will ensure that we treat each other respectfully and come to better understand each other, which is key to building friendly, peaceful relations. Learning about Indigenous culture and language also supports Indigenous revitalization efforts, which are vital for Indigenous Peoples' identity, well-being, and survival.

At the end of each podcast episode, I asked my guests for three things that non-Indigenous Canadians could do to contribute to the national reconciliation process. Part of Deborah's advice to the listeners was to meaningfully engage with Indigenous people. She gave the example of visiting a cultural event like a powwow. If you do, I suggest that you think of yourself as an ambassador for your own people: Read about the history and current practice of powwows and the First Nations hosting it, and participate respectfully, in observance of the Protocols, just like a good diplomat would. You will help pave the way for reconciliation.

My friend Deborah Chatsis passed away from cancer in June 2022, a few months after our podcast conversation and only half a year after receiving the Order of Canada for her leadership on advancing reconciliation and Indigenous rights worldwide. I miss her.

Nine Ways to Support Indigenous Cultural Revitalization

Canada's assimilation policies, laws, and systemic discrimination against Indigenous Peoples have resulted in an immense loss of cultural knowledge. Cultural practices and knowledge systems are intrinsic to a people's sense of identity and way of life. Language is one of the main foundations of a culture, as it holds traditions, ceremonies, songs, stories, and unique ways of thinking, communicating, and understanding the world. The loss of culture and language has had far-reaching consequences for Indigenous Peoples in Canada, at both the community and individual level, compounded by the trauma from the residential school system and separation of families that came with it. Today, Indigenous communities are struggling with the loss of social cohesion, a sense of belonging, parental bonding, and with mental and physical illness, addiction, and poverty.

By re-engaging with culture, learning the language, being with nature, attending ceremony, and having it present in their lives, Indigenous people find their way again. Here are nine suggestions to help support Indigenous cultural revitalization, and we encourage you to think of a tenth!

1. When you organize an event, consider contacting a local Indigenous community to see if an Elder is willing to open the meeting by providing a land acknowledgement or other opening ceremony, such as a prayer, smudging, drumming, or dancing. The inclusion of these types of ceremonies brings greater meaning to the event itself, forms relationships with Indigenous communities, encourages the use of Indigenous ceremony, and prompts people to ask their own questions about language and culture.

2. **Consider conducting a smudge, or cleansing, for yourself.** The purpose of a smudge is to spiritually cleanse yourself from negative thoughts or energy, and anyone can do it, as everyone has a direct relationship with the Creator. However, a non-Indigenous person should not perform a smudge for other people unless invited to do so or guided by an Indigenous person, as this could constitute cultural appropriation. Here are some tips for conducting a smudge:

  a. To obtain your sacred medicine, such as ceremonial tobacco, sage, cedar, and sweetgrass, you can grow and harvest it yourself; visit an Indigenous community that may sell it, which supports them economically; check with your local health food store, and suggest they carry it from an Indigenous provider if they don't already; or purchase it online from an Indigenous provider.

  b. There are different ways of smudging. Derek starts with burning tobacco while he sets his intention for the smudge, deciding what to cleanse or let go of from his mind and spirit, with the goal of establishing a personal connection with the Creator. This should be performed outside or within a place that will allow the burning and smoke. When you burn, make sure to use a fireproof vessel such as an abalone seashell or small cast-iron pan, and seek to create a smoke wand, like burning incense, rather than an open flame. After the tobacco, Derek burns sage, or sometimes cedar or sweetgrass, or a mix thereof, for the actual smudge. He uses a feather or his hands to direct the smoke over his head to wash away bad thoughts or to clear his mind. Next, he washes his eyes while thinking that he wants to clear his eyes so that he can see more clearly, then his nose and throat so he can breathe easier and speak his truth, his heart so he can speak from his heart instead of just his mind, and, finally, he washes the rest of his body with the smoke. Remember that it is about intention; just like in meditation and many other aspects of healing, intention and belief are what cause medicines to work for you.

c. Similarly, Derek uses sage, cedar, or sweetgrass to cleanse his home or office. He starts at the front door, leaving the back door open to allow the bad energy a route to leave the home. Again, he begins with tobacco and then, as he enters his home or office, usually burns sage or sweetgrass. He walks through each room, wafting the fragrant smoke, including in closets and even drawers, while consciously asking the Creator to help clean the space of any bad spirits or energies. He imagines talking to any spirits that may be there to ask them to leave and find another place to rest. Essentially, to smudge a space, you move from room to room, guiding the energy to leave through the back door or window that you left open at the outset.

d. There is no set schedule for cleansing yourself or your home or office, but consider establishing a regular routine, such as weekly or monthly. If you work in a field where you encounter a lot of trauma or pain, consider more frequent smudging, and smudge when you feel the presence of negative energy. Sometimes, someone may visit our home and leave negative energy behind; don't ignore it. By consciously taking steps to put ourselves back in balance, we become at peace once again.

3. Seek further learning about the cultural practices of Indig-enous communities near you by reading up, watching documentaries, and, as we have discussed before, attending Indigenous cultural and ceremonial events open to the public, or if you receive an invitation. But remember to observe the Protocols and be mindful that Indigenous people are trying to learn themselves.

4. Consider making a donation to an Indigenous-led organi-zation or fundraising initiative that supports Indigenous culture and language revitalization.

5. Listen to Indigenous music. By seeking out Indigenous mu-sicians on YouTube, Spotify, and other sites and sharing what you find on social media outlets, you increase views, allowing those artists to draw more listeners.

6. Seek out and purchase products from Indigenous artists, whether it be painting, sculpting, jewellery, or clothing. By purchasing and wearing Indigenous products, you support the artist economically and bring attention to their culture. It also counteracts the whitewashing of our culture while normalizing Indigenous culture.

7. Support Indigenous businesses that are often struggling to enter markets dominated by mass-produced goods. By buying from them, you are not only helping them thrive but also contributing to fighting Indigenous poverty. Also consider volunteering or seeking employment in those businesses.

8. Try to incorporate the Indigenous language of your area in different ways in your work and social life, for example, by using an Indigenous greeting before or alongside the French or English one.

9. Learn about Indigenous cuisine and its intrinsic relation to the land, such as the role of seal in Inuit culture. Explore dishes such as Three Sisters soup made from corn, squash, and beans or bannock, both common in most First Nations communities. Cooking and enjoying Indigenous dishes with friends, family, or colleagues can be an excellent way of spending the National Day for Truth and Reconciliation!

Part IV: Education

The Great Explorers

Derek Aronhie:nens Montour

> . . . if anything is to be done with the Indian, we must catch him very young. The children must be kept constantly within the circle of civilized conditions.
>
> —Nicholas Flood Davin, *Report on the Industrial Schools for Indians and Half-Breeds*, 1879

"BABA? WHY DID we kill all the poor settlers?"

My son Achilles was in Grade 3, in the middle of doing his homework, when he asked me this question. He was confused why we—the Kanien'kehá:ka—were so cruel to the poor French settlers. He seemed genuinely upset. I was also confused and asked to look at his history book so I could try to understand what he was talking about. He pointed to the passage where the book referenced the Iroquois savages who murdered the French settlers who were trying to survive in Nouvelle-France. There was little mention of the attacks made by the French. I was shocked. How could this be the standard provincial curriculum?

I looked through the text to see what else the book included about First Nations, and it was minimal, to say the least. I remember a passage about Jacques Cartier's voyages describing in heroic

terms how he "claimed" Canada for France, as well as an explana-
tion that the British had a similar claim. There was no mention
of the First Nations people who were already living here when
the colonizers arrived. *Wow.* Growing up, I had—wrongfully—
assumed that the education I received during the 1970s and '80s
at the Indian day school was the indoctrination that all First Nations kids get so we can become more "civilized" and thus fit into
Canadian society. And I'd naively thought that others would get
a "correct" version. I certainly never thought that by the time my
son was in Grade 3 in 2020 that we'd still be framing the "discovery" of my land in this lopsided way, talking about the great
explorers and the murderous savages that awaited them here.

Reading my son's textbook was a powerful reminder of
just how deeply education and reconciliation go hand in hand.
Education in Quebec, and across Canada, is based on the perspectives, worldview, and beliefs of settlers, and there have been
too few attempts to change the education system to allow for a
greater understanding of an Indigenous perspective and worldview. There's little excuse for this—the information exists, if only
our governments had the will to enact more widespread, meaningful change. Over the years, numerous reports (many of them
Indigenous-led) have called for an overhaul of our colonial education system. They've been mostly ignored. And yet, not only
do these reports illustrate how challenging it can be for Indigenous issues to gain traction, but they also offer an essential starting point for Canadians who want to engage in reconciliation.

One of the first such reports was released in the early 1900s by
Dr. Peter Bryce. Bryce was a physician and public health official
and studied public health and sanitation policy, releasing a series of reports on the health and living conditions of Indigenous
people. His 1907 Report on the Indian Schools of Manitoba and
the Northwest Territories highlighted the staggering death rates
in the schools and exposed their unsanitary conditions. At the

time, his reports were largely ignored, or suppressed, by the Department of Indian Affairs.

Publishing them cost Bryce his career. The administration of Duncan Campbell Scott, who was appointed to be the deputy superintendent of the Federal Department of Indian Affairs from 1913 to 1932 and was a fierce advocate of assimilationist policies, did whatever it could to silence Dr. Bryce, including forcibly retiring him. In response, Dr. Bryce published a book in 1922 called *The Story of a National Crime: An Appeal for Justice to the Indians of Canada.* It provides clear evidence of the government's role in creating and maintaining conditions that led to huge numbers of Indigenous student deaths at the residential schools. Unfortunately, despite this, the government policies on residential schools continued unabated and, in some cases, intensified.

Decades later, in the 1960s and '70s, Indigenous nationalism took off, sparking a rise in advocacy and protest movements. But while Indigenous Peoples were speaking out, it seems that most of the Canadian population continued to largely ignore the so-called "Indian Problem." They saw themselves as unaffected by First Nations issues—or they were simply ignorant. This is what happens when the Canadian population lacks education about both Indigenous histories and present-day realities, despite repeated and various attempts by Indigenous groups, communities, and nations to push for our rights.

I'd argue that things would have stayed the same if not for the 1990 Oka Crisis. Many Canadians reacted negatively when Kanehsatà:ke and Kahnawà:ke closed their borders and community members told the local, provincial, and Canadian governments *no more*. Our people experienced a lot of hate, and that hate continues to be harboured in some people's hearts across Canada. And yet, after Oka, many other Canadians started to pay attention. They looked more closely at the living conditions of the Indigenous people in their area. They started to ask questions. And shortly after Oka, in 1991, Canada formed the Royal Commission on Aboriginal Peoples (RCAP) with the task of investigating and documenting the lives of First Nations, Inuit, and Métis across Canada.

The RCAP comprised seven commissioners, four Indigenous and three non-Indigenous, who spent five years visiting Indigenous communities across Canada. They met with more than 2,000 people and commissioned over 350 research studies to review the evolution of the relationship between Indigenous people, the Government of Canada, and Canadian society as a whole. They organized their research plan in four themes: governance issues, land and economy issues, social and cultural issues, and issues that are unique to the North. Within each theme, they addressed four perspectives: historical, women, youth, and urban. The commission released its report five years later, in 1996. At roughly 4,000 pages, the report is a huge document, but even today it remains a very powerful source of information.

In addition to the main conclusion of the need for a complete restructuring of the relationship between Indigenous and non-Indigenous people, the report included 440 recommendations, some of which would have changed the constitution. Many of the commission's findings focused on Indigenous self-determination and also acknowledged the devastating history of the residential school system in Canada. It is important to note that throughout the 1980s and 1990s, many Survivors of the residential schools had started filing class action lawsuits against Canada to seek compensation for the abuses they experienced. This movement grew until it culminated in 1990 with Phil Fontaine, at the time Grand Chief of the Assembly of Manitoba Chiefs, making a public statement testifying about his abuse.

The RCAP report called for a public inquiry to investigate the residential school system's origins, purpose, and effects, emphasizing the need to address lasting harms. It further recommended remedial action, including compensation for communities and public education programs on the history and effects of residential schools. It also recommended $30 billion in funding, spread out over two decades, to support development in Indigenous communities and to improve education, health, nation-building, and more.

Although many of the recommendations remain unimplemented, the report led to other efforts to change the system, such as the Indian Residential School Settlement Agreement (IRSSA) (which in turn called for the creation of the Truth and Reconciliation Commission). The IRSSA was approved by all parties in 2006, following the federal creation of the Office of Indian Residential Schools Resolution Canada five years prior. The office itself was established to manage the large number of legal claims against Canada related to the abuse of Indigenous children.

The IRSSA process had five different components: financial compensation for all eligible former students who resided at a recognized residential school; an out-of-court Independent Assessment Process (IAP) to resolve claims of sexual and serious physical abuse; measures to address mental and emotional health and support healing, including the Indian Residential Schools Resolution Health Support Program and an endowment to the Aboriginal Healing Foundation; funding to commemorate the experiences of former students and their families; and the Truth and Reconciliation Commission, which was established with a mandate to actually listen to the Survivors, their families, communities, and others affected by the residential school system and to inform all Canadians about the residential school system and its legacy. Most importantly in my mind, the commission was to make recommendations for reconciliation.

This time, as opposed to when the RCAP recommendations were made, the recommendations from the IRSSA were acted upon, and the TRC was officially established in June 2008.

Between 2009 and 2015, the commission visited seventy-seven communities and gathered testimony from almost 7,000 witnesses, including Survivors, their families, and others impacted by the residential school system. They spoke to a wide range of individuals, including First Nations, Inuit, and Métis Survivors of residential schools, their families, and communities, as well as former residential school employees, government officials, church representatives, and other Canadians. And they listened to people describe their experiences.

In April 2013, I attended the commission's hearings at the Queen Elizabeth Hotel in Montreal with the purpose of offering mental and emotional health support to people sharing their testimonials. At the time, I was newly promoted to the position of executive director of KSCS, and while I am not a mental health worker, many of our staff members are involved in healing and wellness. I was there to support our workers in whatever they might need. As I experienced myself, retelling traumatic experiences can be extremely emotional and difficult—often in part because it can feel like a person is reliving that trauma. And it isn't just difficult for the people sharing their trauma; support workers can start carrying the heavy burdens of the stories they hear. I was amazed and awed at the strength, power, and resilience of the men and women who testified.

The TRC published its report in June of 2015. It documented a devastating history of abuse, neglect, and trauma for Indigenous people in Canada. The report concluded that residential schools were a systematic, government-sponsored attempt to destroy Indigenous cultures and languages and to assimilate Indigenous Peoples so that they no longer existed as distinct peoples—this amounted to cultural genocide.

I would recommend that everyone read the report. It includes 94 Calls to Action, framed as demands for change on the part of the Canadian and provincial governments to, in essence, make amends. To me, these calls to action form the basis of the current use of the word "reconciliation." But reconciliation is more than just talking and apologizing; it is doing better. An apology without a change in behaviour is meaningless. And to do that, we need to honour the other important word in the committee's name: truth.

I believe that before we can talk about *reconciliation*, or restoring peaceful relationships, we must first expose the *truth* of what occurred. We must, in other words, educate our populations on the truth of Canada's colonial history and the ways in which it both has caused and continues to cause harm. Otherwise, our societies will continue to live in denial and ignorance, further traumatizing the victims of the country's colonial systems. For most people who have suffered abuse or otherwise have had their rights violated, exposing the truth of what occurred is often as important to the victim as the perpetrator being punished. If the truth is not brought to light, it is very difficult for healing to occur. The "justice" part of the equation can only come after, when we ask: How do we make this right?

I think back to the question my son asked me when he was in Grade 3: *Baba, why did we kill all the poor settlers?* For us to tell our children the truth and thus truly educate people, we need to start from the beginning, before the explorers and settlers first arrived here. The history of Indigenous Peoples should be interwoven with the history of settlers and not be an elective or be supplementary work. The lens needs to shift. There is a famous saying that there is *your truth, my truth, and the real truth*, but I am not sure that the real truth can ever be truly known, especially if we do not want to listen to each other. If we want to try and get close to the truth, however, listening and learning is where we need to start.

Our beliefs, experiences, memories, perspectives, and understandings all contribute and shape what we believe the truth to be. That is true of both Indigenous and non-Indigenous children. If non-Indigenous children are taught that we are savages who killed the innocent settlers, then Indigenous children have been taught that their culture and identities need to be fixed. Both are harmful lies in the guise of education.

History has shown that a people who are taught to believe a certain way can commit unimaginable acts of violence and cruelty, whether that belief is based on a religion, a political ideology, or racism. Perhaps this can help explain why the priests, nuns, and teachers in the residential schools and day schools viewed their actions as justified. Their beliefs dictated they were not abusing children but educating them. But to the child, it sure feels wrong. It felt like you were not good enough in your own skin, or that you should strive to be someone else to hide who you really were.

This is why it was so vital for people to share their experiences through the TRC: The truth is a powerful antidote against the indoctrination they experienced. Many of them experienced trauma twice over; when they were children and again when they were not heard by their own loved ones. They may have even told what was happening to them to their parents, other family members, or people in their community, only to have that trusted adult tell them to forget about it. In this way, the "lie" gets reinforced. The child starts doubting their recollection of what happened.

Perhaps the parent didn't believe their child because of their own shame, their own abuse, or their own fears. Perhaps they were barely coping themselves, and they just wanted to forget. Fear can be a powerful factor to control a people: the fear of poverty and starvation, the fear of shame and being ostracized, the fear of violence and retribution, the fear of loss of freedom and isolation. Breaking those chains of fear is a vital step in self-determination. Only after the schools closed and people were adults, did they find the strength and support to become vulnerable enough to speak out again now and tell their truth.

As we move toward reconciliation, it is important that we continue to listen. We must stop thinking about what we were taught to believe as the *only* truth. We instead need to start asking why we weren't taught about certain subjects and events in school and to seek the information now. There is much that people living in Canada still don't know or understand about residential schools and the harm they enacted. I'd wager, for example, that many people don't know that, between 1831 and the year 2000, there were a total of 699 Indian day schools and 130 Indian residential schools, all funded by the federal government and operated by various religious institutions.

The last federal Indian residential school closed its doors in Rankin Inlet, Nunavut, in 1997, and the last federal Indian day school to be transferred to the rightful community was in Kanehsatà:ke on September 1, 2000. The day schools were in nearly every Indigenous community, whereas the residential schools were usually located outside them. The curriculum taught at both was based on Eurocentric norms, values, and approaches to learning, and was designed to further the effort of eradicating our Indigenous identity. There was no interest in adapting schools to Indigenous norms, values, and ways of learning.

Most people know even less about day schools than they do about residential schools, which also isn't much. The first federally funded residential school opened in Brantford, Ontario, in 1831, which also served as a day school for the Six Nations community. Day schools technically existed long before that, though, in the form of religious schools or mission schools. These religious schools, located in what became Lower and Upper Canada, were also within Indigenous communities as early as the 1600s. They shared the fundamental goal of eradicating the Indigenous child's identity: language, culture, style of clothing, names, anything that would maintain a connection to our identity. They later evolved into the Indian day school system. School systems such as this were built across the colonized world, including in Ireland, South Africa, Australia, New Zealand, and even in Sweden and Norway for Indigenous Sami children.

Most Canadians don't realize that residential and day schools were not in the ancient past; like I have said, the last residential school closed in 1997, and the last day school was transferred in 2000! Nor did most Canadians truly begin to understand until recently the extent of the abuse that went on at both types of schools. Take, for example, the collective shock and trauma that Canadians felt when what is believed to be the remains of children were discovered at the site of the Kamloops Industrial School in 2021. Many Canadians were never taught what really happened at residential schools, and it was like they were finding out about them for the first time. Many Canadians even refused to believe the reports of potential burial sites, despite the documented high death rates and existence of graveyards at residential schools!

New immigrants to these lands are not taught about residential schools either. This is simply unacceptable. It is 2025 as I am writing this, and despite the RCAP, despite the TRC, despite the numerous Canadian human rights complaints, including the 2007 child and family services complaint (that demonstrated that Canada had consistently underfunded Indigenous child welfare programs and services by around 30 percent compared to programs and services afforded to non-Indigenous children and families, proving a distinct and racially based discrimination), and despite all our efforts, the provincial and federal governments are not changing the education system fast enough. Our children continue to be taught about the great "discovery" of our land from a purely European perspective and that the poor

French settlers were slaughtered by the Iroquois savages. This is how systemic discrimination persists.

As I wrote in a previous essay, I grew up during the tail end of the Indian day school system. In 1968, Kahnawà:ke parents formed the Kahnawà:ke Combined Schools Committee to start taking control of education away from the federal and provincial governments and their assimilationist tactics. I was eight years old when our community created the Kahnawà:ke Education Center in 1980 and was in Grade 10 (secondary four) in high school when our community gained full control of all education programs and services in 1988. Taking charge of our own school system and education programs is critical to our self-determination. It gave us the opportunity to integrate our own ways of knowing, instead of being force-fed education from only the settler perspective. But it was still an uphill battle. We needed to build a school system that educated our children with what we felt they needed to know. But we also wanted them to be able to survive in the provincial post-secondary education system and the structures that Canadian society is built on, all of which predominantly rely on knowledge and understanding of the settler perspective. We also had no control of what the rest of Canada taught in their schools.

In Quebec, Bill 101 has also complicated matters. The bill was adopted in 1977 and mandates all children must be educated in French, or receive French instruction, until the end of their secondary education—hence the one hour each of French and Kanien'kéha language instruction I had in school. Later, in 1988, long after I graduated primary school, our community started developing Kanien'kéha immersion programs for our children and, more recently, an option for French immersion. This has been a welcome improvement, but preserving our language remains a huge issue for our community, and many other forced English-speaking communities, because of the eradication of our native language by first the policies of Canada and now the policies of Quebec.

This is an ongoing issue. For example, the 2019 final report by the Viens Commission, which was formed to investigate and document all forms of discrimination in the provision of public services to Indigenous Peoples in Quebec, provided the Quebec government with 142 recommendations to address the underlying causes of discrimination, violence, and differential treatment. In 2025, Quebec's Protecteur du citoyen released a situation report on the implementation of these recommendations that highlighted insufficient progress in supporting the preservation of Indigenous languages in Quebec.

This lack of support has real life implications. When Achilles first started school, I found myself facing the same challenge as so many other First Nations parents: In which language do I choose to educate my son? I had to ask myself many questions. Do I enrol my child in a French immersion program, with English spoken in the home or do I choose to have him educated in English like other Kanien'kehá:ka kids and have him learn French where he can? Or do I request that he attend the Kanien'kehá:ka immersion school in the community and learn English and French where he can? Which road to go down?

Although it was a tough decision, Afroditi and I ultimately chose to send our son to a francophone school, since French is much harder to pick up outside of school than English. But what about Kanien'kéha, how do I ensure he learns that, too? My spouse, Afroditi, is Greek. She spoke French at school and learned English by playing with the other kids in her neighbourhood and Greek by speaking it at home. But I speak only beginner-level Kanien'kéha and am not fluent enough to be able to speak to my son in my own language. Yet, it was Afroditi's ability to speak all three languages—Greek, English, and French—that helped me to realize that parents also have the responsibility to educate, as naive as that may sound. We wanted our son to have the same opportunity to learn as many languages as he could, as the ability to understand and communicate with others opens doors and removes limitations. We decided that he would attend school in French, learn English at home, learn Greek from Afroditi and her family, and we would all learn and practice Kanien'kéha. Imperfect, we knew, but we must do our best to try.

I thought about my job as a parent again when Achilles asked me about our savage practices. Looking back, I remember feeling a sense of powerlessness. How do I try to explain concepts of colonization, broken treaties, and attempted assimilation to an eight-year-old? It felt like the battle for better education was never-ending. How was it my job as a parent, which I am not trained for in any shape or form, to offset the insufficient and even false curriculum taught by his school? And yet, I also realized that I had an opportunity to not only correct what Achilles was learning but what his classmates were being taught as well.

Even so, I still might have let it go if it were not for my wife. With Afroditi's encouragement, I decided to start taking a more active role in our son's school. I am grateful that I found such a wonderful woman to share my life with. Among all her admirable qualities, she is also such a strong advocate for First Nations rights, more so than me in some cases! I can sometimes be too quick to let things go, to not fight, and to choose to take my business elsewhere. She is the first to demand change to the system, the first to insist on recognition for First Nations, and the first to volunteer to help to educate. I suggest to you now—and this is important to understand why being an ally is so important—that it can be easier for someone to challenge the system when they have not been constantly subjected to discrimination, racism, and mistreatment by said system their whole lives.

Together, Afroditi and I contacted the school, asking about the curriculum. We were told the Ministry of Education requires each school to provide a set curriculum, including which books are required to be taught. But they were open to including more First Nations content if we would help them. *Awesome.* And so, throughout Achilles's years at primary school, I volunteered to do whatever I could to teach more about our culture, language, and history.

Over the years, I introduced our traditional dances, music, and drumming; explained our language and had them practice basic words; and educated them about Orange Shirt Day, which acknowledges and honours the experience of Indigenous children in Canadian residential and day schools, and also Bear Witness Day, which honours Jordan River Anderson and invites people of all ages to "bear witness" to ensure Jordan's Principle— a 2007 law that seeks to ensure that all First Nations children could access public services on the same terms as other children, addressing jurisdictional disputes and service gaps—is fully implemented. And on our own, both Afroditi and I have tried to explain our own understanding of history to Achilles.

I believe the impact of all this has been powerful, but also small. Thanks to our efforts, the kids in my son's class had a chance to directly benefit from hearing about our Kanien'kehá:ka culture and traditions. Yet, what about the rest of the school? My son graduated primary school in 2024 and is now in Secondary Two at Collège Jean-de-Brébeuf in Montreal. So how does a model like this carry on after he leaves? How do we reach more schools and change the system? Because we know it isn't just in primary school that miseducation occurs: The same still happens in high school, university, and in the lives of everyday Canadians.

I had another "Huh?" moment earlier this past year when Achilles came home from secondary school. He was so excited to tell me that he learned that the real Jean de Brébeuf, a Catholic missionary in the 1630s and 1640s, invented lacrosse! I was astounded. I explained that while Brébeuf may have coined the name "lacrosse" in 1636, the game itself existed for many years before that and was common among our nations. I'd like to give the school the benefit of the doubt that perhaps Achilles misunderstood his teachers, but it was another reminder for me that it's important to stay involved throughout our child's education.

I truly believe that one of the underlying foundations for reconciliation is education, for all of us. This education is everyone's responsibility. We must all read the RCAP, TRC, and other critical reports. Doing so is particularly important for anyone in a position of authority: teachers, employers, supervisors, religious authorities, parents, and so on. Such reports are also excellent study guides for anyone who wants to become a Canadian citizen. And nobody should be taught about the Great Explorers in the lopsided and straight-out false way that Achilles was. Parents who care about reconciliation must stay involved in their child's education. After all, surely, we all want our children, Indigenous or not, to learn the true story of Canada. I implore every parent who is reading this book to ask your child's school system to add Indigenous content. I was encouraged to learn that Quebec mandated all of its primary and secondary schools to include books from Indigenous authors for the 2026 to 2027 school year; this demonstrates a willingness to change! Parents can easily follow suit by reading or encouraging their children to read books by Indigenous authors. Parents should ask schools to educate their children on the histories of what really happened. If enough voices are raised, change happens.

About Listening

Elin Sandberg Miller

MY FIRST GUESTS on the podcast were Truth and Reconciliation Commissioner Marie Wilson and her husband, Stephen Kakfwi, former premier of the Northwest Territories. Stephen is Dene, born in a traditional bush camp not far from the Arctic Circle, and Marie is non-Indigenous from a small town in Ontario. I had consulted Marie on my idea for *Everyday Reconciliation* before it became a podcast, and she suggested I speak to Stephen as well. I was impressed by their vast knowledge and experience advancing Indigenous rights and reconciliation, so when I later embarked on the podcast, I invited them both to the show. I was also curious to know if in their personal relationship they had encountered any of the same challenges that colonization had brought to our relationships at the national and community level.

It was my first interview for the podcast, and I was nervous. I was not trained as a journalist, had never recorded a podcast before, and was on a steep learning curve about Indigenous perspectives and the national reconciliation process. At one point during our conversation, to help illustrate a point Marie had made about shame and stigma, Stephen spoke of the physical and sexual abuse he had suffered at residential school—and how he had suppressed those memories for years. He spoke matter-of-factly, saying that some terrible things had happened to him when he was nine years old at the hands of a nun and at the hands of a Catholic layman. Yet, it was only later in life that he understood he hadn't merely been spanked for misbehaving but severely whipped.

He recounted to me the exact moment he remembered that he had also been sexually abused. It was a shocking realization, he said. He was already twenty years into his marriage, the Minister of Justice in the NWT, and alone in a hotel room. Some time back, people in his community, including friends and colleagues, had started disclosing what had happened to them, which had triggered him to think harder about his own experiences, reassessing his memories. As his mind worked through many layers of suppression and denial, the memories of his own sexual abuse suddenly hit him, right there in that hotel room. He lost control of his body. He described it as if somebody had taken their hand and reached down into the pit of his stomach and started to pull, and it all came out: This is what happened. This is who did it. This is what they did. This is where they did it.

As he spoke, I got the same feeling I have when I receive really bad news. It's like I'm outside of my body, floating somewhere above the conversation, like someone else is being told the story and I just happen to overhear it. On the show, Stephen didn't provide much detail, but he mentioned a dark room, a storage room, and in my mind, it left an image of him as a little boy being led into the darkness of that room. During the conversation, I searched for the right words to express my sympathy, but what do you say to someone who was so brutally betrayed as a child? Those who violated him had signed up to take care of him, and he had nobody else to protect him. I felt inadequate and useless.

Even before the podcast, I knew that physical and sexual

abuse had been common at many residential schools. But that knowledge hadn't hit me like Stephen's story did. Hearing Stephen talk about what happened to him made me feel like I was there, outside the room he was led into, and it became part of my own experience. This prompted me to learn more. I wanted to know: What did the abuse that so many Indigenous people experienced and have had to carry with them every day since mean for the reconciliation process?

On the podcast, Marie described how the TRC was able to create a safe space for Survivors. With a mental health support team by their side, many shared things they had spent most of their lives trying to forget. Others spoke about experiences they had previously tried to disclose, but nobody had listened. Still others, like Stephen, hadn't been able to be truthful even to themselves. The commission, she explained, wanted to allow these people to speak up, advocate for themselves, and help them let go of the feelings of shame and guilt associated with psychological, physical, and sexual abuse.

I've heard several times, mostly from non-Indigenous people, that there were teachers at residential schools who meant well, who were kind and caring, and that not all students had a bad experience. People have told me that in those days, students in non-Indigenous schools got beaten, too. Yet, the more I researched this, the clearer it became just how widespread serious physical and sexual abuse was in Indian residential schools.

Following the 1996 report by the Royal Commission of Aboriginal Peoples, which included a chapter on residential schools, residential school Survivors increasingly disclosed the abuse they had experienced. In response, Indigenous groups and law firms initiated legal proceedings across the country to push the government and churches to recognize the abuses and provide some compensation. There were other attempts at addressing these claims, but eventually, discussions between the legal representatives of former students, the Assembly of First Nations and other Indigenous organizations, the involved churches, and the federal government resulted in the Indian Residential Schools Settlement Agreement (IRSSA), which Derek also examined in his previous essay.

To better understand the extent of the abuse, I turned to the IRSSA statistics on the number of claims of sexual and serious physical abuse. As Derek explained, the IRSSA included both a so-called Common Experience Payment for every former student and an out-of-court Independent Assessment Process (IAP) that assessed claims of sexual or serious physical abuse. At that time, there were about 80,000 Survivors still alive, and almost half of them, 38,000 people, submitted claims under the IAP. Most of these claims—more than 30,000—were validated.

This is a shocking number, and the first time I read it, I couldn't help but stare at the numbers on my screen. The abuse had clearly been rampant. I felt nauseated. On top of it, this agreement didn't include Survivors of Indian day schools or of residential schools in Newfoundland and Labrador, which later became part of separate settlement agreements. Having listened to Marie and Stephen for my first podcast episode, I imagined there were also Survivors who didn't come forward to participate in the IAP because of how difficult it is to talk about such deeply personal, hurtful, and often humiliating experiences.

A few months after I recorded the podcast conversation with Marie and Stephen, many Canadians were shocked to learn about what appeared to be the remains of 215 children at the Kamloops Indian Residential School in British Columbia. The discovery should not have come as a surprise. It wasn't new information that children died or went missing at residential schools.

Indigenous families and their communities knew, of course, but when they spoke of it, nobody listened. It also wasn't a secret that residential schools had graveyards. What's more, the Truth and Reconciliation Commission published its report years earlier, in 2015. While estimating the number to be at least double, the TRC was able to document over 3,200 deaths across all of Canada and dedicated a whole section of its calls to action to missing children and their burial information.

Children died from many different causes, including fires, suicide, and freezing to death while trying to run away. But most died from diseases, in particular tuberculosis, because of the dire conditions in the schools: over crowding, poor ventilation, poor diet, and starvation. Dr. Peter Bryce, whom Derek talked about in his essay "The Great Explorers," estimated that the death rate from all causes for those attending residential school was eighteen times higher than that of non-Indigenous people in Canada of the same age.

I've thought a lot about why it was Kamloops that had finally caught Canadians' attention and made them listen. Perhaps it was the sheer magnitude of the number of what appeared to be graves. But I also think people are more likely to tune in when an event feels more immediate. History turns events into abstractions, things that don't concern *you*. But Canadians learned of the Kamloops discovery in real time, which made it relatable, as if this were part of our own ongoing reality, which it is.

I was reminded of the reaction I had when listening to Stephen's story, as the impact of his words similarly became part of my own experience. In the wake of the Kamloops discovery, people from all walks of life came together to show their grief and horror, placing stuffed animals and little shoes to represent the dead children on memorials across the country. Commenting on the discovery, Prime Minister Trudeau said, "Residential schools were a reality—a tragedy that existed here, in our country, and we have to own up to it." This was our story, too.

People's reaction to Kamloops—as if it was new information that children died at residential schools—put a spotlight on our knowledge gap. Canadian schools haven't taught students nearly enough about what happened to Indigenous Peoples during colonization or of the ongoing impacts of colonization. It's not just Canada. When I grew up in Sweden, I learned next to nothing about the Sami people. I wasn't aware of the persecution they suffered or the challenges they are facing today. I should have been taught this in school, but I wasn't. I only became aware later in life because of my interest in human rights and what I saw here in Canada.

Not learning about Indigenous Peoples and our colonial past gives us a skewed version of history, as Derek so poignantly illustrated in the case of his son's schooling. Learning about the whole history of this land, also from an Indigenous perspective, is essential for understanding our country and ourselves—and for reconciliation. I had the opportunity to discuss the importance of this with my friend Deborah Chatsis, whom I talked about in my previous essay, "We Are All Ambassadors." Her father was a member of the Poundmaker Cree Nation in Saskatchewan, established by the famous Chief Poundmaker, who was a diplomat like her, trying to manage relations and prevent conflict with the colonial power. Yet, he was badly treated by the federal government and was unjustly convicted of treason in 1885.

When I later read more about him, I learned that he took part in the 1876 negotiations of Treaty 6 and was instrumental in having a famine clause added to the treaty, which promised that the Canadian government would provide food supplies to signatory nations during times of scarcity. In March 1885, after a harsh winter left many First Nations desperately famished, Poundmaker led a group of Cree to Battleford, about 50 kilometers to the southeast, to plead for more supplies with the Indian agent there.

At this time, Métis leader Louis Riel had launched the so-called North-West rebellion and the government was concerned that the resistance would spread to First Nations. While the Métis and First Nations shared many of the same hardships, most First Nations wanted to honour their treaty relationships with the Crown, and Chief Poundmaker was advocating for peaceful negotiations, not to join forces. But rumours of an imminent "Indian" attack were circulating, and the Battleford residents had abandoned their homes and taken shelter in the Battleford fort. The Indian agent was nervous and reluctant to leave the fort to even speak with Poundmaker. While Poundmaker and his people were waiting for the agent to come out, many grew restless, sensing they would have to leave empty-handed, and some of the abandoned homes and shops got looted. It wasn't clear if it was the Cree who did it.

After Poundmaker gave up the mission and left Battleford to bring his people back to their reserve, several local First Nations gathered there with them, near Cut Knife Creek. Like the Battleford residents, the group at Cut Knife also worried about being attacked, including as retaliation for the looting incident. The camp grew and tensions increased as Riel sent men there to convince First Nations to join his fight, and about a month later, a Canadian officer launched a surprise attack on the camp, inside the reserve, which became known as the Battle of Cut Knife. After inconclusive fighting, with casualties on both sides, the Canadian forces retreated. Poundmaker stopped his people from pursuing the soldiers, likely preventing the loss of many Canadian troops.

The Métis rebellion was defeated a couple of weeks later that spring, after which Poundmaker led his people to Battleford to surrender, explaining to the Canadian general there, who had just defeated Riel, that he had never promised to help Riel. In fact, he had consistently done the opposite, and they were simply defending themselves at Cut Knife. It didn't stop the general from taking him into custody, and a few months later, Chief Poundmaker was tried together with other First Nations leaders and warriors and unjustly convicted of treason for his alleged role in the rebellion. The whole trial was unfair. As an example, the interpretation was so bad that the treason-felony charge was translated as "knocking off the Queen's bonnet and stabbing her in the behind." One defendant was so confused he asked the interpreter: "Are you drunk?" While Poundmaker was released after roughly a year of imprisonment, he died a few months thereafter at the age of forty-four, possibly as an effect of an illness developed in prison.

The Poundmaker Cree Nation has long called for Chief Poundmaker's acquittal and worked to change Canada's official view of him from a traitor to the heroic peacemaker they always knew he was. In 2021, over a century after his death, their tireless advocacy resulted in his exoneration by Prime Minister Trudeau.

On the show, I asked Deborah what his exoneration meant to her, and she stressed the importance of knowing our history. Like so many stories that get passed down from generation to generation, she said, the true story of Chief Poundmaker, his innocence, and his method of seeking justice by peaceful means was not reflected in the official history of Canada. Making sure that everyone knew the truth about this part of history was important to her and her people and an important act of reconciliation. Establishing and acknowledging the truth is absolutely central to a reconciliation process. Such education is a necessary step in granting reparations, including apologies, restitution, and financial compensation, which can allow for healing, forgiveness, and—ultimately—reconciliation.

Listening to Marie Wilson detail the work of the TRC only

further underscored for me just how important it is to establish the truth. We need to know what has happened to understand each other and what the reconciliation process must address. As Derek discussed in his essay "Losing Your Identity, Losing Your Soul," for victims and Survivors, acknowledging their trauma can be necessary for healing to start. Thanks to the tremendous efforts of Marie and her fellow commissioners, Chief Wilton Littlechild and the late Justice Murray Sinclair, criss-crossing the country for years, no doubt all three heavily impacted by what they heard, thousands of Survivors were allowed to speak the truth, and someone listened. Their experiences were acknowledged.

Many of the commission's calls to action focus on education, such as developing mandatory school curriculum on residential schools. Provinces and territories are at different stages of implementing these calls, but I have already seen improvements in my own children's curriculum in the public school system in Ontario. My daughter Eva's Grade 11 English class, for example, centred on reading First Nations, Métis, and Inuit authors. I could see that Eva learned a tremendous amount from this course, also thanks to a wonderfully engaged teacher. But there were still significant gaps in my children's education in other areas. Most importantly, Indigenous history is still largely treated as an add-on instead of being fully integrated into how Canada's history is presented.

And yet, it's simply not accurate to describe Cartier's arrival from a European perspective without also describing what it meant to an Indigenous person. And since Indigenous Peoples were here first, wouldn't it make more sense to describe it from their perspective to begin with? While some of my kids' teachers did a fantastic job bringing in Indigenous perspectives and material to their teaching, many stuck to their old ways. This showed me that we still have a long way to go before we all understand that Canada's Indigenous past is our story, too.

In one of my podcast episodes, I spoke with Member of Parliament Michael McLeod about being Indigenous on Parliament Hill. Michael is Métis from the Northwest Territories, and when he first entered the chambers of the House of Commons in Ottawa, he was shocked to learn that so many of his fellow MPs knew so little about Indigenous Peoples. On the show, he highlighted the connection between ignorance and racism. While many of his colleagues were curious, wanted to learn more, and came to him for advice on Indigenous issues, they would also say things that were insulting, presumably without knowing it.

As he pointed out to me, if someone is not exposed to a culture that is different from their own, they may not even realize that they're being racist. He said he wasn't looking for sympathy, and neither were many other Indigenous people. But he did want people to understand where Indigenous people were coming from when they spoke up and what they were up against. "Everybody should know Canada's history," he stressed, "and Canada's history starts with Indigenous people."

We can't just leave it to school boards and teachers. All generations—including the ones out of school—need to learn. While our lacking education system greatly contributes to our ignorance, it doesn't help that we also don't know each other. If I had known Sami people growing up, I might have reflected upon our very different realities. I used to not know any Indigenous people here in Canada either and many of my friends still don't.

The situation reminds me of the 1945 book *Two Solitudes* by Hugh MacLennan that my father-in-law, Carman, a Canadian historian, gave me many years ago, when I was still new to Canada. The book explores the cultural and linguistic divide between English and French Canadians and how historical and societal forces shape personal lives, as the protagonist struggles to reconcile the two parts of his identity and navigate the tensions between the two cultures. The book helped me understand the divide between Francophones and Anglophones in Canada. But I think the concept of two solitudes could also be applied to the divide between Indigenous and non-Indigenous people, which is so much wider, with few people even talking about it.

During my learning journey, I slowly got to know more Indigenous people, and it confirmed to me how important personal relationships are for achieving reconciliation. If we don't know each other, how can we possibly understand each other and what we need to reconcile? In 2020, during the COVID-19 pandemic, I initiated a collaboration between my daughter Eva's Grade 8 class in a francophone school in Ottawa and an Ojibwe school class in northern Ontario. The kids never had the chance to meet in person, but they learned about each other through virtual exchanges.

It turned out to be an educational experience for me as well, as I came to realize how differently these two schools were equipped and how much better the learning conditions were for the students in Ottawa. The pen pal style exchange was designed to take place virtually, and I didn't expect the COVID restrictions, which saw the kids undergo periods of virtual learning, to be an issue. But I was wrong.

By the time we started the exchange, the Ottawa kids had largely gotten used to periods of online learning, and despite its many shortcomings, the mechanics of it were not a problem. But being set up with a computer and reliable internet connection at home is not a given in every family or community, including, as I learned, on reserves. There was also the issue of matching school classes. Whereas my daughter's school had large classes strictly organized by age group, the Indigenous school had small classes with a mix of ages. This added additional challenges for the exchange. And despite the large number of kids in my daughter's class, her teacher could count on her students' daily attendance, which was not a given for the teacher up North, where, especially during COVID, students often faced more challenges than making it to class on time.

This experience confirmed to me that we have much to learn from communicating across our cultures, and several of my podcast guests stressed the importance of learning not just *about* but *from* Indigenous people. I have learned so much by listening to Derek during the process of writing this book together. Discussing our themes and reading his drafts has allowed me to see the world through his eyes, and every time I got his comments back on my draft essays, I was pushed to challenge my own thinking.

The writing process and the learning journey that came with it were transformative for me. I often had to take a step back and think about my own role and the experiences and actions that informed my own thinking. It also taught me to be more open-minded. Learning *from* other people about their own experiences is also far more engaging than reading *about* those experiences. When Stephen told me about his abuse, it hit me right in the heart, even though I already knew this abuse was common. I think that the human experience allows us an emotional understanding of events, even historical ones, that makes them real.

After my podcast conversation with Marie and Stephen, I read a separate report by the Truth and Reconciliation Commission called *The Survivors Speak*. This report consists of excerpts from some of the statements given to the commission and provides a unique insight into the realities of life at residential school, including what life for these children was like before and after. Reading their personal stories was an experience similar to listening to Stephen. The Survivors spoke to their own experiences, in their own voices. It was easy to picture them in the moment, back in the familiarity of their communities, the closeness of their families, immersed in their culture and speaking their own language, before they knew there was something else. Then the sudden unfamiliarity, austerity, heartless regiment, and violations of their personal and physical integrity, far from home and the love of their parents. Reading it all, I felt like I was hearing their voices speak to me from the pages.

The Survivors Speak is filled with loss and longing and makes for some tough reading. But the Survivors' stories also tell of their accomplishments and bravery, as they risked punishment by speaking their own language, protecting a sibling or friend, or trying to escape. I've heard people talk about the *resilience* of residential school Survivors, and I think it's appealing to use that word because it sounds comforting, implying that children are resilient so they can take a bit of hardship and come out of it okay. I might have used the word myself in this context before I learned about the high number of deaths at residential schools. I find the word "resilient" offensive against this background, as so many children didn't only *not* come through the hardship okay, they didn't even survive it.

Canada's attempt at assimilation failed; Indigenous Peoples are still here. But their survival came at a great cost. The cost—the harm inflicted on the children—didn't end with the Survivors. Twice, I've been in the audience (once at the screening of an Indigenous film, another time at the launch of a book) when the speaker asks the audience to raise their hand if they went to residential school. Hands go up here and there, and no matter how excited the room was before, it now turns sombre. Next, the speaker invites the audience to raise their hand if they have a father, mother, grandparent, or other family member who went to residential school. Most hands go up, and you can feel the room go dark, like someone turned off the lights. These were good reminders for me of the impact the residential school system has had on generations of Indigenous people and of how many are living with the scars, whether they are their own or scars that have been passed on.

The Indian residential school system permeated the lives of Indigenous Peoples in Canada for generations, and it continues to impact them. Together with the loss of land and access to resources, it colours every discussion about reconciliation. If I've learned anything on this path, it's that when you meet an Indigenous person, it is important to understand the magnitude of this experience; it destroyed or nearly destroyed families, communities, and whole nations. When you speak to an Indigenous person, you're speaking to a Survivor. When you visit an Indigenous community, you're witnessing the fragments of what is left.

Throughout my learning process, I often felt sadness, shame, and guilt over what happened here in Canada, even though I had no direct part in it. I believe many non-Indigenous people encounter these feelings when they start to learn about the realities of Indigenous Peoples in Canada. Being ashamed and feeling sad or guilty can be inhibiting, preventing us from wanting to learn more or holding us back from engaging with Indigenous people. It's like we want to protect ourselves from knowing, because once we know, our conscience tells us we ought to do something about it, and when we don't, we feel guilty.

When I first started reading up, I thought that surely, as a recent immigrant, I couldn't be responsible for any of this. And in a direct way, I wasn't. But the more I learned, the more I understood that as long as I benefited from the lasting impacts of colonization—living on stolen land, heating my house with energy extracted to the detriment of Indigenous Peoples, among other things—I was responsible. The situation was ongoing, and I wasn't doing anything about it. It was deeply unsettling and would have been easier not to know about. But I now understand that we must embrace that discomfort of knowing, no matter how difficult, if we want to start our own everyday reconciliation. In a way, this education is its own action. And to live in ignorance is to not only embrace inaction but perpetuate harmful myths and blatant racism.

Every so often, in particular around Orange Shirt Day, articles and social media posts surface questioning Indigenous people's experiences at residential schools, including the extent of the serious physical and sexual abuse they suffered and the elevated number of children who died and were buried there (which the government was aware of but chose to ignore). These articles and statements reek of racism and are part of systematic efforts to deny what happened and distort the public discourse. It is retraumatizing and deeply harmful for residential school survivors and for the communities who are working hard with little means to uncover the truth in their painful search for closure. It also ignores the work of the TRC and effectively challenges efforts to improve Canadians' understanding of our history.

Residential school denialism is part of a larger pattern of downplaying Indigenous people's realities. During a dinner conversation I was part of about ten years ago, a discussion began about the elevated numbers of missing and murdered Indigenous women and girls. I believe it was shortly before or after the launch of the Missing and Murdered Indigenous Women and Girls (MMIWG) national inquiry in 2016. The person next to me leaned over and told me in a hushed voice, "They're doing it to themselves, you know." As in, don't worry about it, it doesn't concern us.

My dinner companion wasn't the only one who felt that way. The year before the inquiry's launch, the federal Minister of Aboriginal Affairs Bernard Valcourt stated that 70 percent of homicides against Indigenous women were caused by Indigenous men. His claim was widely quoted and backed up by the RCMP

Commissioner at the time. The data used to make this claim has since been proved flawed and seems to have been related to the number of Indigenous women killed by an intimate partner or family member. Most murdered women have this relationship with their perpetrator, across all population groups, in Canada and globally. The minister was exploiting stereotypes of Indigenous men as violent, trying to place blame on Indigenous communities for the high rate of murdered and missing Indigenous women and girls.

But it's important to understand why people were quick to believe this deeply racist manipulation of facts. Perhaps they took comfort in it, thinking that since Indigenous people were doing it to themselves, they had no part in it. *Phew, finally, one issue we're not responsible for!* But if a report showed elevated levels of violence committed against white women by white men, would we sit back and do nothing? Or would we think that the government is responsible for protecting women from gender-based violence—whether the perpetrator is an intimate partner or not—and must do a better job at it?

Gender-based violence is a serious problem in all communities. In addition to the harm it causes victims and Survivors and the children of abused parents, it places a costly burden on the health, social, and justice systems. According to a 2009 study by the Department of Justice, intimate partner violence alone had an economic cost of $7.4 billion annually. The government's financial investments to combat gender-based violence are nowhere near that. Yet, as many as 30 percent of women over the age of fifteen have experienced a sexual assault. For Indigenous women, who face intersecting forms of discrimination and violence, this number is 44 percent.

When we talk about this violence, we must also discuss the root causes. Gender-based violence increases in times of crisis, economic hardship, and unemployment, which all tend to hit already vulnerable communities harder. The Indian Act also introduced gender discrimination: most importantly, First Nations women who married non-status men lost their own status, barring them from accessing treaty benefits and living within their communities, near their social and supportive networks.

Throughout this essay, I have explored the importance of finding out the truth, the *whole* history of Canada, and the more I learn, the more I realize how little I know. Within First Nations alone, there are over six hundred communities in Canada, representing over fifty different nations and languages. Learning about them all is not something most of us could do. But while we cannot know everything, we can always listen and be open to increasing our understanding. We must also accept that listening is a continuous process, and when it comes to the reconciliation process in Canada, there is still a lot to unearth, in some cases literally.

It took us generations to create the situation we're in, and it will take us time to address it. But I'm hopeful because a lot of that work is about education, and what we didn't learn in school, we can compensate for now. As the Truth and Reconciliation Commissioners often said when they discussed their findings: "Education got us into this mess, and education will get us out of it."

Five Ways to Help Indigenous Communities Heal from Residential Schooling

The residential school system caused much suffering and has impacted generations of Indigenous people. It also—intentionally—destroyed or nearly destroyed many Indigenous languages and cultures. As we demonstrated in our previous essays on language and culture, both are vital for any person's sense of identity and mental well-being.

This is why efforts to help Indigenous people and communities overcome trauma and reclaim their languages and cultures must go hand in hand. In both cases, efforts must also be collective and involve all of us, as a central part of the healing process is to have Canadians acknowledge the tragic realities of residential schools. In the end, this comes down to education. As Truth and Reconciliation Commissioners so eloquently stated, education got us into this mess, and education will get us out of it. We therefore call on readers not only to educate themselves but also to educate others by raising awareness about the residential school system and its impact on Indigenous people and communities and to actively help them heal from the trauma caused by that system.

Helping Indigenous communities heal from the trauma of residential schools is a deeply meaningful and ongoing process. There are many ways you can help do this. One example is to recognize Orange Shirt Day on September 30 every year, which is also the National Day for Truth and Reconciliation.

Derek's son Achilles, for example, volunteered to give out pins to students in his school on that day, proudly representing his people.

Orange Shirt Day is an Indigenous-led grassroots initiative first established in 2013, inspired by the experience of Phyllis Jack Webstad. When Phyllis was sent to residential school, her clothes—including a new orange shirt—were taken from her on her first day and never returned. The orange shirt is thus used as a symbol of the loss of identity and culture experienced by Indigenous children in residential schools. By wearing it, you affirm that residential schools were part of a broader policy of assimilation that caused deep and lasting damage to Indigenous children, families, and communities and that "Every Child Matters."

In 2021, after the discovery in Kamloops, B.C., the National Day for Truth and Reconciliation was created as a federal statutory holiday to increase awareness about the children who never returned home through public commemoration and to support the national reconciliation process. But many people are still unaware of the significance of Orange Shirt Day. One year, as Derek and his family walked through their Montreal neighbourhood to attend an Orange Shirt Day march, he was shocked to learn this. "Why are you all wearing orange shirts?" strangers asked them. "Is that a thing in your family, you all have the same taste, haha?" Only as they got closer to the march, where everyone was wearing an orange shirt, did people stop commenting.

We encourage you to acknowledge Orange Shirt Day to pay respect to the over 150,000 children who were sent to residential schools, to the many who never made it home, and to the parents and communities who so tragically lost them. Observing this day helps Survivors and communities heal and many schools, workplaces, and communities organize events that day that also offer great learning opportunities.

Here are five simple but impactful ways to help Survivors and communities heal from residential schooling:

1. Educate yourself about the history and legacy of residential schools. For example, find out if there was a residential school in your area, during which years it operated, and how many children were sent there. If the building still stands, go and see it and try to imagine what life there was like.

2. Learn about the trauma that residential schools inflicted on Indigenous children and often on generations to come. A good place to start is a novel such as *Five Little Indians* by Michelle Good or *Indian Horse* by Richard Wagamese.

3. Acknowledge Orange Shirt Day and the National Day for Truth and Reconciliation on September 30:

    a. Attend marches, lectures, and other events organized in acknowledgement of this day.

    b. If you're a federal employee, you have the day off for this purpose. For others, consider organizing an event at your school or place of work.

    c. Make sure to get your shirt from an Indigenous-led organization or a store that donates the proceeds to organizations or initiatives that support Indigenous communities.

4. Donate to Indigenous-led healing initiatives, such as the Indian Residential School Survivors Society (IRSSS), which provides culturally grounded emotional and crisis support, or other initiatives that provide culturally safe health services for Indigenous people.

5. Support Indigenous artists, authors, community leaders, educators, and others who are reclaiming Indigenous narratives, languages, and cultures.

Healing is not a one-time act—it's a journey, just like reconciliation. Also, like reconciliation, healing requires compassion and commitment in a collective effort that takes continuous participation of non-Indigenous people. While we encourage you to act on an everyday basis, don't miss the opportunity on the next Orange Shirt Day to learn and raise awareness about the impacts of residential schooling—play your part in the healing process.

Part V: Taking Action

Do You Want to Be an Ally?

Derek Aronhie:nens Montour

A FEW YEARS ago, I was asked to give the keynote speech at the First Nations of Quebec and Labrador Health and Social Services Commission's governance development meeting. At the time, I was the president of our board of directors, and I knew I'd be speaking to dozens of Indigenous and non-Indigenous people from all our communities and partners in Quebec. As I've shared in other essays, the commission's role is to advocate for, advise, and provide technical support to all the First Nations communities in Quebec and Labrador. It was created in 1994 after our health and social service predecessors approached the Assembly of First Nations of Quebec and Labrador with their concerns. They felt that the First Nations communities in Quebec were isolated, not talking to each other, and competing for the same resources, with limited support from the federal government and provinces.

But, they contended, the communities also had strength in numbers. What if they banded at a regional level? That way, they could get support and advice for the issues they were dealing with and have a unified voice when advocating while also still respecting each community's rights, vision, and self-determination. The assembly took up the cause and issued a mandate to create an organization that would have the mission to promote and monitor the physical, mental, emotional, and spiritual well-being of First Nations and Inuit families and communities. The organization would also work to improve access to comprehensive and culturally sensitive health and social service programs.

Today, the commission's network meetings allow representatives from communities and organizations at the federal, provincial, regional, or non-profit sectors to all meet in the same place so that everyone can hear the same message from our First Nations. We meet to share knowledge, collaborate on initiatives, provide input on regional concerns and advocacy, and help each other to improve our communities so we are not alone in our struggles. This work gives us a great opportunity to work with different types of non-Indigenous partners.

In my experience, those partners—and settlers more broadly—often fall into four categories: the ignorant, the racists, the saviours, and the allies. I knew there would be a number of non-Indigenous people in the audience when I gave my speech, and I wanted to help give them some introspection into their motives for wanting to help us (or not).

On the day of my speech, I decided to ask non-Indigenous audience members to truly think about which category they fit into. My questions were not meant to be offensive but rather thought-provoking. "Are you ignorant and just don't know enough, so you need to do some homework?" I asked. "Are you secretly (or not so secretly) racist and don't understand why Canadians should offer any help at all to the Indians? Are you a saviour and want to save Indigenous people from ourselves? Or are you truly an ally and want to help make things right between our peoples?"

Each category I mentioned—even allies, if they aren't operating with good knowledge or understanding—can cause harm through their actions. Most settlers, I think, fall into the category of ignorance, and that's because the system is designed for them to be that way. Colonialism works because it keeps people in the dark. Ignorance and racism sometimes go hand in hand, too, and I suppose that's because some families were brought up to hate. The hate may be in their nature, and it may also be a result of their experiences—as a way to hold on to their own identity, their land, and their beliefs. There is a chance to educate both types of settlers—the ignorant and the racist—and sometimes once that happens, there is also a chance for change.

On the other side of this are the saviours. They may be familiar with Indigenous histories and the current challenges we are facing, but they are also those people who profess to "know better." In their minds, they know what Indigenous people should do and will go out of their way to exert control, effectively stealing the Indigenous person's voice. This saviour mentality is embedded in the idea of superiority, in that a superior person must teach or instill their manners, practices, and beliefs in those they feel are inferior. That is the whole basis behind the religious missions: to civilize the savage and save their souls. It allows people to feel good or charitable while at the same time undermining or even preventing Indigenous core issues and concerns from being addressed. Saviourism fundamentally maintains the unequal balance of power that colonialism put in place.

Then there are the allies: people who go beyond intentions and sympathies and who concretely act to help change this unequal power dynamic. Being an ally requires respect, commitment, humility, and not taking things personally. It begins with the need to establish and build relationships; it is impossible to act as an ally without doing so. The work of good relationships builds trust and ensures people are acting in solidarity. Many opportunities exist for non-Indigenous people to help within our communities, but it is critical that they do so with the intent of being an ally—someone who is in the position of learning, not teaching, and certainly not *saving*. In the long run, allyship supports the conciliation of historical and contemporary wrong-doings and the reforming of previously inequitable colonial systems.

Since giving that speech, I would now add a group of people I call apathetic, meaning those who simply do not care. They know what happened, are aware of the circumstances that caused the challenges in Indigenous communities, and still show little interest, concern, or emotion about the issues. They do not appear racist, yet remain uninterested in engaging; Indigenous issues are simply not a concern of theirs. I think some people do not care about others beyond their immediate circle, and issues do not bother them unless those issues directly affect them. It is only when they become personally implicated in the issue in some way that they become engaged.

After my speech, several people approached me with feedback. Some seemed shocked by the blunt truthfulness, and others were concerned with being perceived as a saviour and not an ally. They felt guilt that they might not know enough. But no one disagreed with my simple categorization. Most of the people in the room chose to be in the room, and they were open to learning. I told them there were many things they could do to become a true ally. The first, as I have suggested throughout this book, is to educate themselves. Allies must understand our history. They must understand our rights and how we have fought to protect those rights. And they must also understand that Indigenous people are not a monolith—to secure the support of one group does not necessarily mean your work as an ally is done. As I explain the task of learning about us, of our history, and of the differences and similarities between our nations, I realize it must be confusing to think of where to begin if you don't have some more context, so let's delve into this background more.

It is vital that people who want to be allies understand that every community and every Nation may hold a different mindset or perspective, even if there are sometimes similarities. For example, the Haudenosaunee are different than the Algonquin. Our methods of decision-making and governance, our ceremonies and beliefs, our food and lifestyle, and our family dynamics and relationships are all different. And this is the same for each nation-to-nation relationship; we are different from each other. These differences are what form the rationale for the right to self-determination, and the legal basis can be found in various sources, such as customary international law, the United Nations Charter, and the International Covenant on Civil and Political Rights. These all preceded the United Nations Declaration on the Rights of Indigenous Peoples (UNDRIP), which was introduced in 2007 and is the first global legal instrument to recognize and elaborate on the content of the right to self-determination for Indigenous Peoples. It is also the basis for an act by the same name that received Royal Assent in Canada in 2021.

The scope and purpose of the principle of self-determination have evolved significantly in the 20th century. In the early 1900s, international support grew for the right of all people to self-determination. This led to successful secessionist movements during and after WWI, resulting in new nation-states in Europe, and laid the groundwork for decolonization throughout the world in the 1960s. In Canada, prior to the 1960s, the prevailing view was that Canada was a white settler dominion that was an extension of the British Empire into the New World, and the systemic obstacles to Indigenous Peoples' struggle for greater self-determination were significant. Status Indians could not even vote until 1960 without losing their status. Before confederation, there seemed to be at least some understanding or acknowledgement of Indigenous Peoples as distinct nations; after confederation, Canada began its assimilation project in earnest, aiming to assimilate the Indigenous and all immigrants into one people: Canadians.

First came the Gradual Enfranchisement Act in 1869, which pushed the assimilation agenda by encouraging Indigenous people to give up their legal status and gain "full citizenship." This became the impetus for the formal creation of the band council system, which was established under the Indian Act adopted in 1876. The fundamental purpose of the band council system was to undermine self-determination and traditional governance, thereby allowing the colonial government to control land, money, and resources. All the many different forms of First Nations governance and decision-making systems were replaced with a system that is subject to the Crown and in which our own decisions can be overruled or disregarded. Make no mistake: The Crown wanted to remove our cultural distinctions and to make Indigenous people uniformly think and act like Europeans.

By imposing a system that subjected all Indigenous people to the same rules and that allowed it to change those rules whenever it wanted to, the federal government effectively rendered all Indigenous people as children, or wards of the state. The parent, Canada, got to decide how to raise them, what food or supplies they received, and what room—or land—they could sleep in. The Indian Act created a position called the Superintendent General of Indian Affairs, and that person and their agents had legal authority to exert extreme control over the lives of Indigenous people. They even decided who was allowed to be Indigenous and who could lose their status, in turn allowing them to determine who would receive band or treaty benefits.

The band council system is a forced political system that imposed the same form of government for each community, often in opposition to the traditional, hereditary laws and government of First Nations. It implemented mandatory elections, in which people voted for who they liked the best, regardless of their qualifications for this important role. This system is unlike the traditional ways, such as in Haudenosaunee communities, where clan mothers decided who would be the Chiefs of their clans. Under the band council system, not only are the councils the only bodies with which the provincial and federal governments communicate, but each community must also often negotiate separately with the federal or provincial governments. And while some communities today have attempted to maintain their traditional forms of governance—and I can only hope they succeed and that more communities are inspired by this—the majority of communities now use the imposed band council system.

The band councils have no definitive connection to traditional culture and govern nothing outside of their respective communities. Under international law, a band council has no substance, meaning, or standing. Any law a council wants to create cannot be passed, enacted, or enforced without the consent of the federal government. What's more, any government funding a community receives must go through the band council or its delegates.

This criticism is not a reflection on the good intentions of the people who became band councillors; from my experience, most of them want to see positive change in their communities and are doing their utmost to preserve the future of our people. But anybody who wants to ally with Indigenous communities must understand the implications of this system, which was imposed on us. Allies often misstep in relationships with communities because they (wrongly) assume that a band council speaks for all the members of that community or nation. That's simply not the case. As an example, does the mayor of Montreal speak for all Montrealers? Naturally, not. But in the case of band councils, there is an extra layer of natural resistance based on the imposed nature of the system. This is what needs to be understood by non-Indigenous people. I'd encourage allies to enter each new relationship with a goal of learning and understanding the dynamics of each respective individual, community, or nation.

The creation of this band council system has allowed the provincial and federal governments to *isolate* and divide communities by creating different agreements, different types of support, different funding levels, and different partnerships with each community. Some communities have benefited from these individual negotiations, while others have stagnated or suffered. In this way, Canada has essentially attempted, and arguably succeeded, to divide and conquer each community. And we continue to feel the repercussions of all this today with much division within our own communities and amongst all the different communities and Nations. We argue, fight, compete, and disagree.

In response to the government's assimilation efforts—and all the pain, division, and isolation that were inflicted as a result— Indigenous leadership across Canada sought a strong and effective collective advocacy organization. Many Canadians may have heard of the Assembly of First Nations (AFN) and its regional bodies. The role of such organizations is to assist Indigenous communities in creating unified direction for all the different communities and nations across this land. They cannot, however, supplant any nation's respective decision-making—meaning they cannot make a decision without the consent of the rights holders. Many non-Indigenous people seem to think the AFN and other regional or national organizations can make decisions for all First Nations. But we do not all speak with one voice. People who want to act as allies cannot simply meet with the AFN, or one of its regional bodies, and get an agreement, believing that all the different nations must then agree. That is not how it works in Canada.

If non-Indigenous people want to truly become allies—and not fall into one of the other four categories—then they must seek to understand these complexities. They must understand how these systems have been built. And, they must at least understand the basics of our rights, their history, how they are defined and protected in Canada—and how they are not. This is a layered discussion but also a vital one for any ally.

From a general perspective, a *rights holder* is an individual or social group that has particular entitlements. These are the rights and freedoms that individuals are inherently entitled to, or that are conferred to them by law or other means, in relation to specific duty-bearers. The duty-bearers are those individuals, groups, and organizations that have an obligation and responsibility to respect, uphold, and protect those rights, such as governments of all levels. Companies, international support organizations, and even individuals, like parents, also fall under this category.

For example, all human beings are rights holders under the 1948 Universal Declaration of Human Rights. While the declaration doesn't grant legally protected rights, it has served as a blueprint for numerous international treaties, regional human rights instruments, and national constitutions and laws that are legally binding. Its thirty articles outline the rights and freedoms to which every person should be entitled, including the right to not be subjected to degrading treatment or discrimination, the right to freedom of movement, to education, to own property, to have freedom of expression, and to enjoy and participate in their culture.

What are rights holders then in the context of Indigenous people? In September of 2007, the United Nations adopted the United Nations Declaration on the Rights of Indigenous Peoples (UNDRIP) by a majority of 143 states in favour, with four states voting against it and eleven abstaining. Canada, the United States, Australia, and New Zealand were the four states to vote against the declaration. As I mentioned earlier in this essay, however, Canada later removed its objector status in 2016 and further passed the UNDRIP Act in 2021 to formally acknowledge it as a human rights instrument under Canadian law.

To explain, UNDRIP aims to defend the survival, dignity, and well-being of Indigenous Peoples (i.e., the rights holders in this case) and was created to recognize and uphold their Indigenous rights worldwide. It contains forty-six articles that outline an Indigenous person's rights, including the right to self-determination; to maintain and strengthen distinct governance structures; to live in freedom; to maintain spiritual and cultural practices, languages, and education; as well as to not have children forcibly removed from care; to not be forcibly assimilated; and more.

Canada's UNDRIP Act obliges Canada to ensure that its laws conform with UNDRIP, but Canada may interpret the key provisions contained in UNDRIP differently than how Indigenous people in Canada may interpret them. For example, so far, Canada has not interpreted UNDRIP's right to free, prior, and informed consent on the use of Indigenous lands and territories as an absolute right for Indigenous Peoples to stop a project. Other provisions in UNDRIP that may also be interpreted differently by Canada and Indigenous Peoples include land ownership and shared decision-making.

To be a better ally, Canadians should take the time to read both the Universal Declaration of Human Rights and UNDRIP. They are core documents when it comes to understanding the situations facing Indigenous people in Canada. The two documents are also in direct opposition to the assimilation policies, practices, and laws of Canada, such as the Indian Act.

From there, there are two types of rights, individual and collective, that require understanding when it comes to Indigenous people. According to the Indian Act, individual rights are based on government status: Is a person an "Indian" or not? This is based on whether they are on the Indian Register, in which case they are granted certain rights and benefits. To address reconciliation is to understand how Canada has systematically eliminated the rights of Indigenous people through its laws and policies and through deciding who has a right to status and who does not.

This issue of status often forms the basis of who has the other type of right: collective or so-called Aboriginal rights. Every Indigenous person with status is connected to a specific community or nation that possesses collective (or Aboriginal) rights, which the individuals belonging to that nation can then enjoy collectively.

One type of collective or Aboriginal rights is the so-called immemorial rights. Non-Indigenous people who want to meaningfully work with us must understand the concept of immemorial rights, which are also sometimes referred to as inherent rights. These rights are not covered within the Indian Act, which has in fact sought to remove them. These rights are affirmed by UNDRIP and, as the name suggests, were inherently ours long before settlers arrived. They have always been ours. They form the basis of our knowledge, culture, traditions, and oral histories. They are not something that any other government, even an Indigenous one, can impose or change. Today, these rights are increasingly being recognized through Canadian legal processes, such as an Indigenous community's right to hunt in a specific area.

A band council doesn't hold a community's or nation's immemorial rights, even though the council is theoretically elected by the people. That's because it is, again, a product of the Canadian government, imposed under the Indian Act. In theory, a band council cannot vote on issues, negotiate, or make decisions on behalf of their community unless they have been specifically given a mandate to do so from the community's rights holders. This means that when a decision is required that will affect community members' immemorial rights, band councils have an obligation to go back to the community's rights holders to obtain agreement.

To help you understand these immemorial rights, I will group them into three categories. The first is communal rights, which include our equal right to live and do what we want with our land; benefit from the use of the land to care and provide for our families; build and manage our own systems and infrastructure; govern ourselves as we want to; and determine our own future. These rights make up our right to self-determination, which is central to UNDRIP and has been recognized in Canada through Article 35 of the Constitution. The second is land rights, which include the right to ensure our territory and Traditional Territory is respected; protect the land and its resources, including earth, air, and water; and economically benefit from the use of the land and its resources. Courts have now started to recognize Indigenous, or Aboriginal, title to land, as Elin discussed in her essay "Should We Go?" The last type is our generational rights, which centre on the obligation of all right holders to ensure our next seven generations are considered in any decisions we are making in the present. The goal in this is to honour our ancestors while also preserving a future for our descendants.

It is important for Canadians to understand the nature of Indigenous rights because it can explain why certain actions within Indigenous territories seem different than outside of our communities; we are exercising immemorial rights. It also helps to explain why the duty to consult with Indigenous communities is so vital: An individual's, company's, or government's actions may be unwittingly impacting these rights. These rights that Indigenous communities and Nations hold have never been relinquished, whether by supposed conquest or assimilation.

In the 1867 Constitution Act, Canada did not formally recognize Indigenous people as having inherent rights, including the right to self-government, which set the stage for its assimilation policies. The Indian Act put these assimilation policies into law, and in the Crown's view at least, all Aboriginal rights in Canada became those enshrined within the Indian Act.

When we talk about these rights, we must also consider fiduciary responsibility.

Fiduciary responsibility is a complex subject, but we can trace its origins to the 1763 Royal Proclamation which stated that only the Crown could acquire land directly from First Nations. Fiduciary responsibility evolved through the British North America Act of 1867 (which created Canada) when the British Crown gave control of Indians (Indigenous Peoples) and Indian lands to the Government of Canada, and then again in the Constitution Act of 1982. Essentially, the federal government's fiduciary responsibility means that it must act fairly and with care when dealing with Indigenous Peoples. For example, it is responsible for providing the same programs and services to Indigenous communities that non-Indigenous communities receive through federal, provincial, or municipal governments.

Those programs and services include education, health, social services, roads, clean drinking water, housing, waste management, and more. The problem is that Canada has systematically underfunded all those programs over many years, resulting in increasing lawsuits after the damage is done to our people. This has created an ever-widening gap between the services offered to Indigenous people and the rest of the Canadian population, translating into worse outcomes in many areas. When the Canadian government does not live up to its fiduciary responsibility, it is violating this fiscal responsibility and its agreement.

Over the years, there have been many notable instances of the federal government failing to live up to its fiduciary duty. This failure was a key aspect of the human rights complaint in child welfare made by the First Nations Child and Family Caring Society and the Assembly of First Nations in 2006 that I mentioned in an earlier essay. Canada was responsible for providing Indigenous communities funding for child welfare services equitable to services that non-Indigenous citizens received. The complaint demonstrated that it instead systematically underfunded the Indigenous programs by at least 22 percent over many decades.

Fiduciary duty is also at the core of many of the unsafe drinking water issues faced by so many communities. If non-Indigenous people receive safe drinking water, why wouldn't Indigenous people be entitled to it as well? These rights also extend to involving Indigenous nations in decisions regarding the use of their territory. When Canada makes a decision involving the use of Crown land or territory that an Indigenous group has an immemorial or inherent right to, for example, they have certain obligations because of these fiduciary duties to involve those Indigenous groups. Spoiler alert: This does not always happen.

In addition to fiduciary responsibilities, our constitutional rights, as defined within the 1982 Constitution Act, are also key to understanding our collective rights. The act includes Section 35, which recognizes Aboriginal people, treaty rights, and Aboriginal rights. The section was not initially included when the Pierre Trudeau government first drafted the act, and its omission would have extinguished these rights. It was only added after the many protests, demonstrations, and activism of Indigenous Peoples and their allies. Once it was enshrined in Canada's constitution, Section 35 began to change the relationship that Indigenous people have had with Canada since the British North America Act; Aboriginal rights were now grounded in the new law. Yet it wasn't all good news: Section 35 only protects Aboriginal rights that already existed when the act came into effect. Meaning, an Indigenous group must prove they practised that activity prior to contact, and that up until 1982 the right had not been extinguished.

The act also gives Indigenous groups a path to seek recourse if an Aboriginal right is infringed upon: the court system. Each time an Indigenous group's Aboriginal rights are infringed upon, or the group is seeking to have a right confirmed, they must prove in court that the activity is in fact an existing right. This includes absorbing all the entailed legal costs. I find it ironic that Indigenous people must use the same court system that enforces the rules that the Canadian government itself put in place, including those laws that intended to assimilate us.

What this all means is that, in effect, although Indigenous people in Canada have constitutionally protected rights, defined as Aboriginal rights, they also need to constantly argue in court for their inherent rights—rights they should and would already have, if not for Canada's assimilationist policies. It often seems like every day brings another fight against the injustices Canada has wrought throughout the last 158 years. And every fight we are forced to use the same court system, against the same government, that enacted those injustices in the first place. What's more, it often seems as if everyday Canadians have no idea that these important battles are happening. Can you imagine how exhausting that is, day after day? Every time a new law or infrastructure/resource project is introduced, and the government responsible doesn't consider our inherent rights, it is another fight. What is truly the value of a right if you must go to the Supreme Court every time to enforce it? This is also what Elin and I mean when we encourage *everyday conciliation and reconciliation*: the need for all Canadians to help find a path toward recognizing and affirming inherent rights as they should be.

Lastly, we must talk about treaty rights. Treaty rights, or negotiated rights, are protected under Section 35. Many treaties promised Indigenous groups certain things in exchange for the right of Canada to use their land. There are around seventy recognized treaties in Canada, all still valid, and new ones (so-called modern treaties) being negotiated. One danger that people need to be aware of when agreeing to a treaty with Canada is that treaty rights may take over the corresponding inherent rights; this is what occurred in the past, as it was a forced extinguishment of rights.

The history of Indigenous Peoples on this land—and the colonial systems and laws that have been imposed on us—is both long and complex. What I have discussed in this essay so far is only the tip of the iceberg, but it is important for allies to learn these parts of our journey if they want to understand what is happening today at the national level. If allies want to help us advocate for equitable funding, preservation of our languages, care of the land, and self-determination, they need to understand the roots of how we got here and how the system still needs to change. Advocating with us can help, in large part because the Canadian government has opposed our own advocacy for so long. The truth, in my opinion, is that we Indigenous people can't change the system alone; it is not our system.

Indigenous people have made many notable attempts to break the division and isolation between communities over the years. Even as early as the 1800s, different First Nations repeatedly pleaded with the Crown in England to address the wrongful and abusive practices, such as land encroachment, not honouring treaties, and the undermining of Indigenous governance. They were ignored. That didn't stop Indigenous people from coming together again and again to fight for their rights and against assimilation.

One of the earliest formally organized movements by Indigenous people against the Canadian government dates to 1918. That year, Onondeyoh Fred Loft started the League of Indians of Canada in his community of Ohsweken (Six Nations). The League was the first pan-Indigenous political organization in Canada. As early as the 1890s, Loft was already an involved activist. He previously attempted to organize Indigenous people to lobby for reforms, including the elimination of residential schools, which he had attended. He was ultimately unsuccessful. The Canadian government under Wilfred Laurier had no interest in implementing positive reforms for Indigenous people. Loft's fighting spirit, however, would not give up.

When WWI broke out, not only did Onondeyoh enlist, but he also encouraged other Indigenous men to join with him. After serving in WWI as a Canadian lieutenant with the 256th Infantry Battalion, Onondeyoh was outraged at the poor and unequal treatment that Indigenous veterans received in comparison to non-Indigenous veterans. Indigenous veterans received fewer benefits and smaller pensions—in some cases, they were even denied their pensions and benefits. Onondeyoh had contact with more Indigenous veterans who had all sacrificed and who all felt the unfairness of their post-war treatment, despite their sacrifice. Together, under Onondeyoh's leadership, they formed the League.

The League advocated for equal schooling and standards of treatment that other Canadians enjoyed. They fought to stop the seizure of Indigenous territory for non-Indigenous returning soldiers and also against the threat of forced enfranchisement, among other things. The League enjoyed wide appeal with both Indigenous people and non-Indigenous allies, particularly in the Prairie provinces, where land and treaty rights were major concerns. This widespread support alarmed Duncan Campbell Scott, the Deputy Superintendent General of Indian Affairs, as it challenged his plans and authority. Scott ordered all agents to undermine and suppress the League and worked tirelessly to undermine Onondeyoh himself, including trying to forcibly enfranchise him. In 1920, the federal government passed amendments to allow compulsory enfranchisement, and although a new Liberal government under Mackenzie King soon after repealed it, the threat that it could happen remained in the minds of all Indigenous people.

Unfortunately, Duncan Campbell Scott's opposition to Indigenous civil resistance hampered the League's growth, and memberships declined everywhere apart from in Alberta and

Saskatchewan. Soon, Onondeyoh was largely alone in the fight. There was little support from the communities and limited funding outside his own pocket. But the League lived on in Saskatchewan as the forerunner to the Federation of Saskatchewan Indian Nations and in Alberta as the forerunner to the Indian Association of Alberta.

Others fought the assimilation in different ways, such as Cayuga Chief Deskaheh Levi General in the traditional Longhouse Council. In the early 1920s, the Longhouse leadership actively opposed many federal policies, including conscription. Instead of working within Canada's systems, however, Deskaheh advocated for the international acceptance of First Nations people—specifically the Six Nations of the Grand River community—as a sovereign entity. They should be recognized as allies of the British Crown, he argued, and not subjects. Deskaheh remained in Geneva for over a year in an attempt to gain access to and influence the League of Nations, the forerunner of the United Nations. While there, he had the support of Swiss non-Indigenous allies, like the writer René Claparède and the Bureau International pour la Défense des Indigènes. But it was to no avail. The British Crown suppressed all efforts to influence the other nations, saying it was a domestic Canadian matter.

It was at this point that Canada began enforcing the band council system more aggressively. In 1924, the federal officials ordered the RCMP to Ohsweken, where Onondeyoh Loft and Deskaheh General were from, to force the community to replace their Chief and clan mothers with a band council. Without consultation, the federal government deposed the hereditary council and conducted an election in which only fifty-six community members voted. A new band council was installed that undermined the leadership of both Onondeyoh and Deskaheh.

Over the following decades, the Canadian government continued to impose laws that either chipped away at or outright attacked different aspects of Indigenous society. In 1927, more amendments to the Indian Act banned Indigenous political organizing and stopped our ability to make land claims. It became illegal to hire a lawyer, illegal to fundraise without government permission, and illegal for Indigenous people to even sue the Government of Canada. These amendments remained in place until 1951, when they were finally repealed. Some Nations continued with their traditional ways, but there was increasingly less dialogue and collaboration amongst different communities. Individual community needs, priorities, and concerns became paramount over everyone's common needs, priorities, and concerns. And systemic discrimination only grew more entrenched.

Yet, as the government continued to move against us, so, too, did we continue to organize. Across Canada, different political advocacy groups formed. In 1945, in another notable instance of trying to find common ground, delegates from different nations across Canada came together to form the North American Indian Nation Government (NAING). The NAING had formed to protest forced conscription during World War II, particularly given that Indigenous people were not considered citizens of Canada and still did not have the right to vote. It started when a Wendat man from Wendake named Jules Sioui invited all the First Nations Chiefs in Canada to a major convention in Ottawa. Although not all First Nations attended, fifty-three delegates did, and the meeting went ahead despite opposition from the Canadian government. At a follow-up meeting the following year, two hundred delegates attended.

The NAING political movement was bold for its time and aimed to establish self-determination for all its members. It proclaimed that NAING members were exempt from military service, exempt from taxes, and had the right to hunt and fish on all North American lands, as well as to set up camps anywhere. They were the first ones to declare and establish an Indian Day on June 21, 1945, which eventually became National Indigenous Peoples Day. The organization was particularly active in the

1950s and 1960s—despite the federal government's arrest of Jules and four other members of the organization in 1947.

The government accused the founders of "having conspired for the purpose of sowing discontent and hatred among the subjects of His Majesty, the Indians of Canada, by leading them to believe he had instituted a special status for North American Indians, who no longer need comply with the laws of the land" and charged them with seditious conspiracy. They were found guilty in 1949 of these charges and sentenced to two years imprisonment. The judgment was quashed on appeal, and the government brought it to the Supreme Court, at which time Sioui went on a hunger strike. After seventy-two days of his strike, the Canadian government dropped its proceedings.

The political movements that followed throughout the 1960s and 1970s helped launch further progressive change. In 1961, the National Indian Council was formed with the mission to promote unity among all Indian people. The council represented both First Nations people and Métis. The Inuit have a different relationship with the federal government. Until the 1971 James Bay and Northern Quebec Agreement, Canada had not been interested in providing support to the Inuit through treaties. They were excluded from the Indian Act, did not possess any treaties, do not have status as Indians, and were not part of the reserve system, yet still subject to residential schools, forced relocations to settlements, and slaughter of their transportation dogs and other assimilationist policies.

By 1967, it became apparent that there were too many issues for just one organization to lobby for effectively. By mutual agreement, the council closed its doors so that each Indigenous group could reconstitute into separate advocacy entities. The organization's non-status Indian and Métis members formed the Native Council of Canada in 1971, with the Métis splitting to form the Métis National Council in 1983. In 1993, the Native Council of Canada was reorganized and renamed the Congress of Aboriginal Peoples (CAP). Meanwhile, following the collapse of the National Indian Council in 1967, the Treaty/Status Indians formed the National Indian Brotherhood (NIB) in 1968, which was the forerunner of today's Assembly of First Nations (AFN).

The NIB was created in a time of immediate controversy. Shortly after its formation, the federal Liberal government, under Prime Minister Pierre Trudeau and his Minister of Indian Affairs, Jean Chrétien, revealed its infamous 1969 "Statement of the Government of Canada on Indian Policy." Commonly known as the White Paper, it essentially proposed to end the legal recognition of Indian status, and subsequently, abolish the Indian Act, remove First Nations from the Canadian Constitution, appoint a commissioner to settle land claims, and gradually eliminate treaties, and thereby fundamentally rejecting immemorial or inherent rights. Its effect would be the assimilation of Indigenous people, as if they had the status of ethnic minorities. The NIB was instrumental in confronting the Liberal government on the White Paper, lobbying both Parliament and the Canadian public, and receiving support from many different groups, Indigenous and non-Indigenous allies alike. A key component of these efforts was NIB's support for a counter-proposal to the White Paper: the 1970 Citizens Plus report, commonly known as the Red Paper.

The report's name comes from a term used in the 1967 Hawthorn Report, which was the first federally sponsored study undertaken to assess the economic, political, and educational needs of Status Indians across Canada. The Hawthorne Report argued that Indigenous people should be considered "citizens plus": in addition to the normal rights and duties of citizenship, they possessed certain additional rights derived from history and their status as original inhabitants of the land. At the same time, the Hawthorn Report was also seen as a major influence in the creation of the White Paper, as while it sought to increase services for Indigenous people, identifying them as the most disadvantaged population group in Canada, it also argued that the significance of treaties should be reduced. The Red Paper and NIB's advocacy successfully killed the White Paper, and it continues to influence First Nations discussions on self-determination.

Throughout the history of Indigenous political activism, non-Indigenous allies have been a constant presence and support. We need non-Indigenous allies to help shift the system so that we can all live peacefully. But the question remains of whether it's best to focus our push for change and decolonization from within the very systems that oppress them or not. While some Indigenous leaders, like Premier Wab Kinew, the late Murray Sinclair, or the recently appointed Minister of Indigenous Services Canada, Mandy Gull-Masty, are making efforts to join the system to make changes from the inside, other Indigenous leaders are holding on to their tradition or hereditary forms of government. Which is the "right" approach?

Do we follow in the footsteps of Onondeyoh Loft and fight from both inside and outside the system to seek reform? Or in the footsteps of Deskaheh General and fight from the outside to seek sovereign recognition internationally? I don't have the answer, but I do know we must remember that Indigenous people are not a monolith; we are not an intractably indivisible and uniform group. While powerful change can happen when communities and nations come together to advocate, at the same time, what may be right for one group, community, or person may not be right for another. Self-determination is an affirmation that each group has the right to exercise choice and act in the manner they think is right. Allies, whether Indigenous or non-Indigenous, should take their lead and ask them how they can support them in their journey.

I was always taught, from as early as a young child, about the 1613 *Teioháte Kaswentha*, or the Two Row Wampum Treaty. This wampum design is two parallel purple lines on a white background, with the white representing a river and the purple representing two vessels. In one vessel is the Haudenosaunee with our laws, traditions, languages, culture, and spiritual beliefs. And in the other is the European's. It is the responsibility of the people in each vessel to steer a straight course so as not to interfere with the other. The Haudenosaunee see the Teioháte Kaswentha as a living treaty and as a way for our people to live in peace with the settlers who have come to this land. Yet the Canadian government had long since crossed into our vessel and forced us to cross into theirs.

Deciding how to untangle our paths now—and if we should or to what extent—is complex work. I was impressed to read one day in 2021 that Queen's University raised the Teioháte Kaswentha, along with the Confederacy flag, to honour Indigenous people as part of its "Extending the Rafters" TRC Task Force efforts. This told me that a major Canadian university could work as a non-Indigenous ally to take concrete action and make a statement. To me, this implicitly stated, "We acknowledge and honour the treaties." This is what everyday (re)conciliation means to me: finding opportunities to actively participate in reconciliation in whatever job, role, or activity you are involved in.

If we believe the Teioháte Kaswentha was a valid treaty, then we have an obligation to continue to honour that treaty, do we not? And if so, that means we all must: Indigenous and non-Indigenous alike. From that perspective, for a Haudenosaunee member to become a Canadian politician and work from "the inside" would be crossing from our vessel into the other one and therefore not honouring our treaty. But then again, would abiding by all, or any, of the rules imposed by the Canadian system and government—such as participating on or voting for a band council, obtaining a driver's licence or Medicare card, filing taxes, and everything else—also implicate us, to a certain degree, within this system? And all the attempts at assimilation are a part of that system, too, so no wonder we are all confused on where we are supposed to stand!

I believe self-determination is a process. It is a process of learning for ourselves, after all the trauma and conflict and suppression of culture, and all the rest. It is a process where we need understanding from non-Indigenous allies that we may not know the definitive answers today, but we are on the right track. That we need help from allies until we are organized enough, unified enough, healed enough, and educated enough to be on an equal footing.

I want to be crystal clear that non-Indigenous people can help. It takes awareness first of where you are in your own knowledge. Are you ready to be an ally? Or are you still a bit ignorant, a bit racist, a bit of a saviour, or a bit apathetic? I am not saying this to make readers feel bad but rather to point out that an ally must always check themselves to determine their motivations, so they are ready and have the tools to help enact real change. It's imperative that they start with listening and seeking to understand. Allies must move past ignorance and not try to save us, but instead work *with* us. They must know how all these laws and policies were put in place over time and why, how they infringe on our rights, and how they continue to hurt us. Every Canadian should know this.

The truth is, by simply being a Canadian, you belong to the people who are responsible for all this, and unless you take a stand, you implicitly accept the abuses and suppressions of our rights to continue. I have heard many Canadians say that it wasn't them who put those assimilation policies in place, or it wasn't them who forced people into residential schools, or whatever. But it was the vast majority and all Canadians benefited from the policies to obtain land, take the resources, the broken treaties, the suppression and oppression, the lack of education, the lack of health care, and all the rest. And Canadians living here today continue to benefit from both past and ongoing injustices, as do new immigrants to the country. All Canadians assume the legacy of their ancestors' decisions, just like I do, and we all have an opportunity to do better as we move forward.

What to Do

Elin Sandberg Miller

THE SNOW HAD fallen all night in Ottawa. Large, damp flakes were piling up on my hat and shoulders and melting in my face as I waded through the thick, soft layer on my way to work. After a snowfall like that, the world was usually calm and quiet, sounds muffled and streets tucked in like they had gone to bed, but the snowplows were already hard at work. In my street, contractors were clearing the driveways, their small green tractors rumbling back and forth, the sound of their backup beepers almost deafening. As I turned the corner, I heard the loud clanking of metal and scraping against asphalt as the city's large trucks cleared the neighbourhood's main thoroughfare.

It wasn't cold but I was glad I wore my high-shafted mukluks to protect my work pants and keep my feet dry. The mukluks had been a Christmas gift from my husband, and I loved them. Their soft, tan-coloured suede, their warm, furry lining, the cute pompoms that bounced around my legs as I walked, and, above all, their elaborately beaded pattern of stylized red flowers and winding leaves. They looked particularly pretty against the clean, white snow, and admiring them, I realized that their beadwork matched the design of the beaded earrings I was also wearing.

Then it struck me that mukluks are of Inuit origin, while my earrings were made by a First Nations artist—was it appropriate to mix and match like that? And wait, my mukluks were produced by a company in Manitoba, which I knew was founded by a Métis person. My particular model, with its pretty floral beadwork, was even called *Métis Mukluk*. Were mukluks also a Métis thing? My own ignorance was discomforting and made me question whether I—a non-Indigenous person—should even be wearing Indigenous jewellery and boots, and *why* was I doing it anyway?

At this point, I was well into my learning journey, having taken several courses and done a lot of reading on my own, but I still had lingering questions about some of the more difficult issues to navigate, such as the lines between cultural appropriation, white saviourism, and allyship. As I was walking there in the pretty snowfall, I went from feeling proud of my beautiful earrings and boots to feeling like a dimwit and imposter. I wondered if I should stop wearing the mukluks and my Indigenous jewellery altogether and perhaps donate them to an Indigenous person.

But, I reasoned, I was wearing them not just because they were pretty and, in the case of the mukluks, warm and comfortable, but also because I wanted to be a good ally by supporting Indigenous artists and companies. Both the artist and company making and selling these products had also marketed them as something everyone could wear, without distinction.

We may not always know how to be good allies. There's a saying that when a white person shows up in an Indigenous community and says, "I'm here to help," everybody runs. Indigenous people have learned the hard way to question our intentions. Even when we mean well, we can do harm. I realized that to figure out whether I was a good ally, I had to have an honest discussion with myself about what was driving me not just to wear my boots and earrings—but also to want to contribute to the national reconciliation process.

On the one hand, I think it was my sense of justice that I developed growing up in Sweden in the 1970s, amid egalitarian policies and social movement activism. I strongly remember the anti-apartheid movement and the boycott of South African goods, which had broad support in Sweden, and feeling embarrassed that my dad still bought this South African orange marmalade that he couldn't resist. I was also inspired by the peace and environmental movements going on around me and by my mom, sitting at her desk at night, writing letters for Amnesty International, asking totalitarian leaders to release political prisoners.

On the other hand, as uncomfortable as it was to realize, I also felt a fair amount of guilt, because the more I learned, the more I realized just how privileged I was and how equally disadvantaged First Nations people, Métis, and Inuit in Canada were. The differences we face in socio-economic conditions, access to land and resources, and biases and attitudes while living in the same country are deeply unfair. I think it's normal to experience a sense of guilt when learning that through colonization, one people benefits from the dispossession of the other, and your people is on the winning (or profiteering) side of this relationship.

But I also don't think that being driven by guilt is necessarily a bad thing. Feeling guilty can be a sign of empathy and is often what pushes us to do the right thing. Mulling over your guilt or looking the other way to avoid feeling it, however, is never helpful. What's helpful is to do something—to turn your guilt into meaningful action.

The more I interrogated myself, I determined I was also driven by a sense of care toward other beings. I think that most of us care. For example, following the discovery in Kamloops in 2021 of what were believed to be the remains of children who died at the residential school there, the Kamloops Aboriginal Friendship Society, which had been fundraising toward a new building for months, saw a sharp spike in donations through its

GoFundMe campaign, increasing from a total of $1,500 raised to nearly $80,000 in less than a week.

To further support this, a 2024 national study from the Environics Institute demonstrates that most Canadians support continued efforts by the government to achieve reconciliation and believe that one of the most important obstacles to reconciliation is the poor socio-economic situation for Indigenous Peoples. A 2022 national survey from Leger shows that the vast majority of Canadians understand why reconciliation is important for Indigenous Peoples. All this indicates to me that Canadians care. So, while there's often a variety of reasons for *why* people want to be Indigenous allies or to contribute to reconciliation, in the end, I think that most of us simply think it's the right thing to do.

Reading the Environics report, I was also heartened to learn that 70 percent of Canadians believe that we all have a role to play in bringing about reconciliation. At the same time, based on the respondents' answers, the report concludes that people are less certain about how to go about it. Therefore, while it is important to reflect on the *why*, I believe it's even more important to focus on the *what*, because all that goodwill (seven out of ten Canadians!) could be translated into action, if people only knew what to do.

I think reconciliation is a bit like climate change in this regard. Doing something about it can often seem daunting or even futile. We might think, "How can I, one single person, really change anything, anyway?" Yet, most of us listen to the experts and follow their advice every day: We compost and recycle, buy local, install heat pumps, and reconsider our means of transportation, even our whole lifestyle. It's the same with reconciliation: There are concrete things that we can do, we just need to listen to the experts, who, in this case, are Indigenous people. Only they can know what their needs and priorities are.

This is why I sought to centre Indigenous voices on my podcast. Rather than decide myself how to be the best ally, I would listen to what the experts—my Indigenous guests—had to tell me and my audience. At the end of each episode, I asked my guests for their top three things that non-Indigenous people like me could do to contribute to reconciliation. What were some simple, everyday actions? And as Derek and I have both previously discussed, the number one thing my guests all brought up was the need to inform ourselves. They told me our knowledge gap remains a huge obstacle to reconciliation and a daily frustration to Indigenous people. My guests recommended a wide range of resources, including reports, books, podcasts, and movies.

If you don't know where to start, they suggested, start small: Pick one report, for example. Almost all my guests recommended reading the Truth and Reconciliation Commission's 94 Calls to Action. This is where I started off myself, doing so roughly the same time I moved to Ottawa, and I tried to integrate Indigenous perspectives into my work on peace and security. I'm glad I did. While the calls to action listed in the report are directed at governments, churches, and other institutions, not individual Canadians, they are extremely well researched, building on years of conversations with Indigenous people. Reading them, you'll quickly get an overview of the challenges facing Indigenous Peoples today.

I also realized through my podcast conversations, that although the calls aren't directed at individuals, I could still contribute to implementing them. For example, several of my podcast guests recommended that we use our power as voters and speak or write to our federal Member of Parliament, provincial or territorial Member of the Legislature, or municipal councillor, and ask what they are doing to implement the calls. We can also explore what our church, school, or employer is doing—they are all responsible for implementing the calls addressed to them. Finally, most of us are part of, or belong to, these institutions as employees, students, or members and can help effect change within them. In fact, at Global Affairs Canada, employees are increasingly taking initiative, in parallel to our employer's efforts to implement the calls, to raise awareness and support reconciliation, for example, by organizing study groups and discussions with invited experts.

Perhaps the most important thing I learned from my conversations with Indigenous people, both in my podcast and with friends I've made during this journey, is that we shouldn't shy away from asking questions—although how we ask them, and who we ask them of, matters. It became clear to me early on that Indigenous people shouldn't have to explain to us the basics of colonization and its continuing impacts. This is our story, too. It would be a heavy burden having to teach all of us about the histories, languages, and cultures that Canada nearly erased, and it's not like Indigenous people came up with colonization.

But once you have done your homework, don't hesitate to ask an Indigenous friend or acquaintance about their views on reconciliation or an aspect of their culture that you don't quite understand. For example, at Sundance, when I was told not to blow on the fire, we were in the middle of the ceremony, and it wasn't the right time to ask questions. Yet afterward, I asked my friend Diane about this. She's Ojibwe and her culture is different from the Cree Nation that hosted the Sundance, but she could tell me what this meant in her culture, which helped me understand.

If you don't know any Indigenous people, consider attending a presentation by an Indigenous speaker, a course given by an Indigenous trainer, or an Indigenous cultural event that is open to the public. While you're there, talk to people. Ask them about their community, where they went to school, if they speak their language. As Deborah Chatsis, my diplomat friend, told me, most people, regardless of their background, enjoy talking about themselves. Personally, I have learned more from listening and speaking to Indigenous people than I have from anything I've read. And share with others what you learn. When I have shared resources with my friends and colleagues, such as an Indigenous book I really enjoyed, a local event to attend on Orange Shirt Day and the National Day for Truth and Reconciliation, or where to purchase Indigenous jewellery, they have always been well received.

I'd also recommend reading a document that's available online, called *150 Acts of Reconciliation*, by scholars Crystal Gail Fraser and Sara Komarnisky. Crystal is Gwichyà Gwich'in (and of English/Scottish heritage), and Sara is of Ukrainian, Irish, and Italian settler ancestry. They created the list in response to the federal government's half-a-billion-dollar spending on Canada's 150th anniversary celebrations, which included splurges on fireworks, branded bandages, and more. How far, they wondered, could that money have gone in Indigenous communities? It was unsettling at best, and creating *150 Acts of Reconciliation* allowed them to respond in a constructive way. Together, they wanted to provide examples of concrete things that anyone could do to contribute to the national reconciliation process.

I first came across their initiative in 2018 or 2019 when I was looking for practical guidance for how I as an individual could contribute (which is what eventually led me to create my podcast). There were very few resources like that back then, and this was exactly what I had been looking for! Reading it, I discovered more insight into the questions I'd had since my pondering about mukluks and beaded earrings on my snowy walk to work. In fact, one of the first acts on the list was to "purchase an item from an Indigenous artist." I could easily understand how that would support the artist, but I was less sure how it advanced reconciliation. And, going back to my initial dilemma, could wearing an Indigenous-made item be perceived as cultural appropriation? While the guide was informative, it generated some new questions for me. For example, I could see how the suggestion to read fiction by Indigenous authors would increase my understanding and support the writer, but how did it advance reconciliation? There were also more challenging suggestions on the list, such as the one to "seriously consider your own position as a settler Canadian and whether you uphold practices that contribute to the marginalization of Indigenous Peoples." I wasn't even comfortable calling myself a settler!

With all these questions in mind, I invited Crystal and Sara on my podcast so I could better understand how some of the acts on their list helped advance reconciliation. And while I had done some thinking about cultural appropriation and whether I—a non-Indigenous person—should be wearing Indigenous items, I hadn't yet figured out the best framework for answering this question.

We started with the easy stuff, like the act of reading Indigenous fiction. Crystal and Sara explained to me that buying a book, or asking your library to purchase it, supports the author financially. Canada also has what's called a public lending right program, which provides financial support to authors with books available at public libraries. Anybody who reads an Indigenous-authored book is also learning about Indigenous perspectives from an Indigenous person. As Crystal and so many others have told me, reconciliation is about relationships. It's about supporting each other and trying to learn where each of us comes from.

We also discussed non-Indigenous people wearing Indigenous jewellery and clothing, like my earrings and mukluks. Crystal and Sara assured me that purchasing Indigenous products—designed, produced, and sold by Indigenous people and companies—ensures artists get paid for their work and supports Indigenous economic development, both of which are a central component of reconciliation. Another challenge that Indigenous artists often face is a lack of recognition. Wearing Indigenous items demonstrates appreciation for their work and provides that recognition. Highlighting Indigenous achievements and contributions also actively counteracts the erasure of Indigenous cultures and the whitewashing of our public spaces. What's more, Indigenous design also plays an important role in preserving and developing Indigenous cultural identity, and by purchasing the finished products we can help support such efforts. Keeping all this in mind, following my conversation with Crystal and Sara, I began to share the artist's name or website whenever I received a compliment for my earrings. While a small thing to do, I have noticed that it makes a difference, as people often take note.

But where to draw the line between appreciation and appropriation? The definitions I had come across were very broad, saying that cultural appropriation entails members of a dominant culture adopting elements from a minority culture and using them outside of their original or intended context. If this wasn't done in an obviously exploitative, disrespectful, or stereotypical way, such as dressing up as an "Indian" at Halloween, wouldn't a lot of things fall in this category? I wondered. During our conversation, Crystal and Sara narrowed it down a bit, explaining that, generally, cultural appropriation is when a non-Indigenous person or company designs, produces, or profits from items that pretend to be Indigenous, or when a non-Indigenous person wears a sacred or ceremonial item, such as a headdress or an eagle feather, in a culturally inappropriate setting. Crystal gave the egregious example of a non-Indigenous person wearing a traditional headdress to a rock concert. Non-Indigenous people should only wear or use an Indigenous sacred or ceremonial item if it has been gifted or lent to them or is otherwise required by the Protocol, and they do this in a culturally appropriate setting.

Their explanations helped and all made sense to me, although I still wondered if I would be able to tell with certainty whether a specific item fell into the category of sacred or ceremonial and whether the setting was culturally appropriate or not. Later, I'd learn that this can change over time.

One example is ribbon skirts. They are considered sacred in

many First Nations cultures and have traditionally been worn in ceremonial settings. The ribbons that are sewn into the skirts can have personal and spiritual significance, symbolizing, for example, resilience and connection to the land, ancestors, and family. At the same time, ribbon skirts are increasingly worn in everyday life, not just for special events, but as everyday expressions of identity, to showcase pride in being Indigenous. I was once gifted a ribbon skirt as an appreciation for something my husband had done, and I also sewed one in preparation for the Sundance ceremony in Ministik-wan. There, I was not only allowed to wear a ribbon skirt during the ceremony but expected to, as part of Sundance Protocol.

On a later occasion, I was invited by my friend Diane to participate in an all-women's Sweat Lodge. A Sweat Lodge is a dome-shaped structure heated by glowing hot rocks that are placed in a pit in the middle of the lodge. Each Sweat Lodge is slightly different, depending on the community or person who operates it and the purpose for which it is used. Sometimes, it is part of preparing for ceremony, such as Sundance, and other times, it is a stand-alone activity. Like a sauna, which I'm familiar with from my Scandinavian upbringing, it has many health benefits, such as promoting relaxation, reducing stress, improving sleep, and relieving pain. But a Sweat Lodge goes beyond promoting healthy living, as it is also ceremonial and involves drumming, singing, and letting go of the negative energy that creates disorder and imbalance in life. In this sense, a Sweat Lodge cleanses both body and soul. Another difference from a sauna is that people are dressed in a Sweat Lodge, with women usually wearing a long skirt. In preparation for the sweat, I inquired whether a ribbon skirt would be appropriate in my case. Diane said yes, and that's what I wore. Yet, I wouldn't dream of wearing a ribbon skirt in everyday life. Me doing that wouldn't feel right and, I'm sure, would be considered cultural appropriation.

Based on my own experiences with ribbon skirts, I can better understand how the cultural sensitivity of items can depend on the setting, while, at the same time, a culturally appropriate setting doesn't mean that anyone can wear a cultural or ceremonial item intended for that setting. In other words, you need to follow the Protocols, and if in doubt, ask. If you have nobody to ask, don't wear it. It is important to consider these questions and the boundaries of cultural appropriation to help ensure that we act respectfully toward each other, avoid feeding negative stereotypes, and protect space for Indigenous people to reclaim and practice their cultural traditions.

I came out of my discussion with Sara and Crystal feeling both comforted and more aware of the challenges facing reconciliation. For example, I've mentioned that one of the *150 Acts* I found most challenging was to consider my role as a settler and whether I upheld practices that contributed to the marginalization of Indigenous Peoples—intentionally or not. Before my conversation with Crystal and Sara, I was ambivalent about using the term "settler" in today's context. It felt like a historic term with negative connotations that had little to do with me.

To Crystal and Sara, the term "settler" is a natural choice. As they pointed out, the colonial government and the Europeans who arrived here used the term to describe themselves. It wasn't something that Indigenous people invented, nor was it even controversial when it was first introduced. If you're a descendant of those settlers, it may feel natural to you, too. I have gotten used to it, and I find that it can be a useful term to differentiate between Indigenous Peoples and the rest of us. It can also help with understanding how we, our families, and communities are part of a larger system that has sought to dispossess Indigenous Peoples from their ancestral lands. But in other contexts, I often find it more natural to refer to myself as an immigrant, as it is today's term for newcomers to this land.

The reason the term "settler" can evoke adverse feelings today is, of course, the various negative impacts that non-Indigenous settlement had on Indigenous Peoples, including the dispossession of their land. In this sense, the term is closely related to accountability, which is a good reason for not avoiding using the term. But accountability is much wider than legal liability, and a reconciliation process aims at something much more comprehensive—to transform the societal systems that allowed the violations, injustices, and discrimination to happen and that allow them to continue. Changing those systems—which are costly for all of society and impact all of us negatively—takes action, and for that we are all accountable. Let's start by being honest with ourselves.

The truth is often uncomfortable, and yet it's important not to shy away but to actively seek out the hard questions. I now understand that while I wasn't around at the time of colonization, I can't just brush it off—I could still be contributing to the problem, including by upholding practices that contribute to the marginalization of Indigenous Peoples today.

Many of these practices are related to land and resources. In Ottawa, I live on land that was essentially stolen from the Algonquin people, and the status quo contributes to their continuous marginalization. Growing up in Sweden, I benefited from the flooding of Sami land, since it allowed the development of hydropower and cheap electricity. As painful as it is to admit, such realizations have shown me that, indeed, I have upheld and continue to uphold practices that contribute to the marginalization of Indigenous Peoples—for as long as I don't take action to change things. As the Royal Commission on Aboriginal Peoples stated in its report, "Remaining passive and silent is not neutrality—it is support for the status quo." And as Sara pointed out during our conversation, it's a privilege to not have issues such as the theft of Indigenous land be part of your daily life. This isn't something that Indigenous people can ever ignore. They are deeply impacted by it, even several generations later.

Changing practices such as these, to the benefit of Indigenous

Peoples, can be challenging and is sometimes even out of our immediate control. But I've learned that there are many ways to effect change, such as speaking with your Member of Parliament, raising awareness, and advocating for a more equitable present and future. I was recently inspired by the successful advocacy efforts of the Atikamekw Nation to combat anti-Indigenous racism and systemic discrimination in the health care system, following the death in 2020 of Joyce Echaquan. Echaquan was a thirty-seven-year-old Atikamekw woman and mother of seven who died from pulmonary edema at a hospital in Quebec. Before her death, she recorded a video that showed her screaming in pain while health-care workers made derogatory comments, assuming her to be a drug user experiencing withdrawal symptoms. Canadians reacted strongly to this event, holding vigils and marches in Echaquan's honour across Quebec. The Council of Atikamekw of Manawan and Conseil de la Nation Atikamekw developed Joyce's Principle, aiming to guarantee equitable access to health care without discrimination for all Indigenous people. In response, and informed by Joyce's Principle, the federal government convened a series of national dialogues and committed funding to foster health systems free from racism and discrimination for Indigenous Peoples. While there is much more to do, it is a start.

While acting can yield results, I also understand that for non-Indigenous people like myself, the knowledge gap can be an impediment. I still worry about saying or doing the wrong thing, something that will offend or hurt an Indigenous person. I also continue to worry about exposing my own ignorance, because there is still so much I don't know or understand and, frankly, it's embarrassing. But Crystal said something on the show that resonated with me, arguing that mistakes are critical to the learning process. "If you aren't making mistakes," she said, "you aren't putting yourself out there."

I certainly felt like I was putting myself out there in my podcast conversations and in many other situations since. I've made mistakes along the way, from mispronouncing Indigenous greetings to overlooking the realities of Indigenous people in Canada to unknowingly violating Sundance Protocols. Most mistakes have come down to my knowledge gap. That's why the *150 Acts of Reconciliation* is so helpful, as it provides concrete guidance for people like me who want to do better but also know next to nothing and don't know where to start.

I have enjoyed working my way through the list of acts. Although I'm far from done, and may never be, I've also learned a great deal from them. I find it comforting that even if we played no direct role in how things became the way they are, we can still do something about it. Every act I've done has increased my understanding of Indigenous realities—and of my own accountability. I've read books by Indigenous authors; visited powwows and events at our local Indigenous cultural centre; participated in ceremony; read my local land acknowledgement; and learned about Indigenous legal orders and about how the current First Nations politics are governed by the Indian Act. I've thought about how our history could be told differently; considered my role as a settler; and come to understand the different levels of funding for schools on and off reserves; among many more of Sara's and Crystal's suggested acts.

As I consider my next steps in taking action, I often think of something another one of my podcast guests told me. Sxwpilemaát Siyám, or Chief Leanne Joe, is one of sixteen Hereditary Chiefs of the Squamish Nation and the first female Chief of her Lackett Joe Family. She taught me a great deal, including one piece of wisdom to which I often return. "We can't do anything about the past, because that's history. But we can do something about the future," she told me. "That's why I say, 'Do your part as a Canadian so that I don't have to do that part for you.'" Ultimately, we're all part of the system, and we're all accountable for it.

Three Questions Every Ally
Must Ask Themselves

In our previous two essays, we wrote about allyship as an important part of reconciliation. An Indigenous ally is essentially a non-Indigenous person who wants to contribute to reconciliation while following the lead of Indigenous people. You don't have to call yourself an ally to be one. What matters is that you contribute to reconciliation to the benefit of Indigenous people. To ensure you do, ask yourself the following questions:

- Why do I want to contribute?
- What can I do?
- How do I proceed?

Start by asking yourself why you aspire to be an ally. Remember that there are many valid reasons for wanting to contribute. You may be motivated by a genuine commitment to justice and equity or by empathy and concern for other people's well-being—simply put, you care. You may also be driven by a sense of guilt. Often, it's a combination of these and other reasons. What drives us may not always be easy to articulate, and that's okay. But you must ensure that you're not motivated by personal gain, such as seeking recognition or business opportunities, or by a sense that you know best. The latter is often referred to as white saviourism, or the white saviour complex.

The problem with white saviours is that they don't listen, thereby ignoring or even invalidating the experiences and priorities of those they want to help. They're also uninterested in dismantling structural inequalities, including in relation to decision-making and access to resources. Meanwhile, an ally listens and ensures they understand Indigenous Peoples' perspectives and priorities, reflects on their own position and whether they benefit from colonization, and considers what they can do to help address existing inequalities. The latter involves acknowledging and advocating for Indigenous Peoples' right to land, equitable access to resources, and being treated as equals in a true nation-to-nation relationship.

Once you have reflected on your own motivations—the why— and concluded that you want to effect change for the right reasons, the second question you need to ask yourself is *what* you can do, and the third is *how* to proceed. The next steps can only be guided by Indigenous people; let their priorities and Protocols guide you to ensure your contribution is both meaningful and respectful. Based on what we've learned during our reconciliation journeys, we have put together the guidance below to help you on your way. Once you're on your journey, you will likely come across other ideas to pursue. Feel free to continue developing this guide.

An Indigenous Ally's Guide:

1. Listen, learn, and amplify

Listen to Indigenous voices through podcasts, books, news articles, reports, social media, music, movies, courses, and lectures. Don't confine yourself to learning about what's happened in the past, but make sure you also understand what's happening today in Indigenous communities and in our nation-to-nation relationship. Once you've done your homework, look for opportunities to listen and discuss directly with Indigenous people. Avoid speaking over their voices and instead amplify their messages. Don't hesitate to share their stories to raise awareness.

2. Take action

We encourage you to commit to some of the acts that we have discussed throughout this book, such as drafting your own land acknowledgement; exploring the Indigenous past and present around you; supporting Indigenous artists and businesses; making a donation to an Indigenous organization; and learning an Indigenous language, if even just a few words. For more ideas, visit activehistory.ca to find *150 Acts of Reconciliation*, and pick an act or more from the list.

3. Stand up for Indigenous rights

Whenever you encounter them, challenge prejudice, stereotypes, mis- and disinformation, discriminatory practices, and injustices. Acknowledge Indigenous rights to land, resources, and self-governance; write to your Member of Parliament to ask what they are doing to implement the 94 Calls to Action; and engage in conversations and advocacy efforts to rally support for creating a more equitable Canada.

4. Discuss with others what you learn

Share what you learn with your friends, colleagues, and family, and encourage them to act as well. Share a book you enjoyed, or suggest that you attend a powwow or other public event together. If you have children, speak with their teachers about what they are teaching in school and, if needed, provide some ideas to ensure your children learn about Indigenous history, languages, cultures, and knowledge.

5. Observe Protocols

When you engage with Indigenous people or attend Indigenous events, respect the Protocols and avoid cultural appropriation. Make clear that you're not Indigenous by stating where you're from. Acknowledge that First Nations, Métis, and Inuit are distinct and heterogenous groups and refrain from making assumptions about their cultures and perspectives. When in doubt, ask!

6. Continue to check your motivations

Finally, continue to check your motivations to avoid slipping into a saviour or self-promotion mood. Always make sure to take your lead from the experts—Indigenous people themselves. It doesn't matter whether you're right or wrong; it is simply not your place to decide what's best for them.

Part VI: Worldview

Giving Thanks

Derek Aronhie:nens Montour

TECUMSEH, THE SHAWNEE Chief and Warrior, once said, "When you rise in the morning, give thanks for the light, for your life, for your strength. Give thanks for your food and for the joy of living. If you see no reason to give thanks, the fault lies in yourself." Many, if not all, Indigenous nations possess the worldview of gratitude. We may have values of gratitude embedded in our Creation Story; thanksgiving ceremonies to honour all that the Creator gives us; or in a worldview that is based on having gratitude in each action we take. By practising daily gratitude for what the Creator has given us, it becomes harder for these gifts to be taken for granted.

Canadians are familiar with the holiday of Thanksgiving, but they may not have heard the story of the first Thanksgiving: the Pilgrims of Plymouth and the Wampanoag who welcomed them to their lands and shared all they had in 1621. Most people were taught of the Pilgrims, while very few know the name of the nation they befriended. The Wampanoag were Algonquian-speaking people who lived in the areas around Massachusetts, Rhode Island, and the other islands near there. They were also the first Indigenous people the English pilgrim settlers made a peace treaty with. Before the settlers arrived, the Wampanoag people had their own traditions of giving thanks for what the Creator had given them, as well as their own harvest festivals and ceremonies.

Many, if not all, Indigenous people celebrate harvest, including the Kanien'kehá:ka people. The harvest ceremony and festival are a special occasion to bring families and villages together to share in the product of all their labours throughout the summer. This event has long been praised and celebrated in the United States and was even made into a national holiday in 1863 when Abraham Lincoln declared the last Thursday of November a day of "Thanksgiving and Praise." Although other examples of thanksgiving events by settlers pre-date the Plymouth thanksgiving, like a St. Augustine, Florida, shared meal in 1565, or thanksgiving services in Virginia as early as 1607, it's the Plymouth event that North Americans remember most.

But after the settlers arrived, death followed. The Wampanoag were devastated by the diseases that the settlers brought with them (as were many of the nations who had interactions with the settlers). Whole villages, and sometimes entire nations, were wiped out by disease and subsequent famine when the fields could not be prepared and harvested. Like all other Indigenous nations, they lost land from treaty cessions, broken treaties, forced migration, and outright land theft. They, like so many others, suffered from the incessant demand for more that drove all the settlers who came here. They were searching for more than what they had in the lands they originated from.

In Canada, Sir Martin Frobisher held a meal to celebrate and give thanks for arriving in Nunavut in 1578, and later, Samuel de Champlain founded a series of feasts in Nova Scotia to fight scurvy in 1606, with the first one held to celebrate the return of one of their party from an expedition. The Protestant clergy organized the first national Thanksgiving in Canada in 1859; it was observed as an annual event after 1879. Finally, in January 1957,

Canada's Parliament proclaimed the observance of the second Monday in October as "a day of General Thanksgiving to Almighty God for the bountiful harvest with which Canada has been blessed." There was no mention of the Indigenous harvest ceremonies and festivals at all.

But practising gratitude should be more than a once-a-year event. Having daily gratitude creates an automatic sense of contentment in our hearts. I am fond of the phrase, "The more gratitude we have in our hearts, the less room we have for sadness and anger." Think about it—whenever you've felt an overwhelming sense of gratitude for something in your life (your relationship, your kids, your pet, your job, whatever), you were likely unable to feel sad or anger at the same time. Gratitude also forms the basis of sharing, whereby we begin to believe that we can all benefit from our gifts and we can all prosper. When we feel more gratitude, we are more inclined to share what we have.

And conversely, when we are not grateful, we tend to hold on to what we have more tightly, we protect it and fight for it, and we begin to only think of ourselves. We complain that we do not have enough, we compare our share to another person's share, we become jealous and envious, and perhaps begin to feel entitled. We think that we have a right to demand what others have or even take by force or trickery what we want.

To me, the fundamental problem with the Eurocentric society is the driving sense of wanting or feeling like we need more. Immigrants from Europe, and yes, other parts of the world, too, were enticed to travel to our lands here in Turtle Island with the promise that they would have more. All the overflowing populations in England, France, Spain, and all the rest were told that there is all this land that is just waiting for you, even though those lands were not actually their lands. It was never their intent to share the land, but to possess it.

Throughout this book, I have tried to think about the most important aspects of everyday reconciliation I would want non-Indigenous people to consider and take action on. In this essay, I want to challenge you to adopt a worldview that centres around gratitude instead of a worldview that centres around wanting more. If any sort of conciliation or reconciliation is to occur between Indigenous and non-Indigenous people, adopting this type of worldview is paramount.

So, how do we move to a perspective of being grateful?

When I served on the minister of national defence's advisory panel, I suggested to my fellow members that we begin our final report with the *Ohén:ton Karihwatéhkwen*, which literally means what we say before we do anything important. It is also known as a Thanksgiving address. I wanted to share this practice from my culture, which, I was taught, ought to be done before any important work is undertaken. I thought a task like ours, to address discrimination and racism in the military, which had been given to us following reports of right-wing extremism and allegations of sexual misconduct among the ranks, was as important as it could get.

The *Ohén:ton Karihwatéhkwen* is a practice of honouring Creation, and we say it daily to restore our mental and spiritual connection with Creation. More importantly, it brings people together to become of one mind. When we have a gathering, or we are about to embark on an important event, it is used as an opening address as we all arrive at that moment from our own journeys and our own perspectives. We are all human, and we are all dealing with our own challenges. We don't really know what someone else may be going through or thinking about. Maybe we have a sick parent, child, or spouse, and our mind is preoccupied with them getting better. Maybe we are hungry because we haven't eaten yet, or we are worried about a problem with our house or job. Some of us are grieving or dealing with trauma. Maybe we are tired, or sore, or achy.

Whatever we are feeling at that moment before the *Ohén:ton Karihwatéhkwen* starts is normal, because we are all on our own journeys and our minds are separate. But as the *Ohén:ton Karihwatéhkwen* is being spoken, we are hearing the same words. We think of the meaning of the words at the exact same time, about the exact same things. We are all picturing the images the words bring in our minds, all at the same time. Our minds are becoming of one mind so that once the *Ohén:ton Karihwatéhkwen* is finished, we are all present: physically, mentally, emotionally, and spiritually.

More than that, the *Ohén:ton Karihwatéhkwen* reminds us that everything we do in this world begins with ensuring we are connected with Creation—or, at least, it perhaps *ought to* begin that way. Each person who says the *Ohén:ton Karihwatéhkwen* may word it slightly differently, adding more detail or less, but the goal for everyone is to try to acknowledge all aspects of Creation. Giving thanks is a common practice amongst Indigenous communities, and many conduct something like the *Ohén:ton Karihwatéhkwen* as an opening ceremony before their gatherings. Usually, we burn tobacco before and during the recital; we think of it as a way to bridge our world and the spirit world, where we imagine the Creator to be. It connects the two worlds, so when we burn tobacco, our words are heard by the Creator more easily. Some opening ceremonies may incorporate the use of other medicines, drumming, singing, or dancing.

Although the *Ohén:ton Karihwatéhkwen* itself is a Haudenosaunee practice, every Indigenous nation has a profound connection to Creation and believes that all of Creation is interconnected. We cannot survive as humans unless all the other aspects of Creation work in harmony with us. This interconnectedness is a central core of all First Nations, Métis, and Inuit worldviews.

I hoped that if we incorporated the *Ohén:ton Karihwatéhkwen* in the advisory panel's report, our readers would go on to act with our fundamental connection in mind. We had been saying the *Ohén:ton Karihwatéhkwen* as our opening and closing whenever we would meet, including when we met with Minister Saajan and, after he left the role, Minister Anita Anand. But I think it takes time for people to adopt a new perspective. We felt that perhaps including it at the beginning of the report, without any context or explanation at first, would detract from the focus of the report. In the end, we decided to include my version of the *Ohén:ton Karihwatéhkwen*, edited and supported by fellow panel members, as an annex to the report. Perhaps more work needs to be done within Canada, like everyday reconciliation efforts, so that leading with such an opening, or saying the *Ohén:ton Karihwatéhkwen*, becomes second nature—not unlike how land acknowledgements are now becoming a common practice.

I often wonder if people read that annex and whether the *Ohén:ton Karihwatéhkwen* and its principles of connection guide their next steps as I'd hoped. Unfortunately, I suspect we failed in that. I must confess that I often do not read annexes unless I am specifically looking for something. It is like the author is telling me, "The story I wanted to tell is finished, but if you are bored and want to do extra reading, try this!"

Looking back, I think I didn't adequately emphasize to my fellow panelists how the connection, or lack of connection, with Creation is affecting our world—and why it mattered for readers of our report. If we want people to understand what systemic discrimination and thus reconciliation look like, understanding and addressing differences in worldview is central to that. We must urge them to begin to see things in a different way. The *Ohén:ton Karihwatéhkwen* reflects a worldview and helps us to both understand and work together to change what is happening in our world. The idea of the interconnectedness of all of Creation, and therefore our responsibility toward all of Creation, ties into the decisions of our ancestors and how they will affect our descendants.

Much of colonialism has historically centred around a settler or so-called western worldview. European countries colonized many different parts of the world, including what we now call Canada, because they were vying for more land and more resources. More land and more resources created more wealth. To get that land and resources, colonists had to remove the people living there through elimination and genocide, marginalize them by denying them the same rights that others have, and assimilate them so they no longer exist as a distinct people. The colonist had to enact the same destruction to clear the animals from the land and access its resources: tear down whole forests, dig giant holes, or reshape the land by redirecting water and drainage—all with no regard for the impact that these decisions have on the environment.

To make these types of decisions—the marginalization and assimilation of Indigenous people, the human slave trade, the forced mining and extraction of the minerals, and so much more—requires that the person be disconnected from the implications of those decisions. It is impossible to subject another human person to pain unless you are disconnected from the emotions tied to that action. You must stop caring about the impact and adopt a worldview that allows for disconnection. And you must also believe in your own supremacy—to those around you, to all other people, to the land, and to everything living on it. This mindset—an assumption of superiority and a prioritization of owning the land—is fundamentally at odds with Indigenous people's relationship with land. Such beliefs drove colonists to clear-cut forests and to hunt animals to extinction.

This difference in worldviews has deeply affected Indigenous communities—from the first point of colonization to present day. Even before colonists came to Turtle Island, as far back as the Early Middle Ages in 500–1000 CE, Europe had a thriving fur trade, and the overhunting of beavers and other animals in Europe led to their near extinction. Prior to coal, fur was the principal way to keep warm in the cold months. After the over-hunting in Europe, Russia became the chief supplier of fur. It remained the world's largest supplier from the 17ᵗʰ to the 19ᵗʰ centuries, providing martens, beavers, wolves, foxes, squirrels, and hares. Later, as Siberia was being settled, they traded lynx, sable, sea otter, and ermine.

At the same time, as far back as the 1500s, European settlers have colonized lands across the world, each time imposing their views on trade (and eventually capitalism), resource extraction, religion, land, their relationship with the natural world, and so on. This has had devastating consequences for Indigenous ways of life around the world, but also for the land we now call Canada. Consider, for example, beaver felt hats. They were all the rage in Europe throughout the 16ᵗʰ century, contributing to the animal's near extinction on the continent. Beaver felt hats were durable, waterproof, and held their shape extremely well—just picture the era's popular top hat. Once the high beaver population in Canada was identified, the hunt for pelts continued from 1610 to roughly 1830, when the fashion declined. By 1900, overhunting had reduced the beaver population in Canada from more than sixty million to as few as one hundred thousand. The loss of habitat due to settlement and changing of the environment also contributed to their decline.

The voracious appetite for pelts decimated whole beaver colonies and left the lands barren for kilometres around any trading post. Conservation efforts, like those led by George Simpson, a governor of the Hudson's Bay Company, began in 1821 and started to bring awareness to the problem and contributed to reducing the demand. Today, the World Wildlife Fund estimates the North American beaver to have a population of around ten to fifteen million, a rebound that is directly the result of conservation efforts. Even European beaver populations are making a comeback today, with an estimated size of one and a half million.

When we think of interconnectedness, the loss of any species can have a profound impact on the environment. Beavers are fundamental to the integrity of the wetlands, and the drastic population loss had a significant impact on the land and environment. Beavers shape and maintain the biodiversity, as their dams and ponds create wetland habitats that support a wide variety of plant and animal life. The loss of the beaver meant these wetlands significantly diminished, negatively affecting biodiversity in such areas, including the loss of clean water and clean air and an increase in flooding and erosion. Although the beaver hat craze ended in the mid-1800s, and beaver populations continue to rebuild, the long-term effects of their decline continue to impact our environment today.

So much of the dominant worldview today centres on power and control. Society has built systems of privilege, superiority, and inferiority, and it has used those systems to justify any number of harmful deeds. These systems influence how we interact with each other and the land around us. Western society seeks to exert power over everything it considers *inferior* and seems to be fundamentally on a quest for resources and more wealth. Under such a worldview, humans can no longer be at peace with our surroundings as life becomes a constant struggle to dominate.

Both Indigenous and non-Indigenous people live in a world dominated by advertisements and images of what we *should* want. We are bombarded with countless attempts to create a demand for products that will supposedly make our lives easier, better, more enjoyable. These products are often made to feel essential to our lives. We lose sight of what we do have in search for something else, and the idea of gratitude, or interconnectedness, is often lost in the constant cycle of consumption.

We search for things that will make us happy, rather than just being happy with what we have. We seek to cover our trauma and feel better about ourselves through buying more things. We are bored, and so we entertain ourselves with acquiring more things. We are constantly told that our lives are unfulfilled unless we have a certain thing: a fancier car, a bigger house, a new purse, a new tool, a new whatever. We judge our own bodies, we are told we must look differently, we must go to the gym, we must wear these kinds of clothes, and we need to get that plastic surgery. It often feels like many of us have stopped learning to create things ourselves, stopped interacting and building a community, and stopped learning, relying instead on the world trade system for fulfillment.

To move forward on reconciliation, both Indigenous and non-Indigenous people must all start to question the colonial worldview—and to see the ways in which it isn't working for us and for the planet. While Indigenous culture is diverse, many communities have shared roots in the belief that humans must be in harmony, or at peace, with nature. There must be a balance, and that is where reconciliation has its place. Many non-Indigenous allies also realize the significance of maintaining this balance, and although our voices are getting louder, they are still small. We must all start to recognize that we are all caretakers, or stewards, of these lands, not rulers. This is not "woke" culture; this is mutual survival. Together, Indigenous and non-Indigenous communities can embrace the philosophy that humans need to preserve the land for our future generations. If we do not, we will be passing on a future that is doomed.

I'm not suggesting that we need to abolish capitalism or all become communists. But I am saying there are better ways to live, including in greater harmony with the rest of Creation, and that we can all be more intentional with how we live our lives. To take concrete action when it comes to reconciliation, we must constantly ask ourselves: How do we change our worldview for the better? There are easy, everyday things we all can do. Prioritize reducing, reusing, and recycling. Conserve energy by turning off electronics and lights. Choose environmentally friendly transportation options. Instead of creating vast lawns of grass, let gardens become full of wildflowers. Shop for sustainable products. Reuse and repair products instead of buying new. Reduce waste and especially food waste. Eat more plants and always be conscious of our consumption habits.

We might also take some cues from the ways in which Indigenous people traded with each other for millennia. We used resources in a way that was intended to be in harmony with Creation. For example, the picking of medicine. Knowledge of medicines is sacred, and they are considered gifts from the Creator with the power to heal. When the knowledge is misused or is harvested for economic purposes, there is a danger in that medicine becoming unavailable. I have heard Elders say that they keep the knowledge close to them because it is something learned after a life of struggle, trial, and commitment, and not everyone is prepared for that kind of journey. The road to understanding and using each of these traditional medicines is long but also requires patience, trust, and belief. It is not just a pill you take, but a process that you undertake.

Once I got sober and started learning traditional knowledge, I was taught that when I pick medicine, I must start with mental preparation, with knowledge and respect for the plants, and with respect for the process I am undertaking. I must know what the medicine I seek looks like in its natural, wild state; where it could grow; when is the right time, in both season and time of day, to harvest it; and why I want to use it. I must know how to harvest it, how to look for signs of healthy plants, and how to ensure I do not over-harvest in one area. Once I find the medicine, I begin by offering tobacco while also saying my *Ohén:ton Karihwatéhkwen*, explaining to the medicine who I am, using my Kanien'kéha name, and asking its help for a specific reason. Once those things are finished, I am to never pick from the same plant. Rather than pick the whole thing, I take a little from one and then from another and so on. I leave enough so that each plant can survive. This process of picking medicine is far different than taking a pill from the pharmacy.

Each Indigenous nation may have a different Creation Story and different aspects of how they believe we came to be who we are, but we all have a deep connection to nature. We believe that if that connection is lost, then life will cease to exist. Think about it. What would happen if insects went extinct? Birds? Fish? This is why, to me, the *Ohén:ton Karihwatéhkwen* is so important: It is a constant reminder that we are only a part of Creation and not a ruler of Creation. The essence of gratitude is being grateful for the life we have that is in harmony with all the things in Creation that make life possible. And that is also the danger of not being grateful for Creation; we lose sight of the fact that with the destruction of biodiversity, interconnectedness is not possible, and plants can no longer flourish and animals die off. We would not be able to find the natural medicines in the world.

Now that I have encouraged you to adopt a worldview based in gratitude, as well as emphasized the importance of our daily recognition of the interconnectedness of Creation, I want to share with you the *Ohén:ton Karihwatéhkwen* itself. I am sharing an *Ohén:ton Karihwatéhkwen* similar to the one we drafted for the advisory panel's final report. The *Ohén:ton Karihwatéhkwen* is a traditional speech, used in both ceremony and in everyday practice. There is no right or wrong way to say the *Ohén:ton Karihwatéhkwen*; every speaker says it their own way. I was taught that we are supposed to say it in our own language so that Creation can hear us.

I believe the point of reconciliation is to be able to peacefully exist together, and if we don't share this practice, in whatever language we can, I think we are missing the point. We are missing that, as caretakers and stewards, we are meant to teach everyone how to think and connect with nature and to be connected with Creation. We are also meant to teach each other as Indigenous people who may have lost our way and our knowledge so that we can reclaim it, and we are supposed to teach it to non-Indigenous folk so they can also follow a good path and live in peace. And so, I am sharing my *Ohén:ton Karihwatéhkwen* with you.

Start by being grounded, with your body calm and relaxed. You can read it anywhere, but I suggest that you sit in a chair, with your back straight, shoulders relaxed, and feet flat on the ground. Before you begin, take three deep, slow breaths while releasing the tension in your body so that you may be able to feel. Imagine yourself at peace with the world, feeling connected to it. When you read it, I want you to think about each of the words. I want you to imagine what you read in your mind's eye and picture it with detail. If it is water, what does the water sound like? If it is a bird, what kind of bird does it look like? Take time while you are reading it, as this is not something to skim over.

Before embarking on any important piece of work, whether it is during a meeting or the creation of a document, many people believe that it is worthwhile to say a few words before all other words that come after. Some call it a prayer, but most Indigenous people have some form of opening. The Haudenosaunee People call this the Ohén:ton Karihwatéhkwen. *We are taught that we say these words to acknowledge and honour our Creator, however we perceive him, her, or it to be. We say these words because we all come to this moment in time from our own respective journeys in life; we all have different experiences that led us to this very moment where we are reading or hearing the words to come. It is important to acknowledge and honour our own journeys, our own challenges and joys. We are taught that we say these words because it reminds us of what truly matters in life and what we should be grateful for every day. We say these words so that we all hear them at the same time and then become of one mind as we begin to conduct the business at hand.*

We begin by first acknowledging all the people in our lives. The Creator sends many people to walk with us on our journeys; sometimes they stay only a brief time, sometimes they are there to give us a lesson. Sometimes they walk with us for a season, and other times, they are with us our entire lives. No matter the amount of time they spend with us, we acknowledge and honour them. We offer our greetings to the people, and we thank the Creator for bringing them into our lives. And now our minds are one.

We now turn our thoughts to our Mother, the Earth. We recognize she provides all that we need in life, as long as we also take care of her. We often take for granted the simple act of walking, sitting, or lying on the ground. As she supports our every move, we are drawn closer to her. We acknowledge and honour her, and we offer our greetings to her. And now our minds are one.

Our minds turn to all the forms of water that flow across Mother Earth. We think of the rains, the streams, the rivers, the lakes, and the oceans. We think of how powerful water can be, and yet it flows and adapts around solid objects. We are taught to let our minds be like water: formless, shapeless. We think of how important water is to all forms of life, and we give thanks for the waters that quench our thirst. We acknowledge and thank the Creator for providing these waters. And now our minds are one.

Our minds turn to all the fish life that live in the water; they were instructed to clean and purify the waters. We think of all the forms of water life, whether it be the smallest plankton that feed the biggest whale, or the leeches that feed off other fish, or the fish that swim amongst the reef. We marvel at their beauty, and we are grateful for how they nourish us. All of these creatures have a place on Mother Earth and have a purpose; we offer our greetings to the fish. We acknowledge them and thank the Creator for making them. And now our minds are one.

Our minds now turn to the plant life that Mother Earth provides, and we next think of all the root life that all growing things have. We think of how it connects them to our Mother, like an umbilical cord. We think of how important it is to have roots in our life because it grounds us to a place, a people, or a time. We think of how the roots stretch and search for life-giving water; our roots nourish us. We rely on these roots because even if the winds take us, when we reach Mother Earth again, we are able to put down roots. We offer our greetings to them, acknowledge them, and honour all the root life the Creator has provided. And now our minds are one.

Our minds now turn to the grasses and small plants, and we think of describing her beautiful dress. Our Mother's dress is made green with lush grasses of every shape and hue. It is the colour of the beautiful flowers growing all around us. It is the colour of the bushes and other plants that we may nourish or grudgingly pick from our gardens. We think of the amazing fragrances that sift through the air if we only just close our eyes and focus on them. We acknowledge and honour these plants, we offer our greetings to them, and we thank the Creator for providing them to all of us, as they sustain so many life forms and show us beauty. And now our minds are one.

We turn our minds to those plants that naturally bear fruit, sometimes at different times of the year. We think of all the varieties of fruit that are found all over Mother Earth. We pick the berries to help sustain us, and we harvest the apples and other fruit to make our desserts and to put in our children's lunchboxes. Sometimes, we simply have to reach out, and the Creator provides us this food. We offer our greetings to them, we acknowledge them, and we thank the Creator for these things. And now our minds are one.

We next think of the medicines that we pick. They say the Creator's medicines are the root of all other medicine. We were taught how to speak to them, how to observe them so we don't harvest too many from one area, how we ask for their help to heal our sickness and pain. We try to remember what our ancestors taught us regarding which medicines are for what purpose, and we try to pass on this knowledge to our children. We offer our greetings to the medicines, acknowledge them, and honour all the medicines the Creator has provided us. And now our minds are one.

Our minds turn to the vegetables we plant and harvest. We grow them from seeds, and we nurture them, feed them, and water them. We consider how they may grow better with other plants or how to protect them from the sun, the winds, and the insects. We are happy when they blossom, and we are sad when we find one wilting or dying. And at harvest time, we are grateful for the food they give us so freely. We offer our greetings to them, we acknowledge these plants, and we thank the Creator for providing them. And now our minds are one.

We turn our minds to the tree life; there are many families of trees on Mother Earth, all with their own instructions and purpose. We think of how they help us with shelter and provide shade on hot days or warmth when it is so cold. We think of their sap that supports us in spring after a long winter. Many people of the world use the tree as a symbol of peace and strength. We offer our greetings to the trees and thank them for being with us. And now our minds are one.

Our minds turn to the little creatures that live everywhere among us, the insect life. We think of the ones in our gardens and the ones that fly. We think of all the creatures that eat the insects, whether it is bats at night or the fish and the birds that fly. They take care of the plants, and they work with the animals. Insects form a cornerstone of life, and without them, other life is not possible. We offer our greetings to them; we acknowledge them and thank the Creator for putting them on Mother Earth with us. And now our minds are one.

Our minds turn to the animals that share Mother Earth with us. Since long ago, they have taught us lessons when we take the time to listen to them. They give their lives to feed us, and they give their skin and fur to clothe us. They work together with all other animals to create a complete system—the cycle of life, as we call it. We offer our greetings to all of them; we acknowledge them and thank the Creator for putting them on Mother Earth with us. And now our minds are one.

Now we turn our minds higher, to all the birds in the sky. We think of their beautiful songs; they say when we are sad, we only need to listen to a bird sing and our hearts will be lifted. We think of the geese that signal the changing of seasons. We think of the woodpecker that searches for food so diligently. We think of the eagle who inspires us to be greater for the good of all. They remind us to enjoy and appreciate life. We offer our greetings and acknowledge all the bird life, and we thank them for sharing the world with us. And now our minds are one.

We turn our thoughts to the powers we know as the Four Winds that constantly flow across Mother Earth. They bring cold air or warm air. They provide a gentle breeze, or they shake the trees to spread the seeds and pollen. They purify the air we breathe, and we think of how to take care of the air so that every breath our loved ones may take is pure. We offer our greetings to them, acknowledge them, and give our thanks to them. And now our minds are one.

We turn our thoughts to what we call the Grandfathers, the Thunder Beings. With their storms and lightning, they bring forth the life-giving rains. They say they keep the evil underground by the roar of their voices. They rage over the Earth and the waters. We offer our greetings to the Grandfathers; we acknowledge and thank them for being with us. And now our minds are one.

We turn our minds even higher to our elder brother, the sun. Our elder brother is with us each day to watch over us, protect us, and give us strength. Our brother works with all living things, and all living things flourish under his watchful eyes. We offer our greetings to our elder brother, acknowledge him, and give our thanks. And now our minds are one.

We next think of our oldest grandmother, the moon, who watches over us every night. She is the leader of all the women of the world and guides them on their cycles like her own. She governs all the waters of the world and shapes and moves them. By her changing face, we measure time, and she announces the arrival of new children into the world. We offer our greetings to her, acknowledge her, and give her our thanks. And now our minds are one.

We give our thanks and think of all the stars in the sky. They help light up the dark nights with our grandmother. When we are lost, they guide us home again. They remind us that we are only a small piece of the Creator's plan. We offer our greetings to the stars; we acknowledge them and thank them for being with us. And now our minds are one.

We turn our minds to the enlightened teachers the Creator has sent to us to help guide our way. They have come to different people, and they speak their truth and instructions. When we forget to live in harmony, they remind us of the way we were instructed to live as people. We send our greetings to these caring teachers; we acknowledge them, and we thank them for their direction. And now our minds are one.

We now turn our minds to our Creator. They have drawn a path for us to walk on from before the time we were born. They chose our parents, and they put the obstacles in our path to help us learn and grow. Sometimes we stumble and fall, but if we are brave enough, we can continue our journey despite these obstacles. The Creator gives us the joy we feel in our hearts and the tears that come from the depths of our sadness. We offer our greetings to our Creator and send them our thanks. We ask them to look after our loved ones as we are occupied with the business at hand so that we are not distracted. And now our minds are one.

We have now come to the end of our words. Of all the things we have spoken of, we did not intend to leave anything out. We ask that if you think we have forgotten anything, you put it in your mind, your heart, and your soul for the good of all of us. Now our minds are one.

And now that we have finished the words, I want you to consider what our world would be like if any aspect of Creation were no longer with us. Try to make a practice of reading the *Ohén:ton Karihwatéhkwen* every day, perhaps when you wake up or when you go to bed. Try saying it without reading it. Try modifying it so that it becomes yours, maybe shorter, maybe longer. Try reading it with someone else, such as your children, your partner, your friend, your students, or your work group. Carry a copy with you, and whenever you feel sad or angry, stop, get yourself grounded, and read it to yourself. Before you embark on a decision or an important action, take the time to read it to yourself or out loud.

Everyday reconciliation is about acting intentionally every day to bring us closer to peace. If you were to regularly read the *Ohén:ton Karihwatéhkwen*, you would begin to know peace with Creation, and you would be actively working to reestablish it.

All My Relations

Elin Sandberg Miller

WHEN I MOVED to Canada, I knew very little about the Indigenous Peoples here and was upset to learn about the reserve system and other inequalities I saw. Perhaps it's easier to see injustice when you think you have no part in it. But once I started to learn more, I realized how little I knew about the situation for the Indigenous people in my native Sweden, the Sami. I didn't even understand that Sweden was a colonial power.

I did know that Sweden had held a couple of small colonies a long time ago, but I can't remember learning about it in school. If I did, it was glossed over quickly. Any reference to our colonial past was framed more as a curious anecdote, told with a sense of pride even: Sweden, too, had colonies! I knew that one former colony was called New Sweden and spanned across parts of what we now know as Delaware, Maryland, Pennsylvania, and New Jersey in the US. The other was the Caribbean island of Saint Barthelemy. Only later did I learn that there were three more colonies, in India, Africa, and a second in the Caribbean. They each only lasted for a few years, with the exception of Saint Barthelemy, which Sweden held for about one hundred years (from 1784 to 1878). During this time, Sweden participated in the slave trade, and the use of slaves was central for making money off these colonies. This was also news to me, and contrary to what I *had* learned in school: that Sweden abolished slavery in the Middle Ages.

As I read about the Sami people, I realized that Sweden's role as a colonial power didn't end with these faraway places. My country had also colonized Sápmi, which today makes up the northern parts of what are now Norway, Sweden, Finland, and Russia. In fact, this colonization process is still ongoing, as Sweden continues to extract Sápmi's resources, including critical minerals and power generated from water and wind, at the cost of the Sami and their traditional use of the land.

During a visit back to Sweden in 2021, I had another revelation. It was Christmas Eve, and my sister, Helena, sister-in-law, Åsa, and I were all out for a walk in a semi-rural area just outside my hometown, Linköping. It was dark and cold out, but our conversation was warm and intimate. At one point, I asked if they remembered learning much about the Sami in school. They didn't, confirming my own recollection. But Åsa shared a story that she had heard from her uncle on her father's side. He had learned about it only as an adult, and it was news to the rest of the family, too. Åsa's family on her dad's side is from northern Sweden, where the men in her family traditionally became priests. In fact, her great-grandfather was the first in centuries to break with that tradition when he dropped out of the theological studies program.

The events she told us about took place in the 17th century during a time when observing the Christian religion was strictly enforced in Sweden and just after the peak of the witch trials, which during a span of only eight years saw nearly three hundred people—mostly women—executed, often accused of dealing with Satan. The Christianization of the Sami, however, was primarily a tool of the colonization process, a necessary part of making them Swedish citizens, and thereby their land Swedish, allowing for taxation and mining of important finds of silver and other metals in Sápmi. In this process, the authorities often seized or destroyed Sami drums and idols called sieidis. The drums were used in religious ceremony, as were the sieidis, which are sacred objects in stone or wood found naturally in nature but can also have undergone some processing. Each sieidi is different. They vary in size from small rocks or wooden figures that fit in your hand to large stones over ten metres high. While they lack a specific form, they can have anthropomorphic features, naturally or man-made, or peculiar forms that make them more recognizable. The Sami prayed and made sacrifices to their sieidis, for example, to get help during sickness or assistance in everyday tasks and duties.

What Åsa told me and my sister during that walk was horrific and gave us a new perspective on Sweden's relationship with the Sami. The story has only recently become more known in Sweden, as the Swedish Church is reflecting on its role in the colonization of Sápmi and the oppression of the Sami people. The following is based on Åsa's story, what I later learned at an exhibition at the Nordic Museum in Stockholm in 2024, and additional sources I was able to find online, including letters and legal records from that time.

The story unfolds during late fall in the year 1686, near Arjeplog, in the Swedish part of Sápmi. The priest Petrus (Pehr) Noraeus Fjellström, Åsa's relative, had decided to pay a visit to a Sami man called Erik Eskilsson. After Pehr stepped out of church one Sunday after a sermon he had given, where he denounced the Sami religion, he overheard Erik commenting to a fellow Sami that he found the hostility against the Sami religion strange. *Was it not enough that they attended church?* The priest should understand, Erik said, that they couldn't abandon the faith of their ancestors. Like many other Sami people, Erik Eskilsson attended church to abide by the law, yet continued to pray to his Sami gods. Erik owned a large reindeer herd, and so was relatively well-off, and he was a respected man in his community. Pehr Noraeus wanted to set an example and decided to take two police officers and another man with him.

Erik lived in the mountains, and the four men walked up the treeless, flat hillside, worn down by the heavy ice sheets that covered the area thousands of years ago. When they arrived at Erik's place, they didn't tread carefully. They tore down an altar and entered Erik's hut and seized a ceremonial drum and a sieidi. But Erik Eskilsson wasn't easily intimidated; he wouldn't have it. He went for help and, together with two neighbours, ran after the four men. It must have been getting dark by then, as the sun sets early that time of year, so close to the Arctic Circle. Erik and his neighbours caught up with the four men and managed to take back the drum. Erik also called the priest a thief. Pehr reported the incident to his religious superiors, calling for the death penalty for such acts. The letter triggered a process that eventually led to the trial of Erik Eskilsson. In the end, Erik was freed of the charges, but only after denouncing his Sami religion and handing over his drum.

While the Christianization of the Sami often took on violent forms, such as stealing and destroying their drums and sieidis, execution for practising their religion was *not* common. So, while the priest Pehr Noraeus was implementing government policy, he was harsher than most. The fact that Erik Eskilsson had offended him publicly and gotten away with it must have been a thorn in his side. A few years later, in 1692, Noraeus had another Sami man, Lars Nilsson, similarly tracked down. Lars Nilsson had lost his grandson in a tragic accident. Heartbroken, he sacrificed two reindeer and sat by the little boy, drumming and praying to the Sami gods, seeking to bring him back to life. The priest heard about it and sent a group of men to investigate. The men told Lars to stop what he was doing, but he chased them off and was later tried just as Erik Eskilsson was. At the trial, he defended his actions, saying that the Christian god had done him no good, whereas his own gods had helped him before. Lars was sentenced to death by burning. He took his drum and sieidis with him into the flames.

This is the only known case of execution of Sami people for their non-Christian religious beliefs in the Swedish part of Sápmi. However, there were more such death sentences in other parts of Sápmi, and there may have been undocumented cases, too. Such stories demonstrate the deeply imbalanced relationship between the Sami and the Swedes. Åsa's story about her relative Pehr Noraeus, who so cruelly denounced Erik Eskilsson and Lars Nilsson, advocating for their death, made this part of Sweden's history very real to me, especially as Pehr could just as well have been my own relative. In all cases, Lars Nilsson died at the hands of my people, and our oppression of the Sami didn't end there.

Let me take you back to one beautiful spring day in Sweden, roughly a century ago. The sky is tall, the sun feels warm on your face, and the snow has all but melted. Inside a large building in Uppsala, an old university town north of Stockholm, a doctor called Herman Lundborg is going through his notes from his last trip to Sápmi. Lundborg is the head of Sweden's Institute for Racial Biology Research. The institute was established in 1922 to provide a scientific basis for eugenic measures, based on the viewpoint that the Swedish race needed protection from inferior population groups.

Herman Lundborg was particularly interested in the Sami people and used the institute's resources for his extensive travels to Sápmi. His notes include information about Sami people's physical attributes, such as their height, eye and hair colour, and skull measurements. He also took photos of his study objects during his trips—many of them naked: men, women, and children who were asked to undress for him. He examined other population groups as well, such as Roma, Finnish, and Jewish people. There were no concrete results of Lundborg's research, as one might expect, and when he retired in 1935, the institute's research came to focus on hereditary diseases instead.

It finally closed in 1959, but its vast collection of 12,000 photos has been preserved, with a disproportionate number depicting Sami people. The conviction that the Swedish race needed protection didn't end with Herman Lundborg and the institute. The Swedish Parliament adopted a sterilization law in 1934 to protect society from people who were deemed to be intellectually disabled or otherwise unfit to take care of their children. Sometimes, doctors would recommend it for people they labelled as "promiscuous." This horrendous piece of legislation was in force until 1975 and resulted in the sterilization of 63,000 people, almost all of them women, and many of them forcibly, under threat, or without informed consent. This time, Roma people were particularly targeted.

When we talk about colonization, we often refer to its "lasting impacts," as if the colonization process is over and we're simply living with the lingering results. But that's far from the truth. In many cases, colonization is still ongoing, and we are reaping the benefits. For example, almost half of Sweden's electricity comes from hydropower, the production of which accelerated in the 1950s. Hydropower is cheap, clean, and renewable. What's not to like? Except that most of the production is in Sápmi, and the Sami have had little, if any, say in the development of infrastructure that now sits on their land. As a consequence, culturally important Sami sites were lost, fishing was destroyed, and large reindeer pastures drowned. To those Sami who were dependent on reindeer herding, a traditional, thousands-of-years-old source of income and way of life, this had catastrophic consequences.

Still today, twice a year, hundreds of thousands of reindeer and their herders migrate from higher elevations, where the reindeer spend the warmer summer months, to more sheltered climates during the harsher winter months. Now, these migration routes are threatened by wind parks, as Sweden hopes to become carbon neutral by 2045. Around two thousand wind turbines are already installed in the Swedish part of Sápmi, and many more are being built, including the largest land-based wind park in Europe. The large turbines aren't just in the way of migration paths; they are also loud, creating stress and keeping the grazing reindeer from coming close, affecting their food intake and well-being.

Sápmi is also rich in valuable metals, and the mining of silver, copper, and iron ore has been critical to Sweden's economy and defence industry since the 1600s. The importance of their extraction goes beyond the nation's borders, as Sweden is Europe's largest exporter of iron ore. In 2023, the government excitedly reported a record-large finding of minerals critical in the production of much technology, including cell phones, computer chips, data centres, solar cells, car batteries, and wind turbines. The find could play a key role in Europe's green transition and decrease its dependence on China. At the same time, if the government approves the exploitation, it may have devastating effects for reindeer herding in the area, again ruining pastureland and cutting off migration routes.

While some Sami communities have taken legal action against the government's extraction decisions, others have accepted offers of financial compensation. After repeated criticism from the United Nations for ignoring Sami rights in approving wind power and mining projects, Sweden passed a law in 2022 to ensure a consultative process. The law has been criticized for not going far enough, as the government still has the last word.

Until I started to learn about Indigenous Peoples in Canada and the colonization process here, I had not reflected on my own relation to the colonization of Sápmi. As mentioned, I didn't even realize that Sápmi had been colonized. I'm not responsible for decisions taken in the 1600s, the 1920s, or even the 1950s, but I belong to the people who are. Like them, I have benefited from those decisions, such as the cheap hydropower that kept our lights burning and our home warm when I grew up, while the Sami continue to suffer the consequences.

I think we all want to protect our environment, and it is clearly something we need to get better at. But this includes ensuring that those who are impacted by our decisions are part of making them and benefit from them equally. Sometimes, this will slow down decision-making processes—in the short run. Because I am convinced that not only will meaningful consultations and co-creation result in better-informed decisions—inclusive processes will ensure that everyone's interests are considered from the outset, avoiding mistrust, conflicts, and time-consuming appeals processes that will slow us down in the long run. Co-creation and co-management of our resources will lead to more sustainable solutions for all of us. All it takes is a different mindset, or if you will, another way of viewing the world.

At the beginning of my reconciliation journey, one of my course teachers, Métis lawyer Peigi Wilson, used the expression "all my relations" as she closed out an email, in the place of "best regards" or something similar. Peigi explained that this was an expression used by many Indigenous nations, and by it, she acknowledged all life on Earth. When I later spoke to my Ojibwe friend Diane to find out more about the expression, she told me that our relations are not limited to people: They include plants, animals, the land, sea, and sky, and, if you believe in it, the spirit world. In short, our relations extend to the entire universe. To Derek, the expression is a reminder of who we are and where we come from, and that we are all part of Creation.

To me, this means that it's not *them* and *us*; we're interrelated and thereby share a responsibility toward each other. The expression is thus a reminder that our actions have an impact, whether we're driven by greed or gratitude, and that we're responsible for living in respectful, balanced relationships with each other and with all other parts of Creation. This encourages, I think, humility, gratitude, and mindfulness in how we live and relate to the world.

The expression "all my relations" makes a lot of sense in the context of reconciliation. We cannot reconcile separately from each other but must learn to live together on the same land. It means that we need to listen to each other; to consider our positions of power; to share land and resources; and to be respectful of each other and of our environment. I cannot think of a better expression to guide us on our reconciliation journey and in all decisions that we make about this land and our future.

With the near erasure of Indigenous cultures, Canada has lost a wealth of knowledge about the environment. This includes scientific knowledge of plants, trees, animal behaviour and patterns, the weather, water, and even space. During my learning journey, I have often been reminded of that. For example, when I stayed at the kâniyâsihk Cultural Camps in Saskatchewan in preparation for Sundance, a young man helped me make the whistle I would need during the ceremony. At one point during the process, he said, "Now, go and get some spruce gum." "Where do I find that?" I said, expecting him to point me to one of the tables with boxes of material around us. But he pointed to the nearest tree. "That one should do." I walked over with my ears burning, realizing I would have gone to the store looking for spruce gum before I thought of the forest.

Learning about Indigenous cultures has taught me a lot about our connection—or, in many cases, our disconnection—to the land. Indigenous Peoples lived in harmony with nature for thousands of years, practising sustainable hunting, fishing, agriculture, and forestry, before Europeans arrived and uprooted this way of living. Many Indigenous people still live in harmony with nature, or strive to, and see themselves as defenders and protectors of the land. Yet, they are often disproportionately impacted by the environmental degradation and climate change brought on by colonial and other non-Indigenous governments.

Sheila Watt-Cloutier is an Inuk activist and writer who has spent a good part of her life advocating for the protection of the Arctic and the survival of her people's culture. Her bestselling book, released in 2015, is poignantly named *The Right to Be Cold*. I invited Sheila to the podcast to talk about life in the North and her decades-long work as a climate activist. On the show, she effectively illustrated what happens when we don't respect all our relations, as she described how pollution and the loss of permafrost and ice caps threaten the whole Arctic ecosystem and the Inuit's very existence.

The truth is that we all experience the impacts of environmental degradation and climate change. One example is the increasing frequency and intensity of wildfires. In 2023, a record-setting series of wildfires ravaged through Canada. All thirteen provinces and territories were affected as more than 15 million hectares (or 37 million acres) of land burned. That's an area larger than England and makes it the most destructive wildfire season ever recorded up till then.

These fires are frightening. Their rapid spread forces people to desert their homes and leave everything behind. They cause significant economic, emotional, and physical loss, sometimes taking lives, and the smoke threatens the health of all of us. But wildfires have a disproportionate impact on Indigenous communities. A 2023 study showed that First Nations communities made up over 40 percent of evacuations due to wildfires, even though the communities themselves only make up 5 percent of people living in Canada. This is partly explained by their remote location, often a result of colonization and the creation of reserves. The wildfires also cause spiritual and cultural loss for Indigenous Peoples, as they lose significant connection to the land when old trees and whole forests are burnt to the ground and important places turned into piles of rubbish and ash. At the same time, we continue to neglect proven Indigenous land management practices, such as controlled burning, which helps prevent wildfire from spreading—to the detriment of us all.

Today, we're lucky to have both modern and traditional science to rely on, and many Indigenous nations are working to restore their traditional knowledge while embracing new knowledge and techniques. My podcast guest Sxwpilemaát Siyám, or Chief Leanne Joe, whom I quoted in my previous essay, talked about this in the context of economic reconciliation, which is key to Indigenous self-governance. I had invited Chief Leanne Joe to the show to discuss economic reconciliation, for which she's a leading advocate.

There is no commonly agreed definition for the term, and before my discussion with Chief Leanne Joe, I thought of economic reconciliation as addressing socio-economic disparities, treaty violations, and land claims to ensure that Indigenous Peoples have access to land and other resources to support their self-governance. But Chief Leanne Joe took a much wider, more holistic perspective. Economic reconciliation, she said, isn't just about having Indigenous people participate in the current economic system as it stands today, which, she stressed, has stripped Indigenous Peoples of everything they once had and continues to oppress them. True economic reconciliation, she said, must allow space for Indigenous worldviews to contribute to shaping the economic system. In other words, economic reconciliation must be a transformative process toward a values-based economy. To her, that means that wealth and well-being go hand in hand and financial wealth is only one tool toward well-being. In this system, we're all responsible and accountable to each other, our ancestors, and all living creatures, as well as Mother Earth for seven generations to come.

In our discussion, I had the chance to learn more about Sen̓áḵw, an interesting Indigenous housing project being developed in Vancouver by Sḵwx̱wú7mesh Úxwumixw, the Squamish Nation. While

Indigenous economic development opportunities are usually thought of in terms of resource extraction in rural areas, opportunities exist in urban settings as well, surrounded by non-Indigenous communities, as in the case of Senákw. The name for Senákw is representative of its place, which can be interpreted as "the place inside the head of False Creek." Once a thriving Coast Salish village, in 1877, Senákw was transformed into Kitsilano Indian Reserve No. 6, as the federal government allotted around 80 acres of the Squamish people's ancestral lands for this purpose. Despite this, in 1913, the provincial government forcibly removed the Squamish from Senákw, as the settler population grew around them. The Squamish fought for over three decades to have the Senákw lands returned to them. In 2002, following a land claims settlement, a small portion, just over 10 acres, of the original reserve and the Squamish Nation's traditional territory was finally returned to them as reserve land, today's Kitsilano Indian Reserve No. 6.

The Squamish are now building 6,000 residential rental units there that are also available for other Vancouverites, with a portion designated as affordable units. The Senákw development is Squamish-led, and its planning, architecture, construction, and operations incorporate Squamish culture, history, and values, including by aspiring to net-zero greenhouse gas emissions. The project was made possible thanks to the Squamish's long and hard-fought legal battle to have what was rightfully theirs and will provide them with a steady revenue source while helping to solve Vancouver's housing crisis in a sustainable way.

When I asked Chief Leanne Joe about the building blocks for achieving economic reconciliation, she stressed that it is about building relationships. "How many Canadians," she asked, "can say that they have a true, meaningful relationship with an Indigenous person? And what kind of actions do you need to take to make that happen?" Her point was that for reconciliation to happen, we must create space for that relationship-building. "But," she added, "if we don't have an equal footing in the relationship, at the end of the day . . . reconciliation is like sprinkles on the cupcake. We haven't really changed the foundation of the cupcake."

If successful, the Senákw development will be an example of how the cupcake itself can change, allowing for the kind of relationship and transformation to which Chief Leanne Joe aspires.

Another example of how we can achieve foundational change is the Chiixuujin / Chaaw Kaawgaa "Big Tide (Low Water)" Haida Title Lands Agreement signed by the Haida Nation and Canada in December 2024. The agreement concluded decades of negotiations between the Haida Nation, the province of British Columbia, and the federal government about title—essentially ownership—of Haida Gwaii, a group of about two hundred islands off the northern coast of British Columbia. The agreement affirms that the Haida have Aboriginal title to the islands' lands, beds of freshwater bodies, and foreshores to the low-tide mark. For centuries, colonial governments and non-Indigenous people have exploited the resources on and around Haida Gwaii, including through logging and fishing, generating revenues and profits that haven't been invested back into Haida Gwaii. The agreement will make sure this no longer happens.

About a year before the agreement was signed, in the summer of 2023, I had the opportunity to visit Haida Gwaii, as I tagged along with my husband, who in his role as Minister of Crown-Indigenous Relations was heading there to sign a preceding agreement that recognizes the Haida Nation as the holder of Haida title and rights. I had heard of Haida Gwaii's beauty, which is partly why I wanted to go, but I also felt it was a not-to-be-missed opportunity for me to learn more about economic reconciliation and Haida Gwaii's path to self-governance.

To get there, we boarded a small airplane in Vancouver to Sandspit on one of the main islands, from where we'd take the ferry to Skidegate, the largest community in Haida Gwaii. The views from the airplane window as we approached Sandspit were spectacular. It felt reminiscent of a fantasy movie: dramatic, steep coastlines rising from the ocean and the lush rainforest of Haida Gwaii's many islands glowing green against the water's blue surface. Later, as we drove past majestic old-growth cedar trees, we encountered miniature deer, something I had never seen before. There were lots of them, quietly stepping out of the forest to cross the highway, ignoring our presence. The Haida people have lived on these islands for thousands of years, and during my visit, I got a sense of their sophisticated culture as we visited the remains of old villages across the beautiful archipelago. Thanks to the Haida Nation's incredible leadership and determination and the federal and provincial governments' long overdue recognition of the Haida's Aboriginal title to the land, the Haida Nation has finally been able to reclaim this land that has been rightfully theirs for thousands of years.

The Chiix̱uujin / Chaaw K̲aawgaa "Big Tide (Low Water)" Haida Title Lands Agreement is a huge step away from colonial practices. In it, reconciliation is defined as *Gud ad T'alang HlGang .gulxa Tll Yahda/Tll yáʾadee G̲ii gud ahl t'álang hlG̲ángulaang*, which means *people working together to make it right*. This definition was reflected by the participants at the signing ceremony in Haida Gwaii in February 2025. Justin Trudeau, on one of his last trips as prime minister, described the agreement as "a new chapter that commits the government to partner as true equals with the Haida Nation." The President of the Council of the Haida Nation, Gaagwiis Jason Alsop, whom I had the pleasure of meeting during my visit in 2023, described it as "a move from an era of denial and occupation and resistance to an era of acceptance and peaceful coexistence."

In this new era, the Haida Nation will be able to ensure not just the wealth but also the well-being of its people in a governance system based on their worldviews, founded on their values. A 2024 documentary by the CBC's *The Current*, called *Haida Gwaii's Future, Haida Gwaii's Past*, demonstrates the importance of recognizing the Haida Nation's inherent right to the land. In it, Guujaaw, an Elder and Hereditary Haida Chief who has fought to protect the forest against excessive industrious logging, says, "The most valuable thing we have here is nature." To him, protecting nature was a key objective of securing title to the land: "There's no sense having rights to fish if there's no fish, or right to a culture if there's no cedar and no land to relate to." This brings me back to the expression "all my relations" and Chief Leanne Joe's approach to economic reconciliation: The importance of land rights goes beyond wealth, and our own well-being is closely related to the well-being of the land.

My very last podcast conversation was with Her Excellency the Right Honourable Mary Simon, Governor General and Commander-in-Chief of the Canadian Armed Forces. Despite her top rank, Mary Simon was easy to speak with. My nervousness about making a Protocollary mistake, such as using a wrong title to address her, soon dissipated. As she told me on the show, she grew up in a small village in northern Quebec, in Nunavik, across from Baffin Island. She described it as a peaceful upbringing in a place where everybody knew and supported each other to keep the community going. She spent a lot of time with her family out on the land. She described how, even as a child, she contributed to the work of hunting and fishing, and in the summer season, picking berries and gathering plants needed for the rest of the year. She stressed that having her own roles in food harvesting and other daily tasks instilled in her a sense of responsibility for her family's survival and well-being: "It was a hard lifestyle in many ways, because we had to do everything manually, and at an early age, I realized that part of my role was to help keep everything moving forward," she said. "So, during my career, I've always had a sense of that."

She went on to describe her long experience as a negotiator for Inuit rights and control and how, when she got older, she saw herself as more of a diplomat. Then, when she got the offer to become Canada's first Indigenous governor general, she thought of how she could contribute to bringing a better understanding between Indigenous and non-Indigenous Peoples in Canada. The relationship between the Crown and Indigenous Peoples, she emphasized, is something that's still sacred to many Indigenous people today, and many Indigenous nations are working to build their relationship with Canada. The role as governor general, she felt, would allow her to help improve the conditions for healing and reconciliation by acting as a bridge. If we can build that relationship in a more positive way, she said, and have a better understanding and compassion for people who have been through some very, very difficult periods in their lives, then that relationship will continue to grow. "I have realized that reconciliation is a way of life. It's continuous, with no end date," she said.

Throughout this book, we have highlighted many meaningful acts of reconciliation and ways to contribute as an individual. Numerous times during my own learning process, I have felt frustrated because there's no easy solution, no ten-step approach to reconciliation. It can be tempting to give up. During these moments, I think it's important to look at the progress we've made and can continue to make. When I find it difficult or even hopeless at times, I think of a word Mary Simon chose for her motto as governor general, and a word she explained in our conversation: *ajuinnata*. It's a word in Inuktitut that she learned as a child, that her grandmother and others said when facing hardships. It means to never give up, to keep going, no matter what. Reconciliation is like that, making a commitment to continue to make change for the better, to keep going, no matter what. "There's great meaning to perseverance in the face of adversity," she said.

I think that if we can all aspire to that, then there's hope for reconciliation.

One Final Tip for Your Reconciliation Journey

In our two essays on worldview, we highlighted the importance of gratitude and the concept of interconnectedness. Both are fundamental to many Indigenous cultures and integral to the expression "all my relations" and a more holistic worldview where wealth and well-being go hand in hand. Gratitude and interconnectedness present an antithesis to the colonial focus on power, control, and exploitation—forces embedded in Western culture that have led us to a world that today can be characterized by increasing income inequality, a steadily growing number of armed conflicts, and a triple planetary crisis: climate change, pollution, and biodiversity loss.

The alternative to this world doesn't require that we go back to pre-colonial or pre-industrial ways of living—it is fully within our reach as we can reconcile our modern lifestyles and technologies with traditional knowledge and ways of life. Such a world would be respectful of the early peace and friendship treaties between Indigenous Peoples and settlers, such as the 1613 Two Row wampum belt, which symbolizes a relationship based on mutual benefit and respect where no nation would exert control over another. This world would be characterized by peace and stability, economic fairness, and responsible environmental stewardship.

If everyone adopted this worldview, the transformation could be profound—touching every aspect of life from personal well-being to global systems. So how do we get there? On a nation-to-nation level, whether within or between countries, we would rely on diplomacy instead of force, respectful and transparent collaboration instead of competition, and decision-making aimed at building resilient, equitable, and healthy communities that factor in generations to come.

You can contribute to this world on a personal level by adopting a holistic worldview yourself, where you see yourself and your actions in connection to the land and other human beings. As a final tip for your reconciliation journey, we challenge you to adopt this worldview.

Here are seven ways to get you started:

1. Practice daily gratitude

Keep a gratitude journal, draft your own thanksgiving address, express appreciation to others, or take moments to reflect on what you're grateful for.

2. Strengthen your relationships

Check in with loved ones, offer kindness and forgiveness, and build meaningful connections that reach beyond your own community and existing circle of friends.

3. Engage with nature

Spend time outdoors, acknowledge the beauty of the world, and be mindful of your impact on the environment and on all living creatures.

4. Give back

Volunteer, help those in need, and support ethical practices that benefit communities and ecosystems.

5. Contribute to reconciliation with Indigenous Peoples

Listen, learn, and act, and be a good ally by ensuring your contributions are informed by Indigenous people.

6. Shift from scarcity to abundance thinking

Instead of focusing on what you lack, celebrate what you have and what can be shared.

7. Cultivate mindfulness and presence

Slow down, appreciate small moments, and reflect on how everything is connected.

Living this way fosters stronger relationships, respect for the environment, and mental wellness. It's a shift from colonial and Western individualism to a world where gratitude fuels action, and interconnectedness guides choices. We expect some readers will find that such a worldview is merely aspirational or that, if adopted at the national level, it would compromise economic and national security. But this worldview is grounded in real practices, reflected in Canada's and many other countries' long-standing belief in multilateralism, conflict prevention, international development assistance, protection of human rights, and collaboration to address environmental degradation and climate change. In recent years, these beliefs and efforts have started to fray, as some countries overtly assert their national self-interests over the welfare of all of us.

But there is still hope. For example, in June of 2025, Mexican President Claudia Sheinbaum Pardo spoke to the power and potential of this worldview as she attended the G7 Summit in Kananaskis, Alberta: "All citizens, of all countries, must have the possibility of a life of well-being, and although it may seem like a dream, it is possible. This would mean moving toward a more equitable, peaceful, and sustainable international community. Economic well-being and development cooperation are acts of shared responsibility of all nations. In a world marked by interdependencies, no country can isolate itself and prosper at the cost of the sacrifice of others. To bet on cooperation is ultimately to bet on a common future based on justice."

The challenge is not imagining this world, but listening, learning, and aligning our lives with these values.

Our Approach
to (Re)conciliation

WRITING THIS BOOK felt challenging at times. The truth
is still unfolding, many issues remain unresolved, and there is
so much trauma. What we learned along the way impacted us
deeply, and instead of simply writing about our reconciliation
journeys, our journeys continued as we learned more about Canada and its long history of colonization, often from those who are
living with its impacts.

Reconciliation is a complex concept. As Derek discussed in
his first essay, "Reconciling with Hate," it's debatable whether
we should even call this process *reconciliation*. Many Indigenous
nations have never had peaceful relations with Canada. In those
cases, it isn't about re-establishing peaceful relations, but rather
about establishing them in the first place. It's about *conciliation*.

Key ingredients in establishing peaceful relations between
people are learning about each other, establishing meaningful
communication, and demonstrating that we are listening by following through on agreed actions. This is how we build trust,
secure peace, and make friends—between people and nations.

At the same time, the process is also one of *re*conciliation, as we
must reconcile with the past, with our different beliefs, and with

the truth. In a sense, the process of writing this book has been one of reconciliation in action, as the many experiences and conversations we've had along the way have brought very different perspectives to light—some that didn't at first align with our assumptions or beliefs. We had to find new ways of relating to ourselves and to the process of reconciliation itself. For example, during Sundance, Elin found it difficult to reconcile the ceremonial gender roles with her conception of gender equality. And Derek found he had to reconceptualize his idea of a successful land claim settlement. Before he started this journey, he thought of the Land Back movement as land being handed back to Kahnawà:ke and his people, plain and simple. But once he learned and thought more about it, he realized that even if they got their land back, it wouldn't be the end of the story—his people would have to find ways of collaborating with the non-Indigenous families who had now lived on the land for generations. Even if things are not as simple as we first thought or would like them to be—including matters of cultural norms and practices, land ownership, governance, and resource management—we firmly believe more than ever that these conversations must be held and that our actions will be worth it.

We also came to this project from very different backgrounds. It's unlikely that we would ever have come to know each other had we not embarked on this journey together. But over the course of the writing process, through our many discussions, we developed a warm and solid friendship. This became an important part of our shared reconciliation journey.

To reconcile doesn't mean to always agree with each other. Like in any multicultural society, or any friendship, we must learn to accept our differences and respect each other's practices and beliefs. This means that we cannot begin from a place of superiority, and nor can we believe that our way is the only way. After all, such rigid hierarchal beliefs are exactly what underpin the entire colonial system.

At the same time, understanding *why* we're different and how our different experiences have shaped our views is vital for reconciliation. To understand the *why* requires active listening. In our case, writing a book together forced us to listen closely to each other. We had to understand our respective perspectives and the views that we expressed in our draft texts; otherwise, we wouldn't have been able to agree on the final result.

Writing about your own experiences and beliefs is also a highly self-reflective process. Describing your own actions and reactions, or developing your arguments, requires you to challenge yourself—why do I have this opinion, or why did I react that way? Elin had to think hard about her reasons for embarking on this book. As she read more about white saviourism, she found it difficult to know if she was even being honest with herself about her motivations. And as she reflected on her reasons, she realized that she would have to continue to check in with herself to be sure she wasn't driven by personal ambition or a sense of having all the answers, but that her actions were continuously informed by those she was trying to support.

Derek, before sharing certain moments of his life, had to first understand the feelings attached to those memories. Seeking this clarity of thought often cast his experiences in a new light, sometimes challenging his long-held perceptions. The memories of his relationship with his father were often clouded in pain. But as he examined and, in a sense, relived those memories, he discovered some positive moments, too—happier memories that had been crowded out by the darker ones. Writing down such personal and once-private memories, and reviewing them again and again as we edited our texts, was also at times deeply unsettling. But in the end, the writing process increased his understanding of his own role in those experiences and of the roles we all play in the context we have been dealt. In reconciliation, listening can be just as much about listening to ourselves as it is listening to the other person.

We both found it hard to accept that there is often no perfect solution to a conflict. We cannot reverse history. When it comes to land claims, which is arguably the most challenging aspect of the reconciliation process, asking all non-Indigenous people to simply leave isn't necessarily the best solution for anyone. It may not even be the right one morally, when you consider that many people have purchased their home in good faith, or grown attached to the land over generations, with no other place to go "back" to. We still haven't had an honest discussion about this in Canada, if there's a right and wrong and what that looks like, and perhaps it is time. Just like in all areas of a reconciliation process, we must identify our respective interests, including those that we may share, before we can discuss and reach mutually acceptable solutions.

For non-Indigenous people, to whom we direct this book, mutually acceptable solutions may involve letting go of the idea that they must control everything. Sharing your power, or ceding control over something you care about, can seem scary at first. But as our peoples get to know each other better, we will build the trust this will take. While writing this book, and as we learned more and more about reconciliation, we became increasingly optimistic and bolder in what we believe that Canadians can achieve.

For example, we have seen a growing openness to Indigenous beliefs around wellness, as the interconnectedness between body and mind is becoming more widely respected in medical and mental health sciences. This is an important milestone because adopting these types of holistic practices brings benefits to everyone involved, including taxpayers, as studies show that mindfulness-based health programs can lead to significant savings in healthcare costs, whether it involves an Indigenous patient/practitioner or not. An Indigenous worldview that centres around the interconnectedness between humans, animals, and plants, or One Health, likewise offers a win-win for everyone involved, as we become more mindful of our impact on those with whom we share this planet: animals, plants, and whole ecosystems. Mutually acceptable solutions can also be seen as win-win solutions, rather than compromises, as we begin thinking long-term for everyone.

Individual, positive action is always meaningful and often more powerful than we anticipate. Our actions can have a direct impact on people, and they can also inspire others to act. One single act can spread like ripples across a lake as your friends, family, and colleagues follow your lead. In the beginning of her journey, Elin once shared an Indigenous reading list with colleagues, and several went ahead and purchased some of the books, including for children. Those children got a chance to learn about Indigenous Peoples and cultures through the stories their parents read to them. What a wonderful way of learning.

Derek will often begin communication, such as emails or texts, by using Kanien'kehá:ka greetings, like *Wa'tkwanonweráton* or the simpler form of greeting, *Kwe*. Recently, he noticed his son's schoolteachers in their email replies are now using those same words of greeting. It may seem small to some, but such teachers work in a traditional French language high school, and so using Kanien'kéha is an encouraging indicator of peaceful relations. And with time, even small solutions can grow to have a big impact on all of us, proving that being determined to carry on brings positive, notable change. We are confident that reconciliation is fully feasible and within our reach if we want it to be.

Our understanding of what (re)conciliation is—or should be—developed over the years it took to write this book and became more concrete and comprehensive as the book progressed. If we were to now define it in one sentence, based on what we have learned and tried to express throughout our essays, we would say that: *Reconciliation is an ongoing process in which we seek to establish and maintain friendly, mutually respectful rela-tionships that allow us to share this land peacefully and on equal footing.* There's a lot that is packed into or just assumed in this one-sentence definition. To share this land on equal footing, for example, many of us will need to change our colonial mindsets. It's our hope that building friendly relations will bring about this change, but it will also take listening, learning, and self-reflection. Were we to provide a more comprehensive and in-depth explana-tion of our approach to reconciliation, these are the key compo-nents that we hope you will take away from reading our essays:

Reconciliation is everyone's responsibility: While institu-tions bear significant responsibility, reconciliation must also be pursued by individuals. It involves listening, learning, and reflect-ing on our own roles and positions, and taking meaningful action.

The role of education: Education is both a tool of coloniza-tion and a path to reconciliation. Indigenous perspectives must be integrated into school curricula, and historical narratives must be corrected.

Truth before reconciliation: Acknowledging the truth, in-cluding about residential schools, intergenerational trauma, sys-temic discrimination, and other historical and ongoing injustices is a prerequisite for genuine reconciliation. This is our shared his-tory, present and future, and we must own it.

The centrality of land: Land is a vital resource, and access to land and its resources is a must for any nation's survival. Land is also a source of identity, culture, and spirituality. Reconcilia-tion must include addressing land theft, broken treaties, and con-trol over resources.

Cultural revitalization and language: Reclaiming Indig-enous languages and cultural practices is essential for identity, well-being, and nation-building. While learning basic elements of an Indigenous language, or visiting a powwow, is important, that is only one small step in understanding someone's culture.

Little by little, step by step, we must all ensure that our work-places, schools, and public places are inclusive and reflective of all peoples in Canada.

Indigenous worldview: Gratitude and interconnectedness are essential to well-being. By approaching life with gratitude and embracing the concept of mutual coexistence with other aspects of Creation, we can redefine how we view prosperity and security. This will allow us to value what is truly important in our lives and to hand over the world to the next seven generations without shame. We took care of it—of all our relations—the best we could.

Everyday actions matter: Reconciliation is not only about grand gestures but also about everyday choices—how we speak, what we learn, and how we engage with Indigenous communi-ties. Each act of reconciliation helps foster a culture of respect and understanding.

Reconciliation is not a destination: Reconciliation is not a destination but a continuous effort where each act contributes to a broader movement of awareness and change toward a more inclusive and equitable society.

We have finished writing this book, but our reconciliation journeys continue. For Elin, who moved back to Montreal as we were completing this project, this means getting to know the Indigenous past and present of the Montreal area. She will do that out of respect for the Indigenous people still living there, but also to feel more at home, just like learning about the Algon-quins in Ottawa made her feel more rooted there. Having grown up in Sweden, a country that was universally renowned for its egalitarian society and whose diplomats, including herself, rou-tinely championed human rights around the world, Elin is also committed to learning more about Sweden's aggressive assimila-tion of the Sami and ruthless exploitation of their territory. This will likely involve some hard learning, including through self-reflection, but also offer opportunities to be an ally from afar.

Derek will continue to serve his community within holistic wellness services at the local, regional, and national levels. He will not only help address the negative impacts of colonization but also contribute to changing the systems that continue to oppress Indigenous Peoples. His efforts will require him to continually reach out, teach, and engage with non-Indigenous Canadians, because Indigenous people cannot change these systems alone. They need the collaboration and support of the non-Indigenous people who, through municipal, provincial, and federal governments, control decision-making and governance. This collaboration must be at the core of the reconciliation process, and we must all contribute to it.

What we each discovered on our journeys and have done our best to reflect in this book wasn't always pleasant, and the truth can sometimes be hard to accept. But our deep dive into the issue of reconciliation also allowed us to reflect on it from so many different perspectives, to grow our understanding of it, and to grow ourselves. In that sense, this has been a wonderful and truly transformative experience. We look forward to our next steps, as we know there are many more inspiring stories to learn about, rich cultures to discover, and new friendships to be made. We hope that this book will inspire you to act. Your own journey is waiting.

Acknowledgements

IT TOOK US over two years from when we first talked about writing a book together in the spring of 2023, until we sat down to draft our final chapter. After all the research, drafting, editing, and many bouts of self-doubt, to think that we would soon see our names on the cover and feel the weight of the book in our hands—our words printed onto tightly packed pages—was difficult to believe.

We have many beautiful souls to thank for helping us get this far. They offered their expertise, advice, and support, and believed in our idea when we hardly did ourselves.

First, we thank our agents Lisa Rambert and Rob Firing at Transatlantic Agency for seeing the potential in our concept. Lisa and Rob set us on the right path toward something more ambitious and challenging than we had originally envisioned, and supported us in finding our way there.

Second, without Lauren McKeon, our editor at HarperCollins Canada, there would be no book. We cannot thank her enough for her encouragement, expert guidance, and patience. She believed in us, yet challenged our thinking, ensuring our words expressed our thoughts, and answered our multitude of questions about the publication process, always with grace and attention.

We extend our thanks to everyone else at HarperCollins who helped make this book a reality; the editing, design, marketing, legal, and production teams, as well as everyone who operated behind the scenes to bring our book to fruition.

Derek offers thanks to the Creator, as our paths have crossed each other's for a reason, and he is forever grateful to have been given the chance to write this book. He never would have imagined his journey would take him here. He thanks Afroditi for her encouragement and unwavering support, for sharing her experiences and love as a non-Indigenous psychologist working with—and for—First Nations for decades, and for all her fire, determination, compassion, tenderness, and acceptance. And to his mom, Isobel. A woman who has taught him that it is never too late to make changes in our lives. A woman who has been the pillar of his family. Small in stature but built like a strong wall that they have all leaned on throughout their lives. Thank you for loving and believing in your boys no matter what.

He thanks his two brothers, because regardless of where they are at today, David was there when he needed him the most, and Craig was the inspiration to follow a good path. Derek thanks his children, Achilles, Trevor, Kati and his granddaughter Amilia, his whole family, and his extended family for their patience, support, and understanding, especially where his memories of the past may differ from theirs. We are a powerful family!

Finally, he is grateful for the many friends he has made along his journey; school mates, fellow service members in Canada and the USA, all his co-workers and the Board at K.S.C.S., the community members from Kahnawà:ke who showed him what it means to be a proud Kanien'kehá:ka man, Rakwirenhtha and the other healers who helped free his spirit, and all the friends and peers he has met in his travels across Quebec, Canada, and the world. Thank you for your friendship, for believing in me, trusting me, inviting me to your table for conversation, for teaching me so many lessons, and for taking a chance to do things differently in this world of ours. We are all in this together, and although I may not have named you specifically, when we crossed paths, you have remained in my heart.

Of all the people who helped inform her thinking about reconciliation, Elin first acknowledges Marc and thanks him for their many discussions about the reconciliation process, for his unwavering dedication to it, and for his love and support while she took on this second job of writing a book amid the busyness of work and family life. She thanks her children Marius, Lukas, and Eva, and her grandchild Magnus, for their encouragement and inspiring, infallible sense of right and wrong.

Elin is also grateful to her podcast guests who generously shared their stories, perspectives, and recommendations with her and the listeners. She thanks Anna, Alex, Caroline, and Aisha at Canada 2020 for believing in her and for working with her throughout the ten episodes. This was a truly unique opportunity to seek answers to all her questions and have conversations that generated many new, and often more difficult, questions. Without her podcast guests and their insights, intelligence, and inspiration, Elin wouldn't have been able to write this book.

She especially thanks Marie Wilson and Stephen Kakfwi, who took their time to discuss the concept of *Everyday Reconciliation* back in the summer of 2020, for sharing their significant experiences and great wisdom, and for encouraging her to move ahead with the idea. She also thanks Crystal Gail Fraser, Sara Komarnisky, Aubrey Charette, and Alisa Lombard, who likewise took their time to listen and share their thoughts about the concept of *Everyday Reconciliation.*

To Kevin, Matilda, Kevin's wife Jody, his late father Andrew, and his kokum Elder Margaret Crookedneck, and Kevin's whole beautiful family, Elin feels deep and sincere gratitude for hosting her in Ministikwan. Sundance was an exceptional experience, and she is deeply obliged to Sundance chief Wilfrid Waterhen, who allowed her to write about her experience, to

Annie Waterhen, who gave her a Cree name, to Ministikwan Lake Cree Nation for accepting her presence, and to everyone who graciously put up with her faux pas. She is also grateful for the chance to get to know the other guests at kâniyâsihk Cultural Camps who were all warm and welcoming and contributed to making her stay there so memorable.

Elin also acknowledges the course instructors at the Canada School of Public Service, in particular Peigi Wilson, who taught her the expression "all my relations" and led her to the talented artist Janet Kaponicin. She thanks Janet for generously sharing her grandmother's story about the horrific crime committed against the young Algonquin girl below Parliament Hill and for providing important cultural, historical, and personal context.

While she has undoubtedly made some factual errors in her essays, for which she apologizes in advance, it is thanks to the expertise and kindness of law professor and author Douglas Sanderson (Amo Binashii) that she was hopefully able to correctly explain the Doctrine of Discovery in Canada and how Indigenous Peoples here lost their land.

Elin is deeply grateful to Diane Gauthier for her patient explanations of Indigenous culture and spirituality and for welcoming her into her life. She thanks Verla Chatsis, the late Deborah Chatsis's sister, for sharing her own insights as well as their father's stories about the trial against Chief Poundmaker. She also thanks her sister-in-law Åsa Sandberg (born Fjellström), for sharing and encouraging her to write about the horrific death of Lars Nilsson, instigated by Åsa's ancestor, the priest Pehr Noraeus Fjellström.

Finally, Elin is deeply grateful to all the excellent Indigenous fiction writers she has read over the years, too many to name here, for her beautiful reading experiences and the improved understanding of Indigenous cultures and realities they brought.

Before concluding, we want to acknowledge some of the

books, articles, and reports that helped inform this book: *The Report of the Royal Commission on Aboriginal Peoples*, 1996; *The Final Report, The Survivors Speak*, and the *94 Calls to Action* by the Truth and Reconciliation Commission, 2015; James Daschuk, *Clearing the Plains: Disease, Politics of Starvation, and the Loss of Aboriginal Life*, 2013; Andrew Stobo Sniderman and Douglas Sanderson (Amo Binashii), *Valley of the Birdtail: An Indian Reserve, a White Town, and the Road to Reconciliation*, 2023; Blair Stonechild and Bill Waiser, *Loyal Till Death: Indians and the North-West Rebellion*, 2010; Stuart Banner, *How the Indians Lost Their Land: Law and Power on the Frontier*, 2007; Ronald Wright, *Stolen Continents*, 2015; Noreen Kruzich, *The Ancestors Are Arranging Things: A Journey on the Algonkin Trail*, 2011; Jim Stone, *Chief Pinesi and His Pursuit of Justice*, presentation to the Historical Society of Ottawa, 2023, and *Grand Chief Constant Pinesi: Fighting a Losing Battle in a Turbulent Era*, article published online by Kichi Sibi Trails, 2022; and Alastair Sweeny, *Thomas Mackay: The Laird of Rideau Hall and the Founding of Ottawa*, 2022.

Last but not least, we feel deep gratitude toward each other for agreeing to walk this journey together, for the good humour when the challenge of completing this book at times felt insurmountable, and for our resulting friendship.